Women, Reading, and Piety in
Late Medieval England

Women, Reading, and Piety in Late Medieval England traces networks of female book ownership and exchange which have so far been obscure, and shows how women were responsible for both owning and circulating devotional books. In seven narratives of individual women who lived between 1350 and 1550, Mary Erler illustrates the ways in which women read and the routes by which they passed books from hand to hand. These stories are prefaced by an overview of nuns' reading and their surviving books, and are followed by a survey of women who owned the first printed books in England. An appendix lists a number of books not previously attributed to religious women's ownership. Erler's narratives also provide studies of female friendship, since they situate women's reading in a context of family and social connections. The book uses bibliography to explore social and intellectual history.

MARY ERLER is Professor of English at Fordham U~~~~~~~~ ~~~~~~~
work c
Power
Hellin~~
(1999).
Modern

This series of critical books seeks to cover the whole area of literature written in the major medieval languages – the main European vernaculars, and medieval Latin and Greek – during the period *c.* 1100–1500. Its chief aim is to publish and stimulate fresh scholarship and criticism on medieval literature, special emphasis being placed on understanding major works of poetry, prose, and drama in relation to the contemporary culture and learning which fostered them.

A complete list of titles in the series can be found at the end of the volume.

Frontispiece. St. Anne teaching Mary to read, in "a domestic interior that also includes other students," and illustrates women reading in groups. Roger S. Wieck, William M. Voelkle and K. Michelle Hearne (eds.), *The Hours of Henry VIII: A Renaissance Masterpiece by Jean Poyet* (New York, 2000). Pierpont Morgan Library MS H.8, f. 186v.

Women, Reading, and Piety in Late Medieval England

MARY C. ERLER

CAMBRIDGE
UNIVERSITY PRESS

CAMBRIDGE UNIVERSITY PRESS
Cambridge, New York, Melbourne, Madrid, Cape Town, Singapore, São Paulo

Cambridge University Press
The Edinburgh Building, Cambridge CB2 2RU, UK

Published in the United States of America by Cambridge University Press, New York

www.cambridge.org
Information on this title: www.cambridge.org/9780521812214

First published 2002
This digitally printed first paperback version 2006

A catalogue record for this publication is available from the British Library

ISBN-13 978-0-521-81221-4 hardback
ISBN-10 0-521-81221-6 hardback

ISBN-13 978-0-521-02457-0 paperback
ISBN-10 0-521-02457-9 paperback

Contents

Illustrations

Acknowledgments

Like many others, I have benefited immensely from the magisterial work of A. I. Doyle, to whose generosity everyone studying medieval books is indebted. Similarly, I was one of many people to whom Kitzi Pantzer extended her detailed and painstaking help on matters connected with early printing.

Caroline Barron has taken an expert interest in this book and has guided all my ventures into London's medieval history with her characteristic care and openheartedness. Lotte Hellinga's encouragement and the model of work she provided made a great deal possible. The brilliant research skills that Sheila Lindenbaum commands have regularly been put at my disposal for many years.

To my surprise and pleasure Marilyn Oliva kindly gave me the fruits of her years-long collection of information on nuns' books. My interest in the details of London lives was sustained by Anne Sutton. Jocelyn Wogan-Browne's joyful enthusiasm has consistently provided welcome support to her struggling colleagues. I am extremely grateful to these and to many other friends, especially Maryanne Kowaleski whose faithful comradeship can now be measured in decades. I acknowledge, too, my debt for institutional support from the John Rylands Research Institute, Manchester; the Folger Shakespeare Library, Washington D.C.; and Fordham University, New York.

Abbreviations

BIHR	*Bulletin of the Institute for Historical Research*
BJRL	*Bulletin of the John Rylands Library*
BL	British Library
BRUC	Emden, A. B., *A Biographical Register of the University of Cambridge to 1500*, Cambridge, 1963
BRUO	Emden, A. B., *A Biographical Register of the University of Oxford, 1501–1540*, Oxford, 1974
CCR	*Calendar of Close Rolls*
CIPM	*Calendar of Inquisitions Post Mortem*
CP	*The Complete Peerage*, ed. G.E.C., 13 vols. in 14, London, 1910–49
CPL	*Calendar of Papal Letters*
CPR	*Calendar of Patent Rolls*
CUL	Cambridge University Library
DNB	*Dictionary of National Biography*
EETS	Early English Text Society
EHR	*English Historical Review*
ELH	*English Literary History*
IMEP	*Index of Middle English Prose*
IPMEP	*Index of Printed Middle English Prose*
JBAA	*Journal of the British Archaeological Association*
JBS	*Journal of British Studies*
JEH	*Journal of Ecclesiastical History*
JMH	*Journal of Medieval History*
JRUL	John Rylands University Library
KCC	King's College Cambridge

L&PH8	Brewer, J. S. (ed.), *Letters and Papers . . . of . . . the Reign of Henry VIII*, 22 vols. in 38, London, 1864–1932
MED	*Middle English Dictionary*
MLGB	N. R. Ker (ed.), *Medieval Libraries of Great Britain*, 2nd edn, London, 1964
MLR	*Modern Language Review*
MMBL	N. R. Ker (ed.), *Medieval Manuscripts in British Libraries*, 4 vols., London, 1969–90
NCC	Norwich Consistory Court
NRO	Norwich Record Office
NYPL	New York Public Library
OED	*Old English Dictionary*
PCC	Prerogative Court of Canterbury
PRO	Public Record Office
RES	*Review of English Studies*
SC	F. Madan, et al., *A Summary Catalogue of the Western Manuscripts in the Bodleian . . .* Oxford, 1895–1937
SPCK	Society for the Promotion of Christian Knowledge
STC	*A Short-Title Catalogue of Books Printed in England . . . 1475–1640*, London, 1976–91
Supplement	A. G. Watson (ed.), *Supplement* to *MLGB* London, 1987
TBGAS	*Transactions of the Bristol and Gloucestershire Archaeological Society*
TCBS	*Transactions of the Cambridge Bibliographical Society*
TE	James Raine (ed.), *Testamenta Eboracensia* 6 vols., Surtees Society 4, 30, 45, 53, 79, 106, Durham, 1836–1902
TEAS	*Transactions of the Essex Archaeological Society*
TLS	*Times Literary Supplement*
TRHS	*Transactions of the Royal Historical Society*
TRP	*Tudor Royal Proclamations*
TWAS	*Transactions of the Worcestershire Archaeological Society*
VCH	*Victoria County History*

Prologue

Bibliography has sometimes been moved by what might seem an especially pure form of the historical impulse: the wish to use physical objects, books, to reveal something about non-physical realities: about intellectual lives, about manners or habits in the past. Viewed in this way, books have continued to signal seductively their potential as guides and markers to another age's sensibility. In fact current fascination with book provenance has perhaps derived from the insight of the *histoire du livre* school that research into book ownership could offer a novel way in to social history, one which might make visible even the elusive matters of personal preference and personal taste, always particularly difficult to recover.

This study began with the wish to provide additional evidence for late medieval female reading and book ownership. Its intention was codicological: to use for this purpose the names and marks in surviving books owned by women. The physical objects themselves and their histories, then, would provide a starting point. But, while interrogating this sometimes cryptic witness, it became clear that additional supporting testimony would be required – that material evidence in the books, while primary, might be insufficient to provide the fuller account of womens' reading which I imagined. Other forms of historical record, in particular the evidence of wills, would have to provide the lived particulars out of which the reading sprang. Despite their unreliability as tallies of books owned by individuals, their insecurity as indicators of what was generally read, and their extremely partial record of women's lives and property,[1] wills remain unparalleled in the social information they provide about networks of friendship and connection. Consequently this book has relied both upon manuscript evidence and testamentary evidence, and both bibliographical and biographical approaches have been used.

In pursuing this inquiry, the line between female states in life appeared increasingly blurred. The cultural ideals offered to women, whether lay or religious, did not differ greatly. And this common female social formation was often based upon texts which were widely distributed and read. As a background to illustration of such reading, the book opens with an introduction that draws attention to the shared elements in female lay and religious lives, and to women's connections with each other.

Until now only one kind of female book ownership has been thoroughly tabulated – that of religious women. As a result, nuns' reading, in what follows, has sometimes served as a point of comparison against which to examine the reading of women in other forms of life: anchoresses, vowesses, widows. Hence this book first offers a bibliographical overview of English institutional libraries for women, based on their surviving books. Using the recuperative work of Neil Ker, Andrew Watson, and David Bell,[2] it attempts to revise slightly upward the estimated number of extant nuns' books, and to summarize what houses owned them and what their subjects were. It notes that book bequests made to women's houses altered their nature in the fifteenth century, and thus is able to support with evidence from female monastic history the changes which the evidence of individual books had earlier shown: the rise of a new female lay readership and the synthesis of this vernacular audience with that of religious women, their common interest being devotional reading. This chapter closes with a brief taxonomy of the structures and occasions which supported exchange of religious books among women.

The book's final chapter returns to the topic of what women read and, like the first chapter, offers an overview. It looks at selected religious incunabula which carry women's names to see what portion of these popular devotional works were female-owned and whether the titles which interested women changed with the coming of print. It thus attempts to carry forward chronologically the first chapter's slightly earlier investigation of women's religious reading.

Enclosed by these two bibliographic chapters whose method is the survey, a different sort of work is presented. The center of the book is the histories of seven women readers. Some of these narratives had their beginnings in the books these women owned which still existed and could be held and examined (Eleanor and Dorothy Fettyplace, Elizabeth Throckmorton, perhaps Margery de Nerford). The impetus to study the other women came from their wills or their histories (Margery de Nerford, Margaret Purdans, Susan Fettyplace Kyngeston, Katherine Manne).

Half of these women, those who made wills, were lay and widowed (or divorced, as was Margery de Nerford). The other half, whose books instead witness to their reading, were for the most part nuns who would have been less likely to own the possessions usually bequeathed in wills (unless, like Syon, their order required such arrangements at entrance, as with Dorothy Fettyplace). What married women or young unmarried women read is altogether more difficult to trace, since such reading has no *systematic* conduit to the present, either documentary (these women seldom made wills) or institutional (their books do not survive as part of collective holdings). The scarcity of such evidence is reflected in this book, which includes no accounts of such female readers.

For several reasons the focus here has been on religious texts. Their preponderance, as earlier research on book bequests in wills has shown, makes it possible to see in them the common currency of book exchange. Though at least half the books mentioned in medieval wills were liturgical or devotional,[3] this does not, of course, mean that half of all medieval books fell into these categories. Books bequeathed in wills were those considered especially valuable, either economically or spiritually, and in both of these categories secular books could be less highly regarded. Consequently the use of wills, as in this study, may be thought to weight the results in favor of religious reading. In addition, though Ker and Watson's work has provided numerical evidence for religious women's book ownership, no comprehensive effort has yet been mounted to trace the survival either of secular women's books or of secular texts owned by women.[4] Indeed it is difficult to see how such a study would proceed. Thus both the disproportionate testamentary mentions of religious books and the valuable identification of nuns' surviving religious books – both wills and codices, that is – may overemphasize religious reading.

Nevetheless it is hard to deny the cultural centrality of a literature of spiritual formation. Indeed devotional books make their presence visible in other places besides wills. In the last quarter of the fifteenth century, for instance, devotional works constitute the largest subject category in the surviving output of English printers.[5] This collective judgment about such works' economic power underlines devotional books' social importance.

In fact, reading with a spiritual intention was more widespread than we find it easy to realize. The division of books into religious and secular is a recent phenomenon, and it has often been observed that categories which we judge secular such as conduct literature or romance could be read as religiously instructive. Conversely, religious texts might be appreciated in various ways. A nuns' manuscript from Barking, for instance, London, BL Additional MS 10596, includes a collection of prayers and meditations in addition to texts of the Book of Tobit and the Book of Susannah. Both these Old Testament narratives enforce a meditative awareness of divine providence's workings in a life of faith. Nonetheless both tales have suspenseful (and, in the case of Tobit, picaresque) elements and indeed a recent judgment that the Book of Tobit can be called "a Hebrew romance,"[6] suggests that the line between secular and religious texts was not always sharply drawn for medieval readers.

In addition to ownership, this study's other main area of interest is circulation, where "we still know remarkably little about the comings and goings of . . . manuscripts themselves across space . . . For a good majority of the texts that have come down to us, a vast invisible network of loans, borrowings, exchanges, sales, purchases and other less formal arrangements underpinned the spatial dissemination of Middle English [texts]."[7] The particulars of book transmission can reveal surprising juxtapositions. Nuns who at the Dissolution returned to their families bearing the remnants of institutional collections; women who read together in a secular household; anchoresses and vowesses who lent each other volumes; laywomen who enriched nuns' libraries with bequests; aunts who presented to their nieces the devotional reading so widely disseminated to both male and female, secular and religious owners; nuns who gave each other books or to whom institutionally owned volumes were assigned within the house – all these make their appearances in the following chapters. The permeability of female lay and religious culture is in fact one of the book's most persistently recurring themes. In the act of reading, as at so many other times, women made connections among themselves, sometimes despite a degree of official discouragement. Indeed one of the ways to read this book is as a study of female affiliation.[8]

It is true, of course, that men feature prominently in all these narratives. Men who made book gifts to women, who read to women, who wrote books for women, are an important part of the story of women's reading, as A. I. Doyle's thesis very early pointed out.[9] But that narrative is not the one told here. Rather, the claims of a female culture of reading have in these pages been allowed to take precedence.

This culture appears often to flow alongside the more visible learned culture, in which sometimes men were responsible for opening a place for women. When Susan Kyngeston received her half-brother Sir Thomas Elyot's translation of St. Cyprian, she was participating as a reader in a patristic tradition which men had for centuries made available to women through translation. At other times two varieties of book ownership are discernible. Elizabeth Englefield, for instance, made a public transfer of book material recognized by society as valuable (her will bequest of her husband's law library to her sons). At the same time she made a private transfer of book material whose worth was primarily personal (her gift inscription in a book intended for her daughter-in-law, one she had herself received from her aunt). Here and elsewhere, scarcity in numbers and, often, privacy in transmission distinguish the record of women's book ownership.

The books and documents examined in this study illustrate both older and newer forms of reading, the public and the private. Hearing a saint's life read in the monastic refectory from a book such as Campsey Abbey's collection, now London, BL Additional MS 70513, or doing needlework in a courtier's chamber while listening to Hilton's *Scale*, as the Duchess of York's daily regimen specifies, one might be part of a group which read together by hearing together, in the traditional fashion common both to religious and lay lives. At the same time, other books make clear their function as private reading: Oxford, Bodleian Additional A.42, for instance, whose small size and humble materials reflect its personal use by a nun of Amesbury for meditation on the Rule.

This study's two subjects, then, are lives and networks. Examining the circumstances under which reading took place – not merely *what* was read – brings these two subjects together. Likewise, the movement of books inevitably illuminates the outlines of a particular community of readers, and such a view of reading coteries can provide a rich sense of what perusing a particular text meant culturally. Through this examination of the ownership and circulation of women's religious books I hope to offer a fuller and more revealing account of a female culture of reading and thus of women's intellectual and spiritual lives.

Introduction: Dinah's Story

Mandate to abbess and convent of Shaftesbury forbidding the nuns
to leave their house except for good cause, approved by the superior,
and in the company of senior nuns of proved character.

It has been reported that several nuns have often been wandering
outside the house in various places longer than is seemly and for
frivolous reason. The abbess and prioress are enjoined to consider
the punishment that overtook Dinah the daughter of Jacob for
yielding to the desire to go abroad, so that the bishop is not forced
to impose punishment himself [sent between September 26, 1411
and November 1412].

Register of Robert Hallum, Bishop of Salisbury 1407–17[1]

Not surprisingly, the punishment which overtook Dinah was rape. The
circumstances of her transgression may now be only vaguely recalled,
since the Genesis story (34:1–2) is not especially well known. Dinah
had gone out "to visit the women of that [Canaanite] region" or "to see
them."[2] Her subsequent violation was thus the direct consequence of
her desire for female companionship. The bishop's letter intends, of
course, a general caution against contact between female religious and
the secular world, but in recalling Dinah the letter may have in mind,
as well, the particular occasion of her downfall – female friendship. The
injunction surprises us in two ways: in its linkage of sexual danger with
women's meeting and also in its illustration of the closeness of female religious life to the world – particularly, as we will see, the world of women.

Perhaps in the scriptural account these two different translations of
the verb – to visit or to see – are responsible for the two different interpretive paths which the story takes, for indeed in the Middle Ages
Dinah's story was frequently invoked. In one tradition, which goes back

at least to John Chrysostom, Dinah appears as an example of the in-judicious use of the eyes. Following this tradition, in a famous passage which condemns Eve not for eating the apple but for looking at it, *Ancrene Wisse* comments, "all the misery that now is, and has been and ever shall be, all this arose through sight . . . The beginning and the root of all this misery was a light glance." Dinah's guilt is defined even more narrowly than Eve's. "Dinah's evil was not the result of her seeing Sichem . . . with whom she sinned, but the result of her allowing him to look upon her."[3] That is, even though Dinah was in fact raped, the author suggests that her guilt lay, first, in her own non-sexual gaze, and then in her willing exposure to the gaze of others.

In the other interpretation, the one Bishop Hallum invokes, Dinah's fault is not her gaze but her movement. Her rape occurs as the di-rect consequence of her wandering. This gloss occurs as early as Jerome, whose well-known letter to Eustochium warns: "Go not out from home, nor wish to behold the daughters of a strange country . . . Dinah went out and was ravished." As late as the last decade of the fifteenth cen-tury Bishop John Alcock of Ely repeated this reading, telling nuns that Dinah "wolde go forth among yonge people and soo was corrupte and rauysshed."[4] Here she serves as a caution to religious women toward whom, from the Carolingian period through the end of the Middle Ages, repeated commands enforcing strict claustration were directed.[5]

Dinah's story can sustain a third reading, however, one in which the focus is her relation with other women. We might look below the commentators' plausible formulation – contact with other women leads to more dangerous contact with men – to discern a substratum of un-acknowledged yet powerful unease with such female groupings. In this reading, the most telling aspect of Dinah's story might be the frequency of its reiteration. This cautionary re-use suggests not only that women continued their attempts to join the world outside with that inside the cloister, but also that they continued to see bonds forged between women as superseding the identifying constructions of lay and religious life.

PERMEABLE PARTITIONS

Medieval women's choices of state in life ranged along a spectrum whose extreme poles were represented by the wife and the nun. Episcopal emphasis on claustration may have had the effect of reducing further the options which lay between these two extremes, that is, of confining authorized forms of female religious life to a single model, the enclosed one.[6] Nevertheless Kaspar's Elm's work has shown how as early as the twelfth century contemporaries described a variety of groups as occupying a middle way between lay and religious states. These groups, which included male and female anchorites and hermits, hospital brothers and sisters, beguines, and religious confraternity members, he called semireligious.[7] John van Engen's masterful survey has made it possible to see how, between the thirteenth and fifteenth centuries, these marginal categories were defined, resisted, and, sometimes, legitimized.[8] Such states of life seem sometimes to admit more readily the possibility of individual construction by the women who preferred them. In late medieval England, women whose choices lay between the two poles might be vowesses – laywomen who had taken vows of chastity and who were most often, though not always, widows. Or they might be anchoresses, whose choice of an enclosed life could be made by either religious or laywomen. Female states in this central area on the spectrum lay close to one another and, often, close to that of religious women. For instance if a widow living with a community of nuns had her dwelling within the nunnery complex, participated in divine office, and wore the dark clothing and *barbe* customary for widows, the physical signs distinguishing her from the rest of the community would surely be minimal. This physical likeness between nun and vowess might in turn be taken as reflecting an underlying similarity in lay and religious women's formation.

The closeness of female secular and religious life is visible in a common spirituality which transcends state in life and which often presents only marginally differentiated ideals to secular and religious women: humility, obedience, some degree of physical enclosure. These ideals are supported as well by common texts, which were read both by laywomen and nuns.[9] Women's religious reading, and particularly the exchange of books which supported such reading, will be the subject of what follows. In order to see these social practices more clearly, however, we must raise a topic which at first may appear only distantly relevant: the narrative of religious women's enclosure.

The great historian of institutional religious life for women, Eileen Power, devotes one chapter in her *Medieval English Nunneries* to the relation of nuns with the world (it is titled "Fish Out of Water") and a second chapter to the encroachments of the world into the cloister. Jane Schulenburg has used B. Dolhagaray's terms to describe these states: active and passive cloister, respectively.[10] The relation of the two has not been much discussed, and whether historically one occurred without the other is unclear.

Power traces the former, the effort to enforce female claustration, beginning as early as Caesarius of Arles' (*c.* 470–543) rule for nuns, but she notes that the first general law on the subject which bound the whole church was Boniface VIII's bull *Periculoso* (1299). For the next two centuries and beyond, nuns who left their institutions to visit friends and family, or more broadly, to view life outside the cloister or to participate in it, were repeatedly reproved and disciplined, mostly by local episcopal authorities. Power comments pithily: "the constant repetition of the order that nuns should not leave their convents is the measure of its failure." She notes that the church's efforts here in fact added a fourth vow, claustration, to the three familiar promises of poverty, chastity, and obedience.[11] It has recently been observed that a Lateran decree of 1215 forbidding new women's orders had already effectively circumscribed the options available to women, and that the subsequent appearance of *Periculoso* effectively reshaped female religious life still further, privatizing it and ruling out active apostolates in the world such as the friars had initiated.[12] It may be, as Elizabeth Makowski has observed, that *Periculoso* represented an attempt to cordon off nuns from contemporary women's religious movements and, if this is so, we might hear an echo of Dinah's story once again in the effort to separate some women from other women.[13]

It is easy to see these strictures as attempts to deal with a central issue: enclosure. But the reciprocal nature of the commands – keeping nuns in and secular women (in particular) out – suggests that instead the issue might be called permeability, the degree to which secular culture influenced religious life. Episcopal injunctions constituted an effort to stiffen and strengthen the membrane which separated the institution from the world. Yet the later Middle Ages saw everywhere an increased interpenetration of these realms. Speaking of male Benedictine monks from the twelfth century on, Barbara Harvey says that, when they looked at the world outside the cloister, "they liked much of what they saw and paid it the compliment of imitation," and she goes on to specify the ways in which these monks' diet, housing, income, and movement in the world were similar to that of their lay contemporaries.[14]

Ilana Silber has described the Middle Ages as characterized by an ongoing negotiation for balance between religious and lay elements of society. Since monasticism was always in tension with the world, this interaction needed permanent regulation, and bishops' supervision of enclosure can be seen as part of this balancing effort.[15]

Recent work has emphasized the relation between English women's institutions and their local surroundings, stressing their interdependence and their intimate connections.[16] The degree of such closeness can be startling: for instance in 1500 the prioress of Dartford, the only house of Dominican nuns in England, was named as master of five neighborhood almshouses, together with the parish priest and churchwardens.[17]

In female lives, the reciprocal relation between cloister and world may have been shaped as much by secular women's introduction into nunneries as by nuns leaving their houses. That is, the important direction of flow may have been inward rather than outward.[18] Though nuns certainly continued through the fourteenth, fifteenth, and sixteenth centuries to leave their monasteries in order to visit "friends," as the injunctions say – male or female is never specified – the ways in which the world entered the cloister seem more varied and complex. The convent appears at the heart of a local network – a position at once immensely useful to its neighborhood (hence valued by locals) and immensely at odds with traditional notions of religious life (hence reprimanded by ordinaries). Sometimes this position must have made the nunnery the focus of conflict between the house's secular and ecclesiastical partisans. For instance at Ankerwyke in 1441, "the prioress did invite several outside folk from the neighborhood to this visitation at great cost to the house, saying to them, 'stand on my side in this time of visitation, for I do not want to resign.'"[19]

This picture of the nunnery emphasizes social centrality, rather than monastic isolation. In 1442 the prioress of Catesby complained:

> secular folk have often recourse to the nuns' chambers within the cloister, and talkings and junketings take place there without the knowledge of the Prioress . . . also the nuns do send out letters and

receive letters sent to them without the advice of the prioress . . . Also
the nuns do send out the serving-folk of the priory on their businesses
and do also receive the persons for whom they send and with whom
they hold parleyings and conversations.[20]

Sending and receiving, the nuns of Catesby were poised at the center of
what seems an actual model of social exchange. Catesby's prioress allows
us to imagine a number of overlapping local systems which converged
at the nunnery. Such social connections – with the neighborhood, or
parish, or farms – must have included, as one of the subsets, Catesby's
contacts with lay women. Nunneries in fact might be thought of as foci
for female interaction, as other institutions were for male meeting. Since
they were not members of choir schools, of university colleges, of law
courts, of military bands, both religious and laywomen found in female
houses a singular opportunity for proximity.

Episcopal reproofs give instances of such coming together and Power's
examples are well known: Lady Audeley with her "great abundance
of dogs" at Langley in 1441; Margaret Ingoldesby with her birds in
the dorter at Legbourne in the same year; Felmersham's wife "with her
whole household and other women of mature age" who gave bad example "by reason of their attire" at Godstow in 1432. Power's list of twenty-
five such injunctions against boarders at nunneries – mostly, though not
entirely female – she calls "only a few examples taken at random."[21]

The flattening of this secular–religious barrier took a particularly
female form in the lives of laywomen who chose to live in female
monasteries. This practice seems to have been widespread in the late
fifteenth and early sixteenth centuries. The "great house" at the London
minoresses and its lay tenants are well known, but, for instance,
Dartford had in 1521–22 a structure called "Nedeham Loggyng" which
had formerly been held by a "Margaret le Vere,"[22] and Carrow's three
surviving account rolls, for 1456, 1485, and 1528, show in the first two
years a named woman renting "a tenement in the monastery precinct."
In the last year the rolls register payments from "Amy late wife of
Thomas Aslak, gentleman, widow, for a tenement by the Granary let to
her for life," while the "Ankeressehous" was being used by the anchoress,
though it had recently been in farm to Dame Dorothy Curson, votary
(*votisse*, i.e. vowess), and a third tenement south of the priory gate had

been "late let to Dame Agnes Appleyerd widow."[23] Mentions of various other kinds of housing show that in the early sixteenth century Carrow had a considerable variety of lay residents, and that at a given time three or four of these might be women.

The political realities of such a life are illustrated in the papal permission which the widowed Elizabeth, Duchess of Norfolk, received. Though she was not vowed, the duchess had earlier received papal consent "in order to live more quietly and to win salvation, to dwell with two or three upright women" at the London minoresses. Now, on August 8, 1506, she received a response to a second request:

> Her recent petition stated that she, now infirm and worn out with age, dwells in the said monastery in an honourable place and separated from the abbess and nuns, without having taken the habit or having made regular profession; that from time to time she requires the counsel of prudent persons for her arduous business and affairs, and a servant especially at table and for writing her business, and also other women. At her supplication, the pope, amplifying his former letter, hereby grants her license and faculty that she may . . . cause men of gravity to attend her . . . that she may have as honourable secular servants one man to serve at table and prepare her food and another to write, and in addition to those women whom she has at present with her, another three or four upright women or maid-servants – since as she alleges no disturbance is caused by them to the nuns – and, as often as the necessity arises, three or four priests, secular or religious, by whose counsel and celebration of divine offices she may receive what pertains to her salvation, and that she may have extensions made, by her industry and outlay or that of her benefactors, to the monastery's garden and ambulatory, which as she alleges is small and rather restricted for the abbess and nuns, extensions, that is, as well in the construction of buildings for the use of the abbess and nuns as in breadth, length and space for walking.[24]

Those overlapping social structures which were perceptible at Catesby here threaten collision. For the abbey, the possibilities both of loss and gain were considerable: a troubling increase of five or six persons as members of the duchess' permanent staff (plus others hired from time to time), and on the other hand the useful building construction which the duchess' wealth could provide and which would outlast her presence.

The attempt to reconcile physically these two forms of female life is nowhere more visible.

The burdens for the house's superior of long-term lay residence are further made clear in the 1530 will of Elizabeth Yaxley, who had been living at Carrow. Asking the prioress to serve as her will's supervisor, Yaxley offers her a stipend of 40 shillings, but delegates to her "the deliverance of all my goods bequeathed and sold," asks her to see that Yaxley's servants have what she bequeathed them "or rather more" shortly after her death, and arranges for her servants' boarding with the prioress a month before

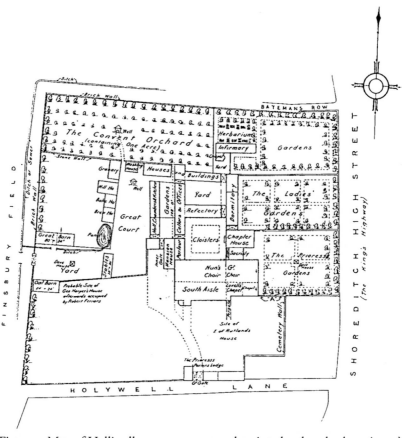

Figure 1 Map of Halliwell nunnery, *c*. 1544, showing the church, the prioress' gardens, two wells, and other features of the indenture between Alice Hampton and Halliwell. Reproduced from London County Council, *Survey of London. Vol. VIII: The Parish of St. Leonard Shoreditch* (London, 1922), plate 83.

her death. Most tellingly, Yaxley requests the prioress to provide a closet within the house "to lay in all such moveables as shall remain ... unto the time they may conveniently be sold."[25] All of these services, though compensated, constitute a substantial administrative burden.

Equally graphic, but more satisfactorily resolved, is the 1492 indenture between vowess Alice Hampton and Elizabeth Prudde, prioress of London's Halliwell.[26] Its detailed spatial arrangements for the vowess' life within the monastery foresee and negotiate possible conflict. In exchange for four pounds of pepper yearly the vowess was to have an entry or passage at the west end of the church which abutted onto the common entry; two parcels of void ground; and a little storehouse adjoining the monastery church and containing two chambers ($18'8\frac{1}{2}''$ × $10'1''$). Here presumably she was to live, since later we are told Dame Alice "shall doo make oute of the Stone-wall atte westende" [of the church] which constitutes "a *particion* betwene" the church and one of Dame Alice's chambers, a "wyndowe therat to here masse and to see the sacrament at an Awter in the body of the said Church." She was to have a door into the garden made with lock and key so she and her servants could "walke and take their pleas*ur*," and she was allowed water for cooking and washing from the prioress' well. (For a reconstruction of Halliwell's grounds see Figure 1). Here a harmonious coexistence between lay and religious forms of life seems viable due to the care with which shared space has been arranged.

CHANNELS OF CONNECTION

John Tillotson has recently examined the visitation records of twenty-five Yorkshire female houses, made in the years immediately after *Periculoso* (1300–40), in order to assess the papal document's impact on English practice. He suggests that the records show a somewhat disorderly situation which was improved by episcopal attention. Nevertheless, the effort at strict enclosure failed, the English bishops being reduced merely to regularizing existing practice (a reading confirmed by Power's many examples extending well into the sixteenth century). Tillotson attributes this limited success to the imposition of an ideal judged impracticable not only by the nuns themselves but by their society, which expected and desired the services they provided.[27]

As often with historical records, it is documents of control which provide the major evidence, and episcopal injunctions have illustrated the frequency with which laywomen visited and even lived at nuns' houses. But such contacts demonstrate only one form in which the tenacity of women's connections manifested itself. A different sort of record can reveal the other side of the coin. In household accounts, the social contacts between lay and religious women, and in particular their exchange of food, offer a more neutral testimony to women's ties than do the strictures of ordinaries.

Female accounts survive both before and after the publication of *Periculoso* in 1299 – that is, during both a freer and a more regulated period in religious women's lives. Some of these examples suggest particular friendship, while others testify to the power of family or regional connections, the necessary soil in which friendships might flourish. Describing the relation between religious institutions and the surrounding countryside, Colin Richmond says, "Most houses were at home in the world in ways which their founders and early benefactors could not have foreseen . . . their religious function was so integrated with other aspects of their existence that they had become veritably part of their environment."[28] Such integration is visible in the mid-thirteenth century when Eleanor, wife of Simon de Montfort, entertained several nuns of Wintney (Hampshire) at her residence at Odiham. Wintney's prioress, whose name is not known, visited separately; the countess later sent her four gallons of wine. Domestic closeness is illustrated by the countess' payment of ten shillings to the nuns for working a cape which she gave her chaplain. The Wintney nuns visited in March; in April the countess entertained Ida, prioress of Amesbury, for four days and when she left gave her three gallons of wine. The accounts show, as well, that the countess wrote to prioress Ida at Amesbury and that she received a messenger from her at least once.[29] Such a variety of contacts within the space of only six months (February to August 1265) testifies to a rich interchange between lay women and nuns.

Other examples can be cited: thirty years later in 1297 Joanna de Valence, Countess of Pembroke, entertained the prioress of Aconbury at Goodrich Castle (Herefordshire). She stayed for about three weeks, and at her February departure was given a salmon. She returned on the Sunday after Easter, and again on a Sunday in May; the accounts' editor refers to her as the countess' friend, perhaps because of her frequent visits.[30]

Extensive accounts survive for the household of Elizabeth de Burgh, Countess of Clare. In the places where she stayed she frequently gave hospitality to the local religious communities, such as the prioress and convent of Usk (Monmouthshire) in 1349. Toward the end of her life the countess lived within the precinct of the London minoresses, whom she regularly entertained.[31] In the summer of 1421 the prioress of the Benedictine nunnery of Westwood (Worcester), perhaps Isabella Russell, was the guest of Elizabeth Berkeley, wife of Richard Beauchamp, Earl of Warwick, in their household at Salwarpe.[32]

A letter from Margaret of Anjou provides an unusual example of lay female intervention in the affairs of a religious house. Written to the subprioress and the master of Nuneaton (Warwickshire), a Fontevrault double house, the letter recommends Dame Maud Everygham as prioress. The letter, though undated, was probably written in the late 1440s; Maud Everygham's name occurs in 1448 as prioress, though she was deposed *c.* 1465.[33]

Gifts of food were regularly passed between lay and religious women. In 1385–86 the prioress of Bungay (Suffolk), Katherine de Montacute, sent to Margaret of Brotherton for her hospice at Framlingham Castle twenty-one partridges, plus twelve ducks and twelve teals, while the countess sent the abbess a pipe of red wine.[34] In the middle of the fifteenth century Isabel, Lady Morley, a widow and the daughter of Michael de la Pole, Duke of Suffolk, was living with her son-in-law John Hastings at Norwich. Her accounts show that in 1463–64 she purchased 2,000 oysters, which she sent to the college of secular priests at St. Mary in the Fields and to the nuns of Carrow.[35] The gift is very much the product of local connection (her will is full of other Norwich bequests).[36] Besides this tie with Norwich's Carrow, Lady Morley was connected with another female house, Barking (Essex) through her sister, Abbess Katherine de la Pole (d. 1473), to whom she left ten marks in her will. Such multiple bonds with more than one nunnery were the common consequence of diverse family and regional ties. In fact Katherine and Isabel's widowed mother had taken the veil at a third nunnery, the Suffolk house of Bruisyard, where she had lived with the child Katherine.[37] Carrow, Barking, Bruisyard, thus each represented different versions of the conventual milieu with which this mother and her daughters were thoroughly familiar.

In the early sixteenth century further gifts between laywomen and nuns appear in the royal accounts: in 1502 Elizabeth of York received rosewater from the abbess of the London minoresses and in 1536 Princess Mary was sent puddings from Syon.[38] The conversational tone of the letters which the French nun Anthoinette de Saveuses sent to Honor Lisle while the latter lived in Calais illustrates their intimacy. When Lady Lisle believed, wrongly, that she was pregnant, the nun sent her a precious piece of medicinal unicorn horn, and Honor's commissions of conventual needlework (caps and baby dresses) recall Eleanor de Montfort and the nuns of Wintney three centuries earlier.[39]

This closeness between female lay and religious life, visible in household accounts, has recently been invoked by Roberta Gilchrist in considering the architecture of women's religious houses. She suggests that, since nunneries were often established near villages and shared their churches with parish congregations, the number of seculars who visited women's houses must always have been large. It may even be that the explicit purpose of female houses was interaction with the local community. Among the various consequences of this exchange between the world and the (female) cloister, was the breakdown of female religious communities into the small groups or households so frequently corrected at episcopal visitations. This development gives further evidence of the closeness of female lay and religious lives, since Gilchrist sees nuns as here imitating a secular domestic model.[40]

The social level represented by nuns has been variously assessed; some work suggests that, rather than constituting "an important part of the social world of the nobility,"[41] by the fifteenth century nunneries more frequently drew their membership from gentry families or considerably lower.[42] Nonetheless, a nunnery certainly had connections at multiple social levels, with local and regional ties more important than class ones. Jonathan Hughes refers to "the close social interaction between the lay nobility and the nunneries of Yorkshire and Lincolnshire," illustrated by the attendance of nuns at lay funerals and by the bequests of laywomen to their friends in religious life – for instance the furred mantle which Margaret Stapilton, a vowess at Clementhorpe in the suburbs of York, gave to Isabel Vavasour, a nun of Sinningthwaite, just west of the city.[43]

Sometimes bequests to nunneries of domestic necessities, either linen or plate, like the exchanges of food mentioned earlier, suggest that the imperatives of household management transcended considerations of lay or religious state. In the middle of the fifteenth century Joan Newmarch, a well-off widow who had served the Countess of Warwick and who lived in London's St. Bartholomew Hospital enclosure, left a pair of sheets to Christine St. Nicholas, the abbess of the London minoresses. Each of these friends owned books. Joan Newmarch's name is written in a manuscript of *Pricking of Love* and Hilton's *Mixed Life* which is associated with the Dominican nuns of Dartford. The context suggests she was a benefactor of that women's house. Abbess St. Nicholas owned one of four surviving manuscripts of *Doctrine of the Heart* which she gave to the minoresses at her death.[44] Nevertheless the gift that memorializes the friendship of the two bookowning women is domestic, not devotional, and the simultaneous existence of these two preoccupations probably characterizes other female friendships as well.

In addition to horizontal networks in which we see books exchanged between friends, vertical relationships existed too between women. Teaching and learning must have been, at least informally, part of life in religious community, as the devotional text written by one Syon nun for another demonstrates ("myn sustir priei my lord god . . . make me a good woman").[45] That nuns instructed laywomen as well is suggested by a Marian miracle found in another Syon manuscript. The story concerns a nun who taught her cousin, a laywoman in her charge, to say the Ave by counting on her knuckles. When the cousin died, the weeping nun received a vision of the Virgin accompanied by "the wenche . . . that was in my keping, whome y taught to haylse [praise] the by the Juncturis of her hondis." Her knuckles were now covered with jewels.[46]

Frequently in women's monasteries such ties of kinship existed alongside the bonds of religious life. Sometimes these conflicted. When at Catesby nunnery in 1442 the community complained that the prioress' mother "rules almost the whole house," it might seem that the reality of family loyalties superseded those of religious community. At other times the language of religious life dominates that of family connection, as in the 1520 will of Beatrice Tynggelden who was living at Barking as a laywoman while her sister Elizabeth Grene was abbess there, and who speaks of "my lady my syster," invoking both religious and natal relationships. Beatrice twice describes her quasi-religious state, asking to be buried "aboughte the Shryne where it shall please my lady abbes to assigne hit / to whoe I submitte my selfe vnto here obbedience as oone off here systers."[47]

Wills like Beatrice's can illustrate the economic advantage which lay female presence gave to monasteries, but just occasionally it is possible to see the monetary support that laywomen throughout their lives provided for nuns' houses. Because in her will Elizabeth Clere, an East Anglian friend of Agnes Paston's, forgave the sum of £5 owed her by Bungay nunnery, we realize that testamentary bequests of money may represent only the final element in a lifetime of connection and support.[48]

Slippage between societal categories such as religious and lay is nowhere more clearly illustrated than in the liminal vocation which the vowed woman chose,[49] one which contained elements from both lay and religious life. Despite having taken a public vow as nuns did, such a woman remained formally lay. She retained control of what were often substantial economic resources and had freedom to come and go as she liked. Sometimes she simply continued a domestic life in her own home. Sometimes she lived with a community of nuns after her husband's death, as Susan Kyngeston did at Syon from 1514 to the Dissolution.

The literature of counsel for widows, the larger group within which vowesses constituted one category,[50] reveals the restrictions of a vocation conceived as demanding and constrained. For instance in a fifteenth-century miscellany which contains some Wycliffite material, Oxford, MS Bodley 938, a short, unique text addressed to a widow describes a rigorous life which has much in common with that of the nun. The widow is enjoined to live "in holi & deuoute preiers & in abstinence, not oonli abstenyng her self fro alle lusti & vnmesurabale metis & drynkis but also fro al wordli welþe and fleschli daliance" (fol. 266).

Do such injunctions to widows and vowesses represent an effort to conform secular women's lives to a model nearer that of religious women? Or does this literature for widows, together with episcopal injunctions aimed at correcting nuns' behavior, attempt to impose on *both* secular and religious women a common pattern of behavior? Outside marriage this pattern, for both lay and religious women, would be remarkably similar: it is sexually abstinent and it values enclosure, whether in home or cloister. The anchoress's life constitutes the most radical formulation of this ideal: physical stability, enclosure, indeed semi-invisibility, here attain a most elevated expression.

The female behavior which is admonished, on the other hand, is not abstinent and – more relevant for our purposes – it continually crosses physical boundaries, while it elides taxonomic ones. Wandering nuns, on the one hand, and secular women sleeping in the monastery's dorter, on the other – nuns who behaved like seculars and laywomen who temporarily comprised part of a community – demonstrate the ease with which female lives could move from one definition to another. Such facile gliding between categories seems to require recognition of female life states as often contiguous. The modern divide between religious and lay experience may conceal from us the earlier opportunities for shifts and exchanges between these two.[51]

The presence of such liminal women, both in female religious houses and in the secular world, meant that women's religious life was never crisply outlined. Rather it carried about it a nimbus of radiating, less-firmly defined forms. Well after such possibilities had vanished, in the seventeenth century John Aubrey recalled how such a constellation of women might have looked. Describing the members of the female house of Kington St. Michael (Wiltshire) at their work in the field, Aubrey's old shepherd tells how he had seen this crowd of women:

> come forth into the nymph-hay with their rocks and wheels to spin, and with their sewing work. He would say that he had told three-score and ten, but of nuns there were not so many, but in all, with lay sisters and widows, old maids and young girls, there might be such a number.[52]

SHE DESIRED A BOOKE OF YOU

Aubrey's pleasing vignette confirms our sense of the variety of female lives and of their juxtapositions. This book attempts to illuminate some of the ways in which such lives were constructed, and to examine the written texts which such women shared. Four states seem often to correlate with religious bookowning: widowed laywoman, anchoress, vowess, nun. Of the women whose lives are illustrated here, Margaret Purdans was a widow, Katherine Manne an anchoress, Margery de Nerford a vowess, Elizabeth Throckmorton a nun, while the Fettyplace sisters fall into the latter two categories.

As the categories themselves seem often to melt into one another, so movement among these states may have been a more familiar phenomenon for medieval women than for modern ones. Women were more likely to be widowed than were men, since they were often younger than their spouses. English male wills which mention a surviving widow range from a low of 53 percent to a high of 82 percent in two different samplings.[53] These wills span the thirteenth to the fifteenth centuries, suggesting that widows were always more numerous than widowers.

Indeed, the option of remarriage appears to have been less frequently chosen by women than by men.[54] If that is so, the question of a form of life alternative to marriage would have been more urgent for widowed women than for widowed men. One of the reasons for St. Anne's great popularity in the late Middle Ages, for instance, may have been that the legendary reconstruction of her life included marriage to three different men, the birth of a child by each husband, and finally vowed chastity. Her example thus supported and legitimized the dramatic changes of ordinary life. John Mirk says, "And soo, when scho had getyn her iii chyldyrne yn þe worschip of þe Trinite, scho wold haue no mor. But aftyr all her lyue scho ȝaf her to chastyte and to holynes."[55] Similarly, Osbern Bokenham's fifteenth-century life of St. Elizabeth of Hungary, written for his married contemporary Lady Elizabeth de Vere, remarks on this saint's triumphant passage through seven different life states:

> Seuene statys wych she was yn vnderstonde be moun:
> As maydenhede, maryage, & also wydewede,
> Actyf & contemplatyf, þe relygyoun;
> The seuente, where she now dwellyth, ys heuenly regyoun.[56]
> (9517–20)

Such exemplary role-shifts can be found in other female saints' lives in the later Middle Ages. St Etheldreda, whose iconic meaning from the tenth to the thirteenth century had been variously defined,[57] in the fifteenth century may have offered women a pattern of successive self-transformation. Four panels probably executed in 1455 by Robert Pygot as part of the Ely shrine of St. Etheldreda show paradigmatic moments of transition from the saint's life: her marriage, her separation from her

Figure 2 St. Etheldreda's stages of life. Panel paintings, probably from the retable of St. Etheldreda's shrine at Ely *c.* 1455, probably by Robert Pygot, painter of Bury St. Edmunds, showing the marriage of Etheldreda to Egfrid, King of Northumbria in 660; Etheldreda taking leave of Egfrid to enter a nunnery; Etheldreda building her church at Ely; the translation of Etheldreda's body to a stone coffin in 695. Each panel: $3'10 \frac{1}{2}'' \times 1'9''$.

husband to enter a convent, her subsequent building initiatives, and the translation of her body (Figure 2).[58]

In whatever state in life they found themselves, women read the texts of spiritual formation which represented the period's most popular books. Susan Cavanaugh's survey of privately owned books mentioned in wills shows that about half the book bequests listed are liturgical and devotional ones.[59] Describing the books in Norwich lay wills between 1370 and 1532, Norman Tanner says, "most of them were standard liturgical books, chiefly missals, breviaries, primers, and psalters."[60] Of course these were the books most likely to be willed because of their spiritual and economic value. Such books, however, predominated in life as well. Speaking of northern reading, Jo Ann Moran comments: "the literature that the student of today usually associates with late medieval England [*Piers Plowman*, Chaucer, Gower, even romances] was in fact the preserve of a very few . . . in marked contrast to the devotional and liturgical literature which circulated widely among almost all the classes of clergy and laity in all parts of the diocese."[61]

The ways in which such texts found their new audience, as traditional monastic spiritual reading (*lectio divina*) was modified for vernacular readers, have received considerable attention. Their modifications could be systemic ones, changes in existing schemes of textual arrangement and the development of new ones, in order to make the work more accessible, for instance.[62] Equally important, texts might be explicitly recommended to a new readership. P. S. Jolliffe pointed out that, in the manuscript which the anchorite John Lacy wrote between 1407 and 1435, he says of Jerome's letter to Demetriade on vowed chastity: "And ȝe mowe vndirstonde & fynde in þis pistull confort & turnynge to all oþer woo þat wol take intente and heed to þe vndurstondinge þerof, be he religius or seculer, wedded man or woman or songul, or in what þe gree he stondit in."[63] Later in the century, probably between 1489 and 1494, a manuscript of the *Myrrour of Recluses* was owned by the chaplain of William Browne, a wealthy merchant of the staple who founded an almshouse in Stamford. The chaplain gave this anchoritic text to the almshouse (presumably for reading by its inhabitants), where a contemporary hand has noted that it is "a good boke ffor holy men or wemen."[64] It has been suggested, in fact, that laypersons now took a place in the educational hierarchy similar to that which had long been occupied by nuns, "and this partly explains the extensive links and literary exchanges between [them]."[65] This shift in reception provides a background for the present study, though its interest in these "links and literary exchanges" is often specifically object-centered: the physical circulation of devotional books from hand to (female) hand.

How exactly did it take place? Sometimes, apparently, in the homeliest of ways: one got books by asking one's family for them. Between *c.* 1450 and 1455 Katherine Chadderton wrote to her brother George Plumpton, a retired priest, requesting a very ordinary book, the common currency of everyday reading, for her daughter. Then she wrote again:

> I trow, & so doth my daughter, that ye be desp[l]eased, denyeing that [disapproving of] my writing afore, because she desired a booke of you, and as ever I be saved, she praied me write for either salter or primmer . . . But I had knowne ye wold haue bene despleased, I wold not haue writt, for as much as I haue speuled [?annoyed] my best brother.[66]

For both men and women the exchange of books in a manuscript culture depended heavily upon whom one knew. Felicity Riddy has pointed out that "when the possibility of owning a text depended on procuring an exemplar for copying, the personal relationships between members of the reading public themselves must to a large extent have formed the routes along which knowledge of particular works travelled."[67] The density of these personal connections means that, even though the book may not say it, "every name in or on a book has an implicit 'et amicorum' after it [and] the community around the named owner must be comprehended."[68]

This book tries to reconstruct such a social context for female reading. As Katherine Chadderton's letter demonstrates, family connections were important in the movement of women's books, but the human "routes" which Riddy speaks of along which books travelled were diverse. Hence the strong emphasis, in what follows, not only on relationships of blood, but on religious ties, and especially on female friendships.

To a surprising degree, in fact, examining women's religious book use has made it possible to view a subject which has not received much notice: female networks and female connection, particularly across the divide of secular and religious life. Though the influential presence of male friends is visible in several of the narratives that follow, nevertheless the social and intellectual ties between women that Dinah sought are the subject of this book.[69] While all these women sustained exchanges with men which were of central importance to them, with the exception of Katherine Manne all had, as well, female connections which we might judge of equal or greater significance. Christine de Pizan tells the story of the Roman orator's daughter Hortensia who, educated by her father in the quintessentially male arts of oratory and rhetoric, became entirely his equal through her apprenticeship in this *techné*.[70] Like Hortensia, the women in this book participate to various degrees in a male tradition of learning – but they remain Dinah's daughters as well.

I

Ownership and transmission of books:
women's religious communities

In the 1460s or 1470s the abbess of the London minoresses, Elizabeth Horwode, acquired a volume containing three texts of Walter Hilton's authorship. An inscription, probably somewhat later than the book's purchase, allows us to see with unusual fullness the way in which the abbess' community constructed the act of reading. On the verso of the volume's last leaf is written:

> Dame Elyzabeth Horwode Abbas of the Menoresse off London to her gostle Comfforthe bow3th thys boke hyt to Remayne to the Vse off þe Systerres of þe sayde place to pray for þe yeuer & For þe sowles off hyr Fader & her moder Thomas Horwode & Beatryxe & þe sowle off Mayster Robert Alderton[1]

These words place reading firmly within a network of reciprocity. Acquisition of the book is itself meritorious, a preliminary to virtuous reading, and that preparatory act will radiate its benefits backward in time to the abbess' parents and forward to future members of her house. Book purchase is placed in a context doubly familial: both the abbess' natal family and her religious one are invoked in a way which makes it impossible to view reading as individual work. Indeed the inscription, coming as it does a little later than Abbess Horwode's acquisition of the book, and probably written by someone else, is itself a work of *pietas* which sets out the house's past for those still to come. This vision links the buyer, her personal and her institutional history, and the reading of multitudes of other women, in a network of "common profit." Though this rubric has been applied to a small group of manuscripts intended for broad circulation, it might with equal accuracy describe Elizabeth Horwode's book, and indeed many other volumes whose owners likewise make clear, through their statements in wills and their inscriptions in books, their understanding of reading as an element in spiritual obligation toward others.

The arrangement which Abbess Horwode made – to commemorate the souls of the dead and simultaneously to provide for the spiritual progress of the living – was one of the many social consequences produced by belief in purgatory. This doctrine has been described as a "system of solidarity between the living and the dead [which] instituted an unending circular flow."[2] Arrangements for book ownership and circulation provided one way in which that solidarity could be reinforced, and the forms which such arrangements took were various. Abbess Horwode's is only one of many such books, given in exchange for prayers to all sorts of institutional libraries: Oxford and Cambridge colleges as well as male and female monasteries.[3] Bell has provided other examples from women's institutions: for instance, a thirteenth-century psalter was given to Goring, "ut ipse orent . . . in uita quam in morte" for Robert and Joan Heryard.[4]

Perhaps, however, Abbess Horwode's gift to her monastery had something to do with more recent currents as well. Other schemes for transmission of books among a variety of owners – and hence for multiplication of prayers – have been traced by Wendy Scase. She describes arrangements to provide books for secular priests in particular need of them, books for laity in danger of heretical contamination, and books for a less firmly specified audience which included lay persons (the common profit books).[5] So many forms of book transmission suggest that systematized book exchange was by the mid-fifteenth century a widespread practice, established through mechanisms which were becoming more and more common – or at least more and more visible to us. Abbess Horwode's purchase, coming as it did about the same time as similar efforts in other *milieux*, may be considered part of this development of structures for book transmission which was making books more accessible to newer audiences, including women. But the abbess' initiative also reflects well-established traditions: the Franciscan interest in books and more generally the monastic practice of institutional book acquisition.

Indeed, it is this institutional tradition, to which the minoress inscription testifies, which provides substantial evidence for women's reading.[6] Institutions' power of endurance is so much greater than that of individuals that it is here, within a communal female culture, that we may ask first about women's intellectual and spiritual lives. In the chapters which follow this one, we will see that even women who were formally lay, like anchoresses or vowesses, were often connected physically with women's religious houses, and we may judge the forms of female secular and religious life to have been mutually influential. Thus exploration of women's reading finds a convenient starting place in the record of institutional book holding – that is, first, in the history of religious women's houses, then of their libraries, and finally of female networks of exchange, based on books' inscriptions.

WOMEN'S HOUSES: AN OVERVIEW

Female communities were, throughout their history, fewer, poorer, and smaller than male religious houses. The degree to which all three of these descriptive adjectives can be applied is perhaps surprising. Based on the poll tax of 1377, J. C. Russell estimated that in 1377–81, the immediate pre-plague era, there were in England 2,054 nuns to 8,564 male religious, a ratio of about one to four. This ratio changed only slightly at the Dissolution (1530–40), when the number of nuns was 1,576, of male religious 6,740. Russell comments on his figures: "The opportunities for women in religious life were not great . . . Yet the number of nuns seems amazingly small."[7] The estimates of R. Neville Hadcock are not very different. He suggested that the total number of male religious during the period from 1350 to 1534 ranged between nine and ten thousand. During these years the number of nuns remained fairly constant at about two thousand – a ratio of roughly one female to four and a half or five male religious.[8] If we were to add the large number of male secular clergy, the disparity between men and women religious would be still wider. It has recently been estimated that in Chaucer's period, given the immense variety of male forms of celibate life, "the celibate male population must have outnumbered nuns by, probably, 20 to 1 or more: say 40,000 men to fewer than 2,000 women."[9]

The number of women's houses, like the number of nuns, was also small: in 1922 Eileen Power called the number 138.[10] Later Hadcock agreed, positing 136–37 houses during the years 1534–40, or about 16.5 percent of the total number.[11]

Assessment of these houses' wealth is possible only sporadically before the Dissolution, but the survey of church resources ordered in 1535, the Valor Ecclesiasticus, is revealing. Summarizing this information, John Tillotson points out that "two-thirds of all nunneries had gross incomes of less than £100 a year; whilst 39, more than a third of the total for which we have figures, enjoyed gross revenues of under £50 a year."[12] Tillotson's comparison of male and female Benedictine institutions' income underlines the disparity between comfortable monks and poor nuns. In the 1535 survey 68 percent of Benedictine women's houses had incomes below £100 yearly, while 4 percent had incomes over £400. By comparison, only 25 percent of male houses had incomes under £100 yearly. The more surprising information, however, comes from the other end of the scale: "More than half the male houses had revenues exceeding £400 a year; 21 had over £1,000; and the incomes of the six wealthiest exceeded £2,000 a year. Indeed these last six houses actually owned lands and rents to an annual value *in excess of all English nunneries put together*" (italics in original).[13]

Finally, the number of nuns at a typical women's house was not large. One authority refers to "the usual twelve nuns under a prioress."[14] At the Dissolution almost half had a population under ten, and all but thirteen had less than twenty members. Some female houses stood out from the rest. Power's listing of the most notable of these would still receive general assent: "the old established abbeys of Wessex: Shaftesbury, Wilton, St. Mary's Winchester, Romsey and Wherwell, which together with Barking in Essex were all of Anglo-Saxon foundation"; Dartford (Kent), the only English Dominican house for women, founded by Edward III (1327–43); and Syon, the only Bridgettine house, founded about 1415.[15] To these might be added the Franciscan house of Denny in Cambridgeshire, the London minoresses, and perhaps Carrow and Campsey in East Anglia, all notable for a developed spirituality, all possessed of surviving books. The correlation of wealth, size, and influence is inescapable. For the most part it is at such advantaged female houses that the record of bookowning and reading can be traced.

WOMEN'S LIBRARIES: A SURVEY

We might begin then by looking at evidence for religious women's libraries. All religious houses, no matter how small and poor, possessed some service books. Such a collection is illustrated by a 1450 inventory from Easebourne, Sussex, a house of Benedictine nuns which can never have had more than ten members, and in the early sixteenth century had at various times a population of six and of eight. Thus its collection of twenty-four books is an impressive one. With the exception of one French bible, however, all of the books possessed by this female house – missals, portases, antiphoners, a troparium, a book of collects, and so on – were connected with performance of the liturgy, perhaps because Easebourne shared its church with the local parish.[16] While we cannot underestimate the liturgy's power as an instructive force, it is extra-liturgical reading on which this inquiry will focus. Whether a female house possessed a collection of non-service books extensive enough to be termed a library must have depended upon several factors – the house's date of foundation, its wealth, its characteristic spirituality, for instance. It is not surprising, then, that the evidence for substantial collections comes from the largest and best-known women's houses.

The Barking ordinal's account of book distribution within that community on the first Monday of Lent is well known because its physical circumstances are so graphically described. (The Benedictine Rule says merely that at the opening of Lent, community members are to receive a book from the library which they must read from beginning to end.[17]) On the chapter house floor the Barking librarian spread a carpet and placed on it all the books from the book cupboard (the word used is singular, *armario*, which might signify "chest" as well as book-case or cupboard).[18] She then read each nun's name aloud, together with the name of her borrowed book from the previous year and, if the sister had finished the book she placed it on the carpet with the others.[19] It has not been previously noted that since the ordinal says the Barking community numbered about fifty in these first years of the fifteenth century, the abbey must have had a book collection at least that large.[20]

Among Barking's obedientiaries, besides a librarian, were two *circuitrices*, also specified by the Rule. Dame Laurentia McLachlan says that their duties were "to go about (*circumeant*) the monastery at times appointed for reading and see that all were engaged in that duty."[21] They were warned neither to spare a defaulter nor to accuse any without just cause.

Another text which points both to the existence of a library and to the care of books in a female house has recently been published:

> Ore dunke soit eschewe of ech and of alle, and nameliche of these younge ladies. That thei be nougt negligent for to leue here bokes to hem assigned, behynde hem in the quer, neyther in cloystre; nether leue here bokes open other vnclosed, ne withoute kepinge, neither kitte out of no book leef, ne quaier, neyther write therinne; neyther put out withoute leue, neyther lene no book out of the place, ho so vnwitinge or [*sic*] his negligence or mysgouernaunce lest or alieneth. Bote al so clene and enter that thei ben kept, and in same numbre and in the same stat, or in bettre, yif it may, that thei be yolde vp agen into the librarie, as thei were afore in yer resseyued. Yif there is eny agens these poyns that had trespassed, of that he be in chapitele changeled [*sic*] and corrected.[22]

The piece is appended to a Middle English translation of the Benedictine rule for nuns, made from French (Washington D.C., Library of Congress MS Faye-Bond 4). Its language locates it in Essex, near Hatfield Broad Oak, the home of a Benedictine male house. The verse colophon says its scribe was a Benedictine, male or female, commissioned by a nun of the same order who might have been Abbess Sibyl de Felton of Barking (1394–1419) or the unknown prioress of the Essex house of Castle Hedingham, a sister foundation to Hatfield. A marginal drawing of a nun's head and armorial, perhaps Lucy de Vere, Hedingham's foundress, together with a bird carrying another shield in its beak, provide tantalizing clues to the manuscript's provenance (Figure 3).[23]

Latin and French versions of these strictures on the care of books are found in the Barking ordinal also, though it seems that this English version is not derived from those appearances.[24] Like the ordinal, however, this manuscript seems to be the product of a female superior's wish to make texts of governance available to her nuns – in English, rather than in the ordinal's Latin or French. What is most significant about the "care of books" text is its incorporation in two manuscripts written especially for a female house or houses, contexts in which strictures on care of

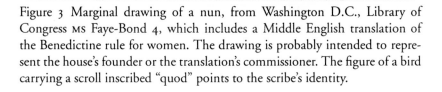

Figure 3 Marginal drawing of a nun, from Washington D.C., Library of Congress MS Faye-Bond 4, which includes a Middle English translation of the Benedictine rule for women. The drawing is probably intended to represent the house's founder or the translation's commissioner. The figure of a bird carrying a scroll inscribed "quod" points to the scribe's identity.

books were thought appropriate. It seems unlikely, in fact, that these two efforts to supply documents of rule for a female community could have proceeded unknown to each other, since they were so closely joined in time and place. Ms Faye-Bond 4 may also be from Barking, but if it is not, we might speculate about the loan of manuscript exemplars between two female Essex houses, Barking and Hedingham.

At Syon, too, we can be confident that a women's library existed, with its own librarian, in addition to the brothers' great collection of over 1,400 volumes. A 1482 contract made by Syon's abbess with a bookbinder, Thomas Baille, refers to "ye kepar of ye brethrenes librarie [and] ye kepar of oure ye sistrenes librarie."[25] To the explicit mention of Barking's librarian at the beginning of the fifteenth century and Syon's at the century's end we may add the visitation account of St. Mary's Winchester in 1501, where librarian Elia Pitte is named.[26]

Additional evidence for nuns' libraries comes from the *Registrum Angliae*, a union catalogue of monastic books in England, Scotland, and Wales which the Oxford Franciscans compiled on the basis of site visits in the early fourteenth century.[27] For St. Mary Winchester the *Registrum* reports a library of thirty-nine titles. The other Hampshire female houses of Wherwell and Romsey have been included in the survey by being assigned identifying numbers – hence presumably the compilers understood them to possess libraries – but were never reported.

So far evidence of reading has come from sources outside of the books. By contrast Neil Ker's recuperative work and its continuation by Andrew Watson bring together the surviving monastic books themselves as witnesses to their ownership.[28] In identifying extant books as monastic holdings, this research makes it possible to speak with some certainty about particular libraries.

Internal evidence of an institutional collection takes two forms: press-marks and *ex libris* inscriptions. Pressmarks, the signs of a book's place among other books, provide the volume's class and its shelf letter. They seem not to have been in general use until the fourteenth century.[29] David Bell notes three examples in nuns' books, one from Barking (B. 3) and two from Campsey (O.E. 94; D.D. 141).[30] To these may be added another Campsey book, which carries the notation C 32 – perhaps a pressmark – at the top of the second folio in an early sixteenth-century hand (Cambridge, Corpus Christi College MS 268).

Bell has found evidence of *ex libris* inscriptions in fifteen volumes from nuns' houses.[31] Most are fifteenth-century notations, except for two thirteenth-century examples from Barking and two fourteenth-century ones, from Campsey and Nuneaton. Again, Campsey is distinctive: Ker noted the presence of "a regular form in French, 'Cest livre est a covent de Campisse' "[32]; it occurs in three books. The remaining inscriptions are one-of-a-kind, though some examples look like house formulae: for instance, "Hic liber constat religiosis sororibus de Deptford [Dartford]" in a chronicle, or "Istud Psalterium pertinet domui de Carehowe [Carrow]."[33]

Another kind of physical evidence is found in an early fifteenth-century manuscript almost certainly from Wilton (Wilts.), where a short list of books, about half of them liturgical, has been entered on the verso of the last page. Of the thirty-six items, seventeen are service books, though the list begins with "Flos Bartholomei," "Isodorus" and "Moralium Gregoriii" and ends with "v Redyng bokys for the frayter" and six "bokys of henglys." The list's editors note that at this time the number of Wilton's nuns was about forty (comparable to Barking's approximately fifty at the same period), but caution that what appears to be a "small communal collection" cannot be assumed to represent the entire library.[34]

Finally, some of the great female houses probably employed scribes. A. I. Doyle has pointed out that Winchester College accounts reveal the presence of a scribe from St. Mary's Abbey (Nunnaminster) "where he must have worked for the nuns, copying books between 1398–9 and 1423–4."[35]

SURVIVING NUNS' BOOKS

At this point we must offer some idea of these books' numbers. Ker's and Watson's lists show a residue almost startlingly small.[36] In their tabulations, surviving books owned by nuns total 138.[37] Bell's additions, which utilize Christopher de Hamel's recent work on Syon, have raised this total to 161.[38] The number of survivors is certainly higher than this.

For instance, in listing Syon's books Bell categorizes twelve as belonging either to the sisters or the brothers; had he accepted de Hamel's classification, the majority of these would have been assigned to Syon nuns. Similarly, Ker decided not to include in his list the business books of a house – cartularies, rentals, surveys – and did so only when other material, such as chronicles, formed part of the volume. Bell notes that Ker includes only one female charter (from Godstow). Actually, as Bell's work on G. R. C. Davis's list of cartularies shows, thirty-two business documents survive for female houses.[39] Of this number Bell includes only three in his own list: had they all been included the total number of nuns' volumes would be 190. To this number another twenty-three newly identified nuns' books may be added (see Appendix I, which lists six possible volumes as well), making the total 213–19. In the main, women's houses owned service books, theological and devotional texts, and business books. No doubt discoveries of more religious women's books will continue to be made, particularly as female names in surviving books are identified as belonging to nuns.

Of the female library collections Syon holds pride of place. Christopher de Hamel lists a total of forty-six manuscripts identified either as coming from the women's library (nine) or as representing women's liturgical or semi-liturgical use (thirty-seven).[40] To these can be added the eleven printed books in Ker and Watson which are identified as female-owned (all bear Syon women's names) for a total of fifty-seven. Bell's tabulation of Syon's printed books and manuscripts totals forty-eight; if the twelve books which he labels as either sisters' or brothers' were added, his count of Syon women's books would be sixty – not very different from the alternative total of fifty-seven.[41] With the additional eight volumes from Syon which are listed in Appendix I, the number of surviving women's books from this house would be either sixty-five or sixty-eight (not counting fragments) – just under a third of all the nuns' books which survive.

Other institutions have not received such intense scrutiny. Bell's work altered Ker and Watson's totals for other female houses by only one or two volumes, and my count is likewise close to Bell's. At present, including the books listed in Appendix I, Barking stands second with fifteen volumes (not counting the problematic list of William Pownsett's books). Dartford comes next with eleven books, Shaftesbury and

Amesbury with seven each, the London minoresses with six, St. Mary Winchester and Campsey with five, Tarrant Keynston and Wherwell with four.[42] Other than that the total is made up of ones and twos.

But these rare objects which have survived both the vicissitudes of their own history and the rigorous screening imposed by bibliographers comprise only a nucleus. Other survivors have not met Ker's and Watson's criteria, yet their association with women's houses is often convincing. The unique manuscript of Osbern Bokenham's *Legendys of Hooly Wummen*, for instance, reports in its colophon that it was written in Cambridge and given "onto this holy place of nunnys."[43] The house may be Denny, the Franciscan foundation seven miles northeast of Cambridge, as A. I. Doyle suggested,[44] or another nearby female house, but in the absence of more certain connection with a particular institution, London, British Library MS Arundel 327 does not appear in Ker–Watson or Bell.

Around this core of surviving books whose claims are more or less compelling, another sort of evidence accrues, the record of lost books. In the inventories from female religious houses, made at the Dissolution in the 1530s we might hope to find the record of additional volumes, but for the most part these lists reveal only collections of service books.[45] Minster in Sheppey (Kent), an ancient and wealthy house founded in 675 by St. Sexburga, the niece of St. Hilda, constitutes an exception. Here commissioners found eight service books with silver clasps in the church, seven books in the vestry, variously termed "goodly" and "good," "an olde presse full of old bokes of no valew" in the lady chapel, and a book of saints' lives in the parlor.[46]

Christopher de Hamel's researches have shown that at the Dissolution the Syon nuns took a great many books with them when a part of the community went abroad. The 1495 *Vitas patrum* owned by Dartford's Katherine Efflyn carries a Dutch inscription, indicating that she likewise took it abroad with her in 1559, but evidence of a larger initiative remains to be discovered. It is possible that less comprehensive efforts to save portions of a collection, where one existed in the larger women's houses, may have been mounted – particularly where small groups of religious women continued to live in common and to maintain their religious rule. The record of women who lived together after the Dissolution is beginning to be investigated, and the accounts of several pairs of friends have been recovered. Perhaps the best-known is Elizabeth Thorne of Swine who left her house in Hull to her "well-beloved in Christ," fellow nun Elisabeth Patrike.⁴⁷ Larger groups who remained together include, among others, Elizabeth Throckmorton and several relatives from Denny who lived at the Throckmortons' manor, Coughton Court; Jane Kyppax, prioress of Kirklees who retired to a house in Mirfield with four of her nuns; a group of Dartford nuns including Agnes Roper and Elizabeth Cressener who lived at Sutton at Hone, two and a half miles from Dartford; the several groups from Syon which continued to live together in various English locations when others went abroad; and less surely, since the only evidence is bequests to former sisters, Dorothy Barley with three older nuns of Barking and Elizabeth Shelley, last abbess of Nunnaminster, who left gifts to seven former nuns.⁴⁸

THE CONTENT OF NUNS' LIBRARIES

The Dissolution, however, marks a formal end to religious women's institutional book collections. Not surprisingly, the nature of those collections changed over time. Is it possible to assess their character? If we look at the book bequests made to nunneries in the century and a half between 1349 and 1501, we can see in this series of twenty-nine gifts a number of significant connections between lay and religious women, and can trace some developments in their shared reading.⁴⁹

Most surprising is the increase in books bequeathed during this hundred and fifty years. Such gifts to nunneries are more than twice as frequent in the fifteenth century as in the fourteenth (twenty gifts vs. nine), reflecting a general growth in literacy affecting both givers and receivers. Even more telling is the alteration, around 1400, in the kind of book bequeathed. In the earliest nunnery bequest, 1349, books are included as an element in church furnishings; their significance is liturgical. In that year William de Thorneye, a London pepperer, gave to St Helen's Bishopsgate a hanging cup for the host and a silver–gilt chalice, plus his portifory and psalter.⁵⁰ In this context the psalter seems intended for liturgical use, though psalters could be used both for divine service and for private reading and thus could serve either the institution or the individual. With one exception, a breviary, the next five gifts were psalters, in 1374, 1376, 1391, 1392, and 1398.[51] Since four of these five gifts were designated for an individual (not 1376), they should probably be counted as personal books (though two of them were given to heads of houses). Psalters are thus the most characteristic fourteenth-century book bequest and, we might conclude, the most characteristic form of female reading at that time.[52]

In the first half of the fifteenth century some older patterns continue: a liturgical book bequest in 1412,[53] a psalter given to a prioress in 1431.[54] But along with such bequests, in 1415 one testator left an English *Prick of Conscience* and two books of hours (the most popular book of the fifteenth century),[55] and halfway through the century in 1448 Agnes Stapilton's five vernacular books signal forcefully the arrival of an audience for English devotional works – an audience composed of nuns and laywomen, as her will makes clear. The four Yorkshire female houses in her will, Arthington, Esholt, Nun Monkton, and Sinningthwaite, lay just west of the city and must have provided a network of friends and peers for this York widow, and within that network she left her copies of the *Prick of Conscience*, *Chastising of God's Children*, a book called *Vices and Virtues*, and a text of Bonaventure.[56]

With the Stapilton collection of 1448 we might compare another collection, the books given in 1399 by Duchess of Gloucester Eleanor de Bohun to her daughter Isabel at the London minoresses, where the duchess was living.[57] Recorded just half a century apart and designated for religious women, each collection might be considered typical of its owner's class and period. The duchess' *milieu* was both elevated and literary. Her mother Joan, countess of Hereford, had commissioned Hoccleve's "Complaint of the Virgin," and at her death Henry V spent £73 for books and other things from her estate.[58] Eleanor's father, Humphrey de Bohun, earl of Hereford, and her sister Mary de Bohun, have been asssociated with the production of several illuminated books, and one of Eleanor's own commissions, a psalter–hours made between 1382 and 1396 or 1397, survives.[59] She was married to the most notable bookowner of the age, Thomas of Woodstock,[60] and her own will mentions fourteen books, both secular and religious; most intriguing of these for our purposes is the group directed to her Franciscan daughter.

The collection appears to be intended for an institutional library, and in particular, to meet the needs of a community superior – and indeed Isabel did later become abbess of the minoresses.[61] It includes a Bible; a book of decretals (Bell calls it "the only book of canon law so far traced to a nunnery")[62]; a historical work ("livre de meistre histoires"); *Vitas Patrum*; "les pastorelx Seint Gregoire" which Bell identifies as Gregory the Great's *Regula Pastoralis*; and two presumably Latin psalters glossed in French. Institutional concerns dominate here (canon law; history, a traditional preserve of monastic libraries; Gregory's work, written for those holding pastoral office and advising on the treatment of subordinates; the *Vitas Patrum*, probably for refectory reading), while the fashion for psalters looks backward rather than forward and the vernacular is French.

Half a century later in Agnes Stapilton's collection only one of the five vernacular books was French (an unspecified gift to Denny). Her four English books represent a mix of moral and instructional emphasis which does not appear in the duchess' collection. The duchess' books are thoroughly traditional choices for a monastic library, male or female; they might as easily have been bequeathed in the twelfth century. Further, their aristocratic provenance is revealed in their usefulness for a female administrator. Agnes Stapilton's books, on the other hand, in their shift to a different vernacular – English instead of French – and in their focus on personal devotion, represent the rising interests of a different group of women.[63] Stapilton, whose origins were gentry rather than aristocratic, chose to give to the nuns *she* knew, not the fruits of the patristic tradition (St. Gregory the Great; *Vitas Patrum*), but newer meditative and ethical works. Her gifts are books which originated in the last hundred years (*Prick c.* 1350; *Vices and Virtues c.* 1375; *Chastising* 1382–1408; Love's *Mirror c.* 1410). Her mid-fifteenth-century will illustrates the successful dissemination of work produced in the last half of the fourteenth century.

The Stapilton will has been much cited – because of its total of ten books, because of the books' Englishness, because of the connections it makes with other women. Centrally, however, it makes visible a new kind of reading. Before Stapilton, books bequeathed to nunneries were primarily for liturgical use. After, they were almost entirely for personal use – and almost entirely English.

In the latter half of the fifteenth century, the book gifts which followed Stapilton's were similar to hers. Here is the list of the bequests which women's religious houses received between 1451 and 1501. Taken in sequence, the books are: a primer (book of hours) and *The Chastising of God's Children* (1451);[64] Rolle's *English Psalter* (1467);[65] the *Pater Noster* with other things (1479);[66] a primer, *Doctrine of the Heart*, and an English book of St. Bridget (1481);[67] an English life of Our Lord (perhaps Love's *Mirror*) and an English life of St. Katherine (1485/86);[68] Love's *Mirror* with a text of Hilton's (perhaps *Mixed Life*) and St. Bridget's *Revelations* (1495);[69] the *Legenda Aurea* in English (1501).[70]

Except for the *Legenda Aurea*, these are texts either newly composed or newly translated. Rolle's *English Psalter* is the earliest, written near the end of his life around 1348. Hilton's *Mixed Life* and the *Chastising* are probably products of the 1380s, though *Chastising*'s editors would allow a date as late as 1408. The rest, however, are firmly fifteenth-century work. Love's *Mirror* was submitted for Arundel's approval, as one of its manuscripts says, about 1410, and the *Pater Noster* was likewise written in the early fifteenth century. St. Bridget's *Revelations*, though begun in the 1340s, were not translated until perhaps 1410–20, the date of the earliest surviving English manuscript. Probably the latest of these bequests was the *Doctrine of the Heart*, composed in Latin in the middle of the thirteenth century but not translated into English, to judge by its surviving manuscripts, until 1400–50.

Transmission of these new works, in the fifty years after Agnes Stapilton's signal bequest, was brisk. A gap of about 120 years exists between the date that Rolle wrote his *English Psalter* (c. 1348) and the date it was bequeathed (1467), but in the next four nunnery bequests only forty to seventy-five years elapse between the time of composition and the time of bequest. In other words, these relatively new works were being circulated fairly rapidly. *Chastising*, for instance, composed between 1382 and 1408, was bequeathed in 1451, a span of forty-three to sixty-eight years. Similar figures can be cited for the *Pater Noster* (c. seventy years), Love's *Mirror* (c. seventy-five years), and *Doctrine* (c. fifty-five years). Abbess Horwode of the London Minoresses, with whose bequest we began, is entirely typical; she bought her Hilton miscellany about seventy years after its author died.

In summary: the book gifts to women's houses between 1349 and 1501 show a doubling in the number of books bequeathed, which no doubt reflects the growth of general literacy. The kind of reading alters, notably by the mid-fifteenth century, from liturgical to devotional. The two collections, the duchess of Gloucester's and Agnes Stapilton's, given fifty years apart, illustrate the difference between books for consultation by a religious superior, (embodying an earlier notion of a useful library for a female house), and books for common reading (implying a model of reading more widespread and more directed toward personal formation). Finally, in the fifteenth century, the books bequeathed were authored recently, for the most part within the last hundred years, while the duchess of Gloucester's little library drew on the fathers, canonists, and historians of ecclesiastical tradition.

The record of book gifts to nuns during these years, despite its slender and partial quality, is valuable because it tracks so closely reading evidence from elsewhere. Through the history of religious womens' libraries, of books "to the Vse off þe Systerr*es*," as the minoress inscription says, we can view the most powerful currents in fourteenth- and fifteenth-century book use.

TRANSMISSION OF BOOKS

What shape did women's reading networks assume? Here we will merely gesture toward several kinds of exchange which in the following chapters will receive fuller illustration. The jottings in surviving nuns' books can provide a taxonomy for book transmission: between female houses, within a house, and outside the house among nuns and laywomen. Evidence of intellectual exchange between female houses is so far relatively rare: A. I. Doyle's work on manuscripts belonging to Barking and Dartford provides the paradigm in its suggestion of manuscript transmission between these houses, which may have involved a laywoman with relatives at both places.[71] More recently V. M. O'Mara has pointed out ways in which a devotional miscellany made probably for Carrow was influenced by St. Bridget's *Revelations* and hence, most likely, by Syon.[72]

Currently, the most telling piece of evidence for intellectual and spiritual connection between womens' institutions is a letter discovered by Doyle.[73] Its hand is Thomas Betson's, the Syon brothers' librarian in the late fifteenth and early sixteenth centuries. The letter speaks of (presumably) Syon's dissemination of spiritual writings to another female house. Addressed to "Welbiloued Susturs in our lord ih*e*su crist," it continues: "knowe ye that of such goostly writyng*es* as our susturs haue with vs we send you p*ar*t Consailī*n*g and willyng you for encresse of oure mede to lete thies be com*m*on among you & yif copy of them to other of religion that dwell nygh you." These lines imply that such circulation of texts to other houses may have been common practice. Stronger evidence of shared reading will depend upon future editing work, which can discover patterns of transmission through comparison of textual relationships. Equally important will be a firmer sense of which houses were connected and how: by ties of blood shared among fellow religious, by membership in the same order such as Fontevrault or the Franciscans, or even by geography. The important female houses of Shaftesbury, Romsey, Winchester, Wherwell, Amesbury, and Wilton, for instance, all stood with a radius of twenty miles.[74]

Circulation of reading material among members of the same community, whether male or female, seems to have been developing as part of monastic culture from the fifteenth century on. Although no religious rule provides for such horizontal exchange, the books themselves testify to this practice.[75] Since private property was forbidden by all monastic rules, meticulous individuals or houses recorded the consent of the institutional superior when books were exchanged. The London minoressess, for instance, seem to have had a tradition of such precise assignment, since four of their five extant books have such entries.

Though examples survive of what appear to be gifts from one contemporary nun to another, some of the books which circulated within a female house, as at male houses, must have passed from an older religious to a younger when the senior member died. "At St. Augustine's abbey [Canterbury] the customary specifically stated that . . . it was the precentor's duty to take such books and to write the dead monk's name in them before bearing them off to the library."[76] So the 1493 *Chastising of God's Children* carries two Syon names on f. 3, Edith Morepath and Katherine Palmer. The former died in 1536, the latter in 1576.[77] Re-use of such books, at once the property of the community and yet strongly individualized by the previous owner's name, must have contributed to the formation of collective identity, and certainly to the sense of the individual as part of a collective history – a position which for women was relatively rare. The strength of such ties is nowhere clearer than in a brief inscription written in the back of a Sarum *horae* from Dartford. It asks for prayers for the soul of sister Alice Brainthwaite "who gave us this book" (*qui dedit nobis istum librum*).[78] The informality of the mutual "us," chosen here in preference to a more formal third-person reference ("gave to the monastery of Dartford") acknowledges the bonds of religious community with affecting simplicity.

The day of religious profession often brought book gifts. Enough examples survive to consider such books a recognizable class. The book of hours which Elizabeth Edward's parents gave her on this occasion is personalized first by Syon's insignia and second by her initial: at the foot of the donation inscription the five wounds emblem, represented by four small squares arranged around a fifth central square, appears above a lower-case *e*.[79] Other books carry this symbol as well: in the JRUL copy of de Worde's 1507 *Deyenge Creature*, originally part of a composite volume, next to the colophon has been drawn a majuscule "S" surrounded by four dots and a comma, representing the side wound. The Lambeth Palace copy of the 1530 *Mirroure of Our Lady* bears the same symbol written in ink, accompanied by two initials, on the binding of the lower cover.[80]

Though service books were perhaps given most frequently, other spiritual texts were also presented. James Grenehalgh's well-known profession-day gift, an annotated copy of the printed *Scale of Perfection* made to Syon's Joan Sewell, in its complex fullness was intended to support a lifetime of meditative reading. The profession ceremony itself could become the material for such meditation. The anonymous author of Oxford, Bodley MS Additional A 42, writing to Amesbury nuns identified only as Mary and Anne, refers to "your good and relygyouse desyres to haue hadde sum goostly comforte & som maner off instructyon of me. nowe att ye tyme of your professyon: And specyally a pon the wordes of the same. & the substancyall."[81] Since around 1516 Bishop Richard Fox likewise provided his Hampshire nuns with his English commentary on the Latin profession rite, it appears that meditation on the *ordo professorum* was regarded as an important element in formation.[82]

The books which laywomen gave to nuns often demonstrate the benefits which wealth could confer on female houses. The countess of Oxford's large French compilation of devotional texts presented to

Barking in 1474 or 1477[83] and Agnes Ratcliffe's gift to Marrick of an illustrated English translation of Deguileville's *Pelèrinage de l'Ame*[84] are such grand gifts. Some of these books might have been intended as mortuaries, gifts from a decedent to a religious house in partial recompense for obligations. The cartulary of Marham, a Norfolk women's house, contains a list of sixteen people who died in the house or its jurisdiction between 1401 and 1453. One of them, Sir John Champeney, a priest who lived in the abbey, left as his mortuary a book which was sold for eight marks, a large sum.[85] These gift books, however, also illustrate the power of local obligation. The interest in Barking shown by several generations of de Vere women was at least partly due to their roots in Essex at their seat of Castle Hedingham, while Agnes Ratcliffe was born a Scrope, a member of a family which regularly patronized its Yorkshire institutions.[86]

Such gifts bear a variety of other messages as well. For instance in Beatrice Cornburgh's life-gift of her psalter to Dame Grace Centurio, and then "unto what syster of the meneres that it shall plese the seme grace to gyf it," the inscription asks the community "to pray perpetually for the sawles named in this present Sawter."[87] The gift thus witnesses the familiar use of books as counters in spiritual exchange. It also gives evidence of a spirituality shared between lay and religious women. And, of course, the psalter constitutes a personal remembrance to a friend. Grace in her turn would be remembered and prayed for by the woman to whom she gave Beatrice's book, as the gift passed from person to person within the confines of an exclusively female world.[88]

The occasions on which books passed outside institutional walls, from nuns to laywomen, must have been fewer. What is in fact one of the very few presentation inscriptions written by a nun can, however, be seen in a printed copy of William Bonde's 1526 *Pylgrimage of Perfection*: "of your charyte I pray you to pray for dame Iohan Spycer in syon" (Figure 4).[89] Since Bonde was a monk of Syon, perhaps copies of the *Pygrimage* had been ordered for members of the community or even as gifts to those outside. The book which Elizabeth Hull, abbess of Malling, gave to the infant Margaret Neville at the latter's 1520 baptism yields more information about local ties and local tensions. The gift must have been to some extent a political one since the child's father,

Figure 4 Joan Spycer's gift inscription. The signature of this nun of Syon is found in the British Library copy of Syon author William Bonde's *Pylgrimage of Perfection*, 1526 (*STC* 3277, BL G 11740 [A6v]).

Sir Thomas Neville, was patron of Mereworth, the church where the baptism took place and he displayed a continuing interest in Malling, at the Dissolution attempting to buy the abbey.[90]

Book gifts by nuns became more visible at the Dissolution as institutional collections were dispersed. Sometime in the 1540s the former Barking nun Margaret Scrope gave to Agnes Gowldewell, a gentlewoman of her sister's household, a copy of Nicholas Love's *Mirror of the Life of Christ* which had belonged to Abbess Sibyl de Felton (d. 1419).[91] Another Barking book was for a time in female hands. In the Barking ordinal "the name Dorothy Broke has been written

46

in a sixteenth-century hand. [She] was the wife of a lawyer, Thomas Broke, who appears on an account roll of the abbey just before the Dissolution."[92] In 1542, the *Orchard of Syon* which had been owned by Syon nun Elizabeth Strickland was given by her brother-in-law and executor Sir Richard Ashton to his second wife.[93] His first wife had been Elizabeth Strickland's sister, and like other nuns after the Dissolution Elizabeth apparently left Syon to live with her sister and brother-in-law. That the book was given to Ashton's second wife underlines the *Orchard's* interest as a text for women, whether religious or lay. Finally the 1493 printed copy of the *Chastising of God's Children* which bears the names of Syon's Edith Morepath and Katherine Palmer, mentioned above, is inscribed in a later hand "Dorothe Abington." This owner was perhaps the sister of Thomas Habington of Hindlip (Worcs.). A conspirator in the Babington plot, Habington made Hindlip a center for recusancy from the 1570s.[94] At the end of the sixteenth century, the decade in which the house was built, ownership of the *Chastising* would have represented the family's support of the old religion and its devotions.

Several of these books which changed hands at the Dissolution, the *Mirror*, the *Orchard*, and the *Chastising*, had been widely owned and read by women since the fifteenth century, and their movement now from their former religious owners to secular women would simply have continued a longstanding pattern of book exchange. To some extent also the acquisition of these books may suggest a continuing attachment on the part of women to older forms of female life, now changing radically or passing from existence.

Against this background – a survey of religious women's houses, their libraries, their surviving books, and their networks of exchange – the following narratives of individual women readers are presented. The connections among these women, who were both religious and lay, and the practices through which they obtained, used, and exchanged books, will illustrate in a more particular way the overview offered here.

2

The library of a London vowess,
Margery de Nerford

If institutional libraries have the virtue of visibility across the centuries, private libraries, except at the most elevated levels, are remarkably hard to see, and those belonging to women are most difficult of all to find. A substantial number of lavishly written and illustrated books – twenty-five – remain from Margaret of York's library, a collection which must originally have been even larger, but the practices of collecting and connoisseurship natural to her aristocratic position underlie such survivals.[1] Thus the record which follows of an earlier and less elevated woman's book collection is particularly remarkable. In addition the collection's owner, Margery de Nerford, left the choice of her books to the anchorite outside Bishopsgate, near her Threadneedle Street dwelling. It is likely that in 1417, the year in which she died, the cell was still held by the anchorite Margery Pensax who had been its occupant three years earlier in 1414. Should that be so, this unusual gift, a collection of books made by a woman and given to another woman, might suggest possibilities for female book collection and reading hitherto largely unrecognized.

If the Bishopsgate recluse was indeed Margery Pensax, such a friendship between an anchoress and a woman vowed to chastity, as Margery de Nerford was, is not surprising. Her vowed chastity does not conform to the most familiar pattern, since she was not formally a widow when she vowed, but instead had been granted an annullment of her marriage. The circumstances were dramatic, though the contours of her life after the vow assumed a calm domesticity. As the achievement of her vowed vocation was assisted by several highly placed persons, so her intellectual and spiritual interests were supported by significant wealth. Her life and her will reveal a woman familiar both with court circles and with London's civic bureaucracy, living in London and the country, close friends with the neighboring parish priest, and assisted by staff and servants with whom her ties of affection are clear. Her books and her reading offer more surprises: a personal library of perhaps fifteen or twenty volumes and, it may be, the ability to peruse them in Latin.

THE MAKING OF A VOWESS

Margery's roots were in Norfolk. When she was about five, in 1363, her father John de Nerford was killed while fighting in France. Piers de Brewes was granted her wardship, and she was married to de Brewes' son John, in or before 1375. She was about seventeen in this year, though the marriage may have been made earlier.[2]

Three years later Margery de Nerford requested a grant of royal protection. She was at that time suing John de Brewes for divorce in the papal chancery, on the ground that the marriage had been made against her will. Her petition stated "that she fears injury from the said John and his accomplices."[3] Margery's receipt of the grant of protection, dated June 26, 1378, initiated a six-month period during which administrative records reveal a high degree of turmoil and confusion.

The person who was central to the situation and whose efforts, in fact, saved Margery, was her wealthy and well-connected grandmother. Lady Alicia de Neville was a baroness by virtue of her third marriage to John, Lord Neville of Essex.[4] On the same June day that Margery's grant of protection was issued, in 1378, Lady Alicia succeeded in having royal sergeants-at-arms dispatched to bring Margery before the king and council, and to arrest John Brewes, Sir Robert Howard, John le Heyr, clerk, and "Richard, that was the ladys cook Nevill," who had abducted (eloigned) Margery.

The judicial function which the king's council exercised has been much discussed. Was it really a court of law? The editors of the council's cases say that its function was "to deal with cases of emergency"; that it "gave attention to anything that required . . . exceptional treatment."[5] Certainly Margery's situation fitted this description.

The council's procedures were usually set in motion by receipt of a petition summarizing the grievance, and indeed Alicia de Neville's 1378 petition survives. In it the grandmother asks that the conspirators may be "fust a garde al tour de londres."[6] The writs of arrest which Alicia obtained represented the next step in the process. Pending trial, the parties were committed to prison. Finally, all were summoned before the council, the petition was read, oral pleading was heard, written documents examined, and in conclusion, imprisonment or fines were decreed.[7]

We can trace these stages in the narrative of Margery's case. Since the king's council did not have a record-keeping system of its own, the memoranda of its cases were not preserved except as they survived in other royal departments. The crucial points in Margery's struggle are found among the records of the close rolls – though no final judgment survives.[8]

On August 2 Sir Robert Howard was released from the Tower on £1,000 bail (his imprisonment probably a consequence of the June warrant), as a result of his promise to bring Margery to the council or else "to deliver her to Madame de Bedeford to abide in her custody." He guaranteed not to harm Margery or her grandmother and he stood surety for the unnamed others arrested also, promising to return to prison by October 13.[9] "Madame de Bedeford" was Isabel, eldest daughter of Edward III and wife to Enguerrand de Coucy. On the accession of Richard II in the previous year, 1377, this French courtier had resigned to the king all his English honors and returned to an elevated career in France. His wife remained in England; the invocation of her name indicates powerful sponsorship for Margery's case.[10]

These events culminated in December 1378 when the royal sergeants-at-arms brought Margery before the council which was meeting at Blackfriars on the tenth of the month. Here she asked to be delivered to her grandmother's custody until the resolution of her divorce suit, still pending at Rome. It was so ordered, and on the next day Robert Howard was again released from the Tower, to appear before the council on January 27. Two days later he and John Mareschall posted bond of £1,000, ensuring they would not abduct or hurt Margery before the pending court date.[11]

The situation must have continued to appear dangerous, since Margery three more times applied for an annual grant of protection, in 1379, 1380, and 1381.[12] The last of these requests, made August 7, 1381 would have expired in August of the following year, and nine months later, on May 4, 1383 when she was about twenty-five, she at last made her vow of chastity before bishop of London Robert Braybrooke.[13]

VOWED LIFE IN LONDON

Margery had considerable real property as her father's heir, and in 1383, the same year she vowed, she is recorded as dealing *sole* with that inheritance.[14] At issue were the Suffolk manors of Wyset and Shotisham, the Norfolk manors of Panworth and Nerford, moities of Holt and Cley, plus the advowson of Holt church, and a share in the advowson of Penteney priory. The years 1382 and 1383 saw a complicated series of land transactions designed to secure a settlement from Margery's husband John de Brewes regarding the real property she had brought to the marriage[15] and to assure for Margery a life income from this property.[16] Though in some cases she acted legally for herself, she was repeatedly supported by two men who assumed the role of her protectors.

The first of these men, Sir John de Cobham, was Lord of Cooling Castle, Kent and M.P. in 1391 and 1395 as Lord Cobham. His granddaughter and heiress Joan married Sir John Oldcastle, the Lollard knight. Cobham was related to Margery and to her grandmother Alicia, who in her will described him as her very dear lord and cousin. She left him a standing cup with cover; his wife Margaret received from Alicia an amber rosary and a gold ring with a diamond.[17]

In 1387–88, Lord Cobham had been a member of the king's commission which heard charges against the favorites of Richard II, and consequently he was impeached by the Commons in 1397. His sentence of hanging, drawing, and quartering was commuted to forfeiture and banishment to the isle of Jersey.[18] This forfeiture had consequences for Margery, since Cobham had acted as her feoffee in conveying her inherited manor of Panworth to Thomas Beauchamp, earl of Warwick, for 400 marks. Citing her vow of chastity and her poverty, she appealed to the king lest due to Cobham's forfeiture she should lose the portion of the money which now lay in royal hands. Her suit was successful, and the patent rolls show a grant to her "of what belongs to the king of that sum."[19]

The second man involved in this transaction, William de Bergh, was to become the central figure in Margery's life. He had been connected to Mary de Saint Pol, countess of Pembroke, the wealthy and devout founder both of Pembroke College, Cambridge, and of Denny, the Cambridgeshire Franciscan house for women. The countess's will names him as one of a group of eight executors. In fact, when the will was proved in Hustings court it was her chaplain, William de la Chambre, and de Bergh who oversaw the process, indicating that these two probably stood in a closer relation to the countess than did the other executors.[20]

Mary de Saint Pol died in March 1377; five years later the intervention of another aristocratic woman altered de Bergh's life. Margery de Nerford's grandmother, Lady Alicia de Neville, held the advowson of five City churches: St. Benet Fink, St. Christopher-le-Stocks, St. Margaret Pattens, St. Peter Cornhill, and All Hallows by the Tower.[21] All had been Neville family presentments, as their early fourteenth-century lists of incumbents show. Exactly five months before Bishop Braybrooke accepted Margery's vow, in her capacity as patron of St Christopher her grandmother presented de Bergh as rector of that church on December 4, 1382.[22] (De Bergh subsequently served as one of Alicia de Neville's executors, as he had done for Mary de Saint Pol.)

Several of the principals in this narrative appear to be connected by ties of blood or marriage or friendship, with particular focus on the intimate world of the episcopal palace. Bishop Braybrooke and Lord Cobham were in 1385 executors of Princess Joan's will. During the rule of the Lords Appellant both were members of the five-man committee for supervision of the king. Braybrooke and Cobham were, in fact, both close friends of the eldest Lord Appellant, Thomas of Woodstock, duke of Gloucester. Cobham was one of Gloucester's executors and was included in the circle of friends to be prayed for by the college of secular priests Gloucester founded at Pleshey, while Braybrooke drafted the college statutes and visited Gloucester there.[23]

Bishop Braybrooke's nephew Reginald, who served as marshal of the household for his uncle (probably from his 1382 consecration), ten years later married Joan, the granddaughter and heiress of Lord Cobham, Margery and Alicia's relative and protector. The vowess and her grandmother would have known Joan's husband, the bishop's nephew. Before Margery's death she would see Joan remarried, to Sir John Oldcastle, and would remember Joan in her will; Margery and Joan belonged to the same generation. Finally, the bishop's biographer suggests that Margery's grandmother Alicia was a member of the bishop's circle, close enough to send Braybrooke a pipe of wine for his enthronement feast in January 1382. His indebtedness to her may in fact have extended beyond this graceful gift: she three times presented clerks of his to churches of which she held the advowson.[24]

Other notable women, too, were connected with the bishop and perhaps known to Alicia, and through her, to Margery. Braybrooke's sister Katherine, for instance, was prioress of the London nunnery of Clerkenwell (d. 1383), and in 1393 the remarkable Sibyl de Felton promised obedience to Braybrooke as abbess of Barking. Like Margery she had been married, and her husband Sir Thomas de Morley, who was one of Braybrooke's feoffees in a land transaction, did not die until 1416.[25] She and Margery were contemporaries: both women attempted a spiritually focussed life which superseded their marital ties and which was supported by a substantial personal library.

THREADNEEDLE STREET AND HACKNEY

Soon after she was professed the vowess seems to have taken up residence in a tenement of her grandmother's called the Worm on the Hoop which fronted on Threadneedle Street, then called Broad Street. Perhaps Alicia acquired this house for Margery to live in, since the date of its acquisition was 1384, the year after Margery made her vows. William de Bergh, clerk, is also listed with Alicia in the property transfer, along with two other men. Next to the Worm lay a tenement and garden belonging to the rector of St. Christopher: hence Margery and William were neighbors.[26]

Her grandmother's death in 1394 gave Margery a share in the manor of Houghton (Norfolk). De Bergh was involved, with others, in the transfer of this inheritance.[27] The financial service which he performed for her was only one evidence of their continuing friendship. The culminating expression of this connection came ten years before she died, when in 1407 Margery and de Bergh together paid twenty marks for a license to found a chantry for themselves in St. Christopher-le-Stocks.[28]

This church, which comprised de Bergh's cure and which provided the site of their joint chantry, appears to have been the focus of their two lives. Margery's wealth contributed substantially to the parish's well-being, since she built for St. Christopher's both a vestry and a chapel of Our Lady and St. Anne. This saint's significance for women in the late Middle Ages was various. Though she represented the value of motherhood to married women, St. Anne was also the patron of widows. She may also have been seen as devoted to chastity at the end of her life. The sermon for her feast in John Mirk's *Festial* (fl. 1403) speaks of the period after her multiple marriages, when "aftyr all her lyue sche 3af her to chastyte and to holynes."[29] The dedication of the parish chapel to St. Anne, in fact, may have been recognized by contemporaries as particularly female. The chapel the London Charterhouse was building in those years, which was intended specifically to provide a place for women to worship (and to exclude them from the monastic precincts), was likewise dedicated to St. Anne.[30]

Margery's will asks burial in that chapel "in which I used to sit . . . before the image of the holy virgin Mary." Parish historian Edwin Freshfield notes that in the sixteenth century "the pew numbered 2 in the chapel was 'the foremest pew before our Lady.' It held two persons and . . . it may . . . be reasonably concluded that this was the pew in which Margery de Nerford sat, and together with her, in the other seat, Christine Ipstans, her servant."[31]

This woman was intimately involved in her mistress's life in a number of ways. A family servant, she had been employed by Margery's grandmother before her, and was left the very large sum of 100s by Alicia "for her good service." Margery herself bequeathed Christine a sizeable amount of plate, and she and Robert Chamberlain, another servant, were given the will's residue to dispose as they saw fit.[32] More importantly, these two were included in the chantry which de Bergh and Margery founded, implying a quasi-familial relation.

Margery died on December 21, 1417, and Christine made her own will only six days later, probably just after her mistress's funeral. In it she calls herself "once gentlewoman to the worthy lady Margery de Nerford, deceased." She asks for an enormous number of masses – a thousand – to be said for her soul and those of all the faithful departed. The will reveals a dramatic combination of wealth and humility in the life shared by mistress and servant. The five torches Christine stipulates for her burial were subsequently willed to a list of institutions, each of which possessed particular significance in the two women's lives. The vowess and her servant had known the bishop of London well enough for Christine to bequeath one of her torches to his private chapel, the place where Margery had made her vow (though Robert Braybrooke was now dead). The two must likewise have known the minoresses at Aldgate, whose bonds with wealthy laywomen have been often noted. St. Christopher's, of course, was given two torches and the country parish of Hackney, where Margery had a house, received one.[33] At the same time Christine Ipstans asked that her body should repose on the base earth, covered and wrapped only with "cloth of Westvale," a thin, cheap linen.[34] The will is incomplete, without executors or date of probate.

Margery and Christine are linked once more, after their deaths, by their joint endowment of a cell at the London Charterhouse, an enterprise which had been underway since 1348. Twenty-five cells were planned: Margery and Christine are named in the Charterhouse register as the donors of the twenty-fourth. It was another of Margery's faithful servants, Robert Chamberlain, who was responsible for carrying out this act of charity, which is not mentioned in either of the women's wills. As we have seen, Chamberlain and Christine received the residue of Margery's estate and after the two women's deaths, probably about 1418, Chamberlain made these arrangements.[35] The register says, "Also those living in the cells which . . . Robert Chamberlayn of the goods of Dame Margery Nerford and of Christian Ipstones caused to be built, are specially bound to pray for the same benefactors here named."[36] Since the Charterhouse register contains an account of Guy of Burgh, a saintly monk who was one of the founding company in 1370, it is possible that for Margery and Christine some personal link existed between the Charterhouse and their friend William de Bergh.[37]

Dwelling side by side near their London church, William de Bergh's and Margery de Nerford's lives seem to have been shared domestically. De Bergh's bequests to members of Margery's household may suggest that these persons served him as well.[38] To her cook "dwelling with me" she left four marks, and de Bergh remembered this man too, supplying his name, John Chapman, with his own remembrance of 3 s 4d. Both Margery and de Bergh left money to the woman her mistress calls "Johanne camerario meo"; De Bergh refers to her as "Johanne de camera Margery de Nerford." De Bergh's legacy to Robert Boteler may be intended for Margery's servant Robert Chamberlain. To another man, Thomas Norton, he left 6s 8d if Norton should be with Margery de Nerford at de Bergh's death and he left the same amount to Margery's chaplain whom he calls "Domino David." More lavishly, de Bergh remembered Christine Ipstans with forty shillings. The congruence of household names suggests that the two friends both enjoyed the establishment which Margery ruled.

Perhaps their recreation was shared as well. The vowess had a country house in the London suburb of Hackney, a favorite resort of wealthy Londoners from the Middle Ages through the nineteenth century. Hackney provided a pleasant stretch of open country easily accessible from the city and thus suitable for day trips. For Margery, the journey would have been a short one from Threadneedle Street via London's northeast exit at Bishopsgate. Lysons calls Hackney "not more than one mile from Shoreditch church."[39] Since the Bishop of London was lord paramount of the manor, perhaps Margery's house in Hackney came to her through his intervention. Her city household must have travelled into the country with her, and many members of that household are remembered with a specificity which suggests a certain tenderness. She left her carpenter, John, clothing and board for the rest of his life: "And this wherever and in whatever place he freely chooses to dwell and live, and over this I wish that each year of his life my executors give him 13/4 to spend as he wishes." The household may have included other women besides Margery and her gentlewoman Christine: Margery specifies "my little jewels, that is rings, paternosters [beads] and so forth, to be divided equally between Joan Pritewell and others once dwelling with me, according to the good discretion of the said Christine Ypstans."[40] The will continues: "Item I leave Maud, daughter of Occliffe, to help her, ten marks." The name is an unusual one and it is just possible that a daughter of the poet is meant.[41]

MARGERY'S LIBRARY

The two wills of priest and vowess illustrate a degree of intellectual and spiritual intimacy. Both of course left bequests to St. Christopher's. The chalice, vestments, pax, and cruets that Margery bequeathed are probably among the pieces listed in St. Christopher's inventory seventy-one years later, in 1488, but they are not identifiable. Her missal, however, or the new missal which William left the parish might be the one which survives as CUL Gg.5.24, identified as early fifteenth century and "probably from the church of St. Christopher-le-Stocks, London."[42] What may also be William's bequest are the "ij copes of white bawdelyn" which the church owned in 1488, since his will had left two "albas capas," requesting the rector and parishioners to pray especially for Mary de St. Pol and "my lord of Westminster" (William Colchester, abbot from 1386 to 1420). The copes were still there in 1550 when on May 19 they were marked "parffyt" by the churchwardens. It may even be that in 1488 some of William's and Margery's own books were part of what was then described as "a grete library with ij longe lectornalles theron to lay on the bokes," on the south side of the vestry.[43]

For indeed both their wills were bookish, hers substantially more so. De Bergh died first, about three and a half years before Margery, in June 1414. He left to the prior and convent of Holy Trinity Aldgate, a neighborhood institution, "vnum librum de exposicions [*sic*] euangeliorum," to be delivered after Margery's death. The implication that he thought she would need or want the book for her own reading is clear. Her will subsequently gave to the priory a volume "which was my father's" and a book "de omeliis euangeliorum" – almost surely de Bergh's book, though he is not mentioned. A recent writer points out that such homiliaries have always served a dual purpose: preaching and private reading. "In the late Middle Ages . . . instances of private devotional study are easier to find among people (often women) of rank and position. Such vernacular reading by the orthodox was not necessarily a feminine pursuit, but it seems to have been one thought eminently suitable for gentlewomen."[44]

Was the book of homilies which de Bergh left, first to Margery and then to Holy Trinity Aldgate, written in Latin or English? De Bergh's ownership, his will's description (which does not specify that the book was an English one), and his designation of the manuscript for further clerical ownership, all argue that the homilies were Latin ones. His will also implied that Margery would read the volume after his death. Hence the possibility that she was Latinate cannot be ruled out. On the other hand, H. Leith Spencer mentions "the appearance from the late fourteenth century and later, of homiliaries containing scriptural commentaries in English [due to] a wish to reach a lay reading public," and comments: "the formal vernacular postils being provided in the late Middle Ages seem as likely to address a devout reading public as a congregation."[45]

De Bergh's service to the Countess of Pembroke is recalled in his will, which asks prayers for her soul and which leaves several legacies to Denny, her foundation. He had continued to be interested in Denny after the countess's death: in 1392 he had been involved in the abbey's purchase of the manor of Histon (Colville) and now in his will he left the nuns a manuscript of *Lumiere as lais* (*Light for Laypeople*), a thirteenth-century Anglo-Norman poem by Pierre d'Abernum, also known as *Le lucidaire*. One writer calls it "essentially a teaching book on sin, salvation, judgment, heaven and hell."[46] About the time that de Bergh made his will, a copy of this text was owned by Joan Kyngeston, abbess in 1402 of the Cistercian nunnery of Tarrant Keynston (Dorset). At the end of the fifteenth century another copy belonged to Cecily, Viscountess Welles, daughter of Edward IV,[47] hence the *Lumiere* appears to have evoked some interest on the part of women both secular and religious. In addition de Bergh bequeathed Denny a set of vestments, and gave to the prioress 20d and to each sister 12d.

Margery also remembered Denny with 40s in gold, and with her book called "La ymage de notre dame," a bequest which together with the information that she used to sit before the "image of the holy virgin Mary," indicates a profound Marian devotion. Nigel Morgan has described the fourteenth-century development of linked pictures and texts on the theme of the Joys of Mary and suggested that such juxtapositions were intended specifically for meditation, rather than being simply didactic. The sort of manuscript which Margery bequeathed to Denny might be represented by El Escorial MS Q.II.6, an East Anglian psalter made *c.* 1320–*c.* 1330. It opens with an Anglo-Norman poem on the name of the Virgin and a Latin poem on the fifteen Joys of the Virgin and is illustrated by fifteen miniatures which picture Mary's life from the meeting of Anna and Joachim at the Golden Gate to her coronation in heaven. Another manuscript which might suggest the contents of Margery's gift is London, BL MS Egerton 2781, dated *c.* 1340–*c.* 1350. Here the salutations of the virgin are illustrated with twenty-three consecutive miniatures of Mary's life, and some Marian prayers in which ten historiated initials depict her miracles. Though these two manuscripts have no known connection with nuns, in each case their strongly Marian iconography might justify the appellation "La ymage de notre dame." A manuscript known to have been a gift from a laywoman to nuns, the Vernon Psalter, given to the nunnery of Hampole (Yorks.) by Lady Isabelle Vernon (fl. 1320s) which contains an illustrated hours of the Virgin might likewise provide a parallel to Margery's bequest.[48]

De Bergh's will mentions specifically only one more book, a white portiforium which he left to a clerical friend who had already borrowed it, but to Margery instead of a particular volume he gave "all my books and the contents of my chamber." Besides those already mentioned Margery's will contains several more intriguing book bequests. One volume went to Joan, Lord Cobham's granddaughter, by now the wife of Sir John Oldcastle. Lady Cobham, herself detained in the Tower on her husband's arrest, was freed only four days before Margery de Nerford died. She received a book which had once belonged to her grand-father Lord Cobham: "Domine de Cobham, uxori Johannis Oldcastle, librum meum quondam domini de Cobham."[49] One other book which Lord Cobham owned is known, an apocalypse bequeathed to him in 1361 by Lady Joan, widow of Sir Reginald de Cobham, first baron of Sterborough, a related branch of the family.[50]

To the anchor dwelling at London's Bishopsgate Margery left "a choice from the books not bequeathed elsewhere." It has been suggested that this recipient was the recluse Margery Pensax, who had been the Bishopsgate anchoress since 1399.[51] She was certainly living there in 1414, when William de Bergh had left 6s 8d to "Margerie anachorite iuxta Bishopsgate," and it seems likely that in 1417, the date of Margery de Nerford's death, the same person was still occupying the cell. The likelihood is increased by a gift the anchoress made to Syon monastery. A manuscript of Hilton's *Scale of Perfection*, now British Library MS Harley 2387, it bears on the verso of its original back cover (f. 130v) the inscription "Istum librum legauit domina Margeria Pensax dudum inclusa apud Bysshoppisgate monasterio de Sancti Saluatoris de Syon." The manuscript was written in London in the first decade of the fifteenth century.[52] Since Syon was not founded until 1415 the gift was probably made after this date, implying that Pensax's tenure at the Bishopsgate anchorage may have extended past 1414.

A most suggestive legacy was given to "domino David, rectori de pylkington," her chaplain.[53] Margery forgave him an unspecified amount of money and left him her breviary, her book of Chrysostom, and "all the other books which he has written for me." This clause makes it clear that her own library predated de Bergh's bequest and was independent of it.

R. M. Wilson notes that the works by St. John Chrysostom most often found in medieval libraries are *De Compunctione* and *De Reparacione Lapsi*.[54] The latter text, which the saint wrote to his friend Theodore when the latter left their common ascetic brotherhood and became interested in marriage, stresses the importance of hope by recalling Christ's tenderness toward us. It urges the reader to try at least to begin the move toward repentance. Since another aristocratic woman, Margaret of York, owned the work fifty years later in a French translation,[55] perhaps this is the Chrysostom tract Margery de Nerford refers to.[56] Whichever work of this Greek father the vowess owned, her lettered state is indicated by possession of what was in all likelihood a Latin translation.[57]

Finally, Margery left to her executor a glossed two-volume psalter. John Whatley was a prosperous mercer, four times master of the company and Member of Parliament.[58] The bequest was presumably Rolle's commentary on the psalter which is found in both orthodox and heterodox versions. A two-volume version of this text survives: MS Lambeth Palace 34 and MS BL Royal 18.c.xxvi, whose similarity to each other was noticed by Dorothy Everett, by Hope Emily Allen, and most recently by Anne Hudson.[59] Everett pointed out that a long version of the text, found in Lambeth 34 (to Ps. lxxxiv) and in several other manuscripts, was continued in only one manuscript, the Royal volume (to Ps. cxviii). These companion volumes thus preserve a long version of the text which is unique in its latter portion. The books are large handsome folios with some decoration, substantial and expensive, requiring a wealthy patron who could have commissioned or bought such professionally produced work. Their cataloguers have called them, respectively, late fourteenth and early fifteenth centuries,[60] hence they could have been written before Margery's death in 1417. Their language has not been identified except as non-northern.

The psalter commentary these manuscripts contain has been labelled Wycliffite by Warner and Gilson, by Everett, and by Hudson, who has provided an analysis of this long commentary which differentiates it sharply from the other heterodox versions.[61] In it she sees "a subtler mind" at work; its thrust is not polemical, like the other Wycliffite psalter commentaries, but consolatory. Indeed Hudson believes it "comes closest of any Wycliffite text to a devotional work."

Could Margery have owned these manuscripts? The psalter commentary's disparaging assessment says that religious orders attracted vocations because of the "plentyouse lyuelode" they provided;[62] Margery, however, left money and books to four religious houses, in three cases mentioning their heads.[63] Though the psalter commentary endorses putting one's trust in God rather than relying on the saints or the Virgin,[64] we have seen evidence of Margery's particular devotion to Mary. The psalter commentary is critical of officialdom, judging that out of a thousand, not twenty people would take estate or office "purely for þe loue of god."[65] Yet it seems probable that, like her grandmother, Margery was familiar with Bishop Braybrooke and his ecclesiastical circle.

These points, of course, do not represent absolute oppositions. Recently, in fact, it has been suggested that we need to establish "a complex context within which the tonalities of Lollard discourse ought to be situated" – giving up "a search for Lollard particulars" in order to examine Lollard sources and purposes. "The Wycliffite psalter's interpolations concerning patience under persecution," for instance, "may be judged as sincere efforts to imitate David, rather than . . . attempts to corrupt Rolle's original."[66]

The text's meditative focus would be especially suitable for a woman like Margery, for whom it would provide the same sort of desired challenge as it did for Margaret Kirkby, the recluse for whom Rolle composed it. Nicholas Watson says, "Margaret Kirkby must indeed have been remarkable to elicit such a work . . . a work which leaves so much of the process of learning to the reader, demanding she master such a range of material and of interpretive skills."[67] Behind his characterization of the *English Psalter*'s first reader, we can perhaps glimpse a later female owner, Margery de Nerford.

What was the size of Margery's library? Fifteen to twenty volumes seems a conservative guess. Three years before her death de Bergh had willed her all his books. Her own will names seven books and an unknown number are indicated by the bequest to her chaplain David of "all the books he wrote for me" and, to the Bishopsgate anchor, "a choice from the books not bequeathed elsewhere."

MARGERY'S CIRCLE

When Margery died her age was about 60. Her will, made October 31, 1417, reflected that she was "seeing and pondering the danger of death [which] more and more from day to day looms very close to me." All during December the Oldcastle matter had been agitating London, and the Lollard leader was executed on the 14th, just a week before the vowess died.

Her wishes are revealed in more detail by the 1425 will of John Whatley.[68] He makes it clear that the Worm on the Hoop was to support her chantry, while a second tenement's rents would maintain the chapel and vestry she had built at St. Christopher's. Her chaplain David and her servant Robert Chamberlain, together with Richard Osbern, clerk to the chamberlain of the City of London (who had served as one of de Bergh's executors earlier)[69] were designated Whatley's executors, and he attempted to establish an annual public accounting at which the St. Christopher wardens would disclose their handling of the de Nerford chantry monies, in the presence of these men.[70] The chantry endured until 1548, when it passed to the crown, its endowment then worth £10 4s, of which £1 was to go to "Lady Nerford's priest." At this time the founders were listed as Margery, William, and "Christian Vugham, widow."[71]

It is not clear how Whatley, a prominent member of London's governing class, was connected with the vowess. His recent biographer suggests that he may have provided credit facilities for members of the gentry, and his record of involvement with London real estate transfers is lengthy. (In one of these transactions he held land on behalf of Bishop Robert Braybrooke of London, the man who received Margery's vows.) Whatley, along with Lord Cobham, Bishop Braybrooke, the Baroness de Neville, and Madame de Bedford, are among the representatives of civic, aristocratic, episcopal, and even royal power who provided the assistance needed to support the vowed vocation at this elevated level.

Sometime between 1410 and Margery's death in 1417, her former chaplain David Fyvyan was presented as rector of St. Benet
Fink. This was another neighborhood appointment. The tenement
by St. Christopher's where Fyvyan had lived lay on the north side of
Threadneedle Street, while St. Benet stood on the south side of the street,
only a short distance to the east. Fyvyan died at his parish in 1451. His
surname was Welsh and his former parish, Pilkington, lay just outside of
Bury, Lancs. (northwest of Manchester). Since John Macclesfield, the
master of St. Anthony's hospital who presented him to the living of
St. Benet's, was from the northwest (Macclesfield is southeast of
Manchester), Fyvyan, too, possibly came from this area.[72] The scholarly
and intellectual interests evident in his life as Margery de Nerford's chap-
lain remained constant: about 1441 he was involved in the foundation of
a free grammar school. In that year the revenues of his church, St. Benet
Fink, were appropriated to support a schoolmaster at the hospital of
St. Anthony of Vienne, the fourth grammar school to be founded in
London.[73]

Fyvyan belonged to a bookish and well-placed group; he was friends
with both the well-known fifteenth-century John Carpenters, the bishop
of Worcester and the London town clerk. The former was responsible
for a variety of educational efforts; at the same time he organized a
systematic inquiry and purge of Lollards in 1448. He was master of
St. Anthony's hospital from 1433 to 1443,[74] while Fyvyan was rector
of St. Benet's. Carpenter was the moving force in the appropriation of
Fyvyan's church for the establishment of St. Anthony's school. Long
before Fyvyan became its rector, St. Benet's had claimed part of the
charitable offerings made to the chapel of St. Anthony, and this dispute
between the parish and the hospital was an ongoing one. A yearly grant
of six marks made in 1417 to Fyvyan and his successors was intended
to resolve this quarrel, but it was not finally settled until St. Benet's
was appropriated to the hospital in 1441. This arrangement, for which
Carpenter had had to secure royal and episcopal approval,[75] was apparently agreed to by Fyvyan. The settlement must have been effected
amicably, since Fyvyan's will bequeaths a small bible which he owned
but which the bishop of Worcester "has in his keeping."[76] Indeed it may
have been Carpenter's and Fyvyan's shared vision of the school which
allowed for this accommodation between parish and hospital.

Fyvyan was closer to the other John Carpenter, the London town clerk and bibliophile, since along with Carpenter's wife Katherine and another man, Fyvyan served as the clerk's executor. For doing so, Carpenter left him a "Bibliae abbreviatae" with "Historiae Provinciarum," together with the sum of five marks. This book had been given to Carpenter by John Sudbury, who was perhaps involved in the common profit manuscript scheme, and since Carpenter mentioned this previous owner in his bequest to Fyvyan, we may conclude that the latter also knew Sudbury.[77]

These men, two lay and two clerics – Sudbury, the two John Carpenters, Fyvyan – were all Londoners involved more or less closely with plans for educational establishments or for book distribution. Since Fyvyan lived for over thirty years after the death of his patron Margery de Nerford, he must have been a young man at the beginning of his career when he knew her. That Fyvyan was close to two of the most remarkable bookowners of these years, one female and one male, suggests that he shared their interests, even their points of view. What would his intellectual orientation – and Margery's – have been during the first decade of the fifteenth century? Lollardy was a particularly crucial issue for Londoners both at the beginning of the century and later. To what extent do these educational plans represent an attempt to respond to the Lollard challenge? And to what extent are the strategies of response – circulation of books, the school – themselves inflected by Lollard patterns?

Margery de Nerford's circle, particularly in its connection with Bishop Braybrooke, appears to have been an orthodox one. Yet during these years religious belief was complexly shaded, and an attraction to asceticism or a repulsion at clerical excesses were not confined to the heterodox. Lord Cobham was said to have spoken against clerical abuses in the parliament of 1391, while an incident in 1387, when an Augustinian friar gave an anti-mendicant sermon at St. Christopher-le-Stocks, might imply some sympathy on the part of the church's rector, de Bergh.[78] On the other hand, the poet Thomas Hoccleve spoke out of the most thoroughgoing traditionalism when he composed his "Remonstrance to Oldcastle" in August 1415. We do not know what Joan Oldcastle's sympathies were; it has recently been suggested that she may have wished to distance herself from her husband (particularly after his execution).[79] Not much is known even about Bishop Braybrooke's relation to heterodoxy, since no record of heretical proceedings survives in his episcopal register. Nevertheless it seems that around 1386 he charged the well-known Lollard preacher William Thorpe with giving heretical sermons at the London churches of St. Martin Orgar and St. Benet Paul's Wharf.[80] Braybrooke perhaps had another encounter with Thorpe (or a continuation) since the latter says in his "Examination" that in 1397 "the Bishop of London . . . found in me no cause for to hold me longer in his prison, but at the request of my friends, he delivered me to them, asking of me no manner of submitting."[81]

Margery's narrative provides further evidence for the existence of a group whose outlines are for the most part visible only in shadowy form – a wealthy, devout, theologically questioning, yet finally loyal assemblage. Texts, rather than biography, have provided the principal witness to such readers' presence – notably the intriguing *Dives and Pauper*, a theological dialogue written between 1405 and 1410. Orthodox, yet supportive of vernacular access to scripture, *Dives* and the same author's sermon cycle suggest a readership dissenting in some particulars whose views nonetheless, as J. A. F. Thomson has recently suggested, overlapped with orthodox ones "sufficiently to suggest that many might not have regarded themselves as conscious rebels."[82] This ambiguous stance is illustrated in a will made about ten years after Margery's death which both reiterates the familiar request for a poor funeral and protests that the writer dies "in full belief as holy church teacheth or ought to teach." Its author was Sir Gerard Braybrooke, nephew of the bishop to whom Margery made her vows and brother to Joan Oldcastle's previous husband, Reginald Braybrooke.[83]

David Fyvyan, as well as Margery, might fit this paradigm. Judging by the connections made during his maturity, he retained the interests of his earlier life. His stay in Margery de Nerford's household may indeed both have shaped his intellectual interests and confirmed his orthodox stance. Margery, if she was the owner of the surviving two-volume *English Psalter*, may have shared its reservations about the institutional church while focussing instead for herself on the "personal, immediate contact between the believer and his creator."[84] Certainly, too, her life illustrates a resolution which is to some extent due to the protective power which the institution extended her.

Margery's relation with the other cleric in her life, William de Bergh, has antecedents in the relation of Paula and Jerome. This wealthy Roman widow, whose intelligence and wide reading evoked Jerome's admiration, followed him to the Holy Land, lived near him for twenty years, and supported his projects financially as well as psychologically. Peter Brown has recently recalled the debt which the work of male intellectuals has often owed to the support furnished by women's wealth.[85] Similar elements are visible in Margery's and William's lives, with their shared spiritual reading, their joint recreation, their mutual interest in the parish of St. Christopher – and indeed with her building program for his, or their, church.

But the centrality of this association with de Bergh, and her significant connection with David Fyvyan, should not obscure the many sustaining connections in Margery de Nerford's life with other women. Her grandmother played a crucial role, particularly during the period of her marital difficulties. A similar connoisseurship is implied by the two womens' ownership of luxurious textiles: Alicia gave to her servant Christine a "cou*er*let oue testure blank poudre oue popinayes" while Margery left to the abbot and convent of Beeleigh, Essex, a set of red velvet vestments embroidered with gold stars. Their common piety, shown in the grandmother's gift to her granddaughter of her private chapel's contents, found expression in the collection of these richly ornamented fabric objects. Similarly, Margery's meditative life was shared with Christine Ipstans, as they sat together in prayer before the altar of Our Lady and St. Anne. Both women's wills, in their allusions to the Virgin, their payments of forgotten tithes, their eucharistic focus (the bequeathed torches were to be carried up at the elevation), are formidably orthodox. Yet the world-renouncing character of Margery's vocation is echoed in the particular asceticisms of Christine's will: the cheap cloth, the bare earth, which are so much a matter of current devotional fashion.[86] Finally, Margery's bequest of the choice of her book collection to the Bishopsgate anchorite, if indeed Margery Pensax was intended, gestures toward a common female spiritual and intellectual formation. In all these contacts between women a remarkable similarity of focus is visible, one which transcends the categories of lay and religious. These common elements include a connoisseur's impulse which found expression in the collecting of religious textiles; a devotional inclination toward prayer and reading which were shared rather than individual; and a stance both theological and social in which withdrawal and contemplation provided the shaping direction.

3

A Norwich widow and her "devout society": Margaret Purdans

In 1481 Margaret Purdans put the final touches on the will which she had been writing for several years. It shows her at the heart of a diverse collection of Norwich friends and acquaintances who together compose what we might call a devout society, one which spans the city's larger groupings of parish and neighborhood.[1] The attractive force of her character is illustrated by her many ties: with the men and women who were part of Norwich's governing class; with the city's hermits, anchorites, and priests; with several Cambridge doctors and masters of divinity, representatives of a learned, clerical culture. Most of all, her will reveals her connections with other women, lay and religious, in every walk of life.

Commenting on the importance which wills assume in social relations between women, one writer notes the variety of tasks which such documents often perform: "the naming of women as individuals, the precise delineation of these individuals and their status, the selection of items appropriate to the person, and the description of those items in a text that functions both as a permanent legal record and as a declaration of sentimental attachment."[2] Such attentiveness both to individuals and to objects marks Margaret Purdans' will.

Remarkably, she left four English books to women or to women's monasteries. (Two more books were given to men; her son-in-law and a clerical friend each received psalters.) The book gifts to women were only one aspect of a generosity which seemed to focus its concern on contemporary female lives, and which remembered anchoresses, hospital sisters, and servant women, as well as nuns. The will, with its dense thicket of connections, makes visible too a female culture in which books were owned, lent, and given by women to other women. More cloudily visible, though part of the will's networks of friendship, are several male representatives of learned culture, their presence perhaps less vital than that of the will's several reading women.

Purdans' bequests are thrown into high relief by the survival of another contemporary will, made by a woman who belonged to the same Norwich circle. Like her friend, Katherine Kerre owned, lent, and bequeathed books. The survival of these two wills allows us to compare Margaret Purdans' and Katherine Kerre's interests as readers. The two friends' testaments, in addition, afford us a view of reading which is otherwise somewhat rarely found. Here, loans and gifts of books are familiar practices in women's daily lives.

A LIFE AT THE TOP

Margaret Purdans belonged to Norwich's governing class. Her husband Richard was probably substantially older than she was; his unusual bearded brass survives beside hers in their parish church of St. Giles[3] (Figure 5). Blomefield lists him as one of four bailiffs as early as 1403, and he was twice mayor, in 1420 and 1433. The latter year saw a disputed election in which the outgoing mayor Thomas Wetherby refused to confirm the commons' choice of two aldermen, Richard Purdans and John Gerard. When Wetherby declared that his own favorite had been elected, the crowd cried "Nay nay nay . . . Purdans and Gerard." The bishop was pursuaded to intervene. Purdans served his mayoral year (1433–34), and Gerard after him, but these events were the beginning of deep fractures within the city which required royal intervention and which lasted over a period of five years. Purdans, however, died soon after this, his second term as mayor, on April 25, 1436.[4]

Margaret thus spent most of her adult life as a widow – forty-five years if we guess that she died in 1481, the year her will is dated. The will shows that, like other urban widows of her class, she remained friendly with the men and their wives who belonged to this governing group. Thus she left a short Parisian cape ("mantlet de paryse") to Margaret Elys, wife of Thomas Elys, mayor in 1460, 1465, 1474, and M.P. for Norfolk.[5] The immensely sucessful lawyer Sir James Hobart and his wife Margery were her friends as well. Hobart was Henry VII's attorney-general and

Figure 5 Richard and Margaret Purdans' brass, St. Giles, Norwich. Reproduced from Peter Eade, *Some Account of the Parish of St. Giles, Norwich*. 2nd edn (London and Norwich, 1906), following p. 161.

the man who brought John Paston II and Margery Brews together. He received from Margaret Purdans a hanging candelabrum, while his wife was given a small black girdle decorated with silver and gilt.[6]

It thus seems that during her long widowhood Margaret Purdans continued to play a role in Norwich secular society, rather than retiring, for instance, to the nunnery of Carrow in Norwich's suburbs. A domestic life is further suggested by the will's bequest of "a cupboard standing in the hall of the great house" – presumably her Norwich residence in the parish of St. Giles. Located at the city's western edge, it was one of the poorer sections of Norwich. She was well-off but not wealthy, to judge by the Norwich taxation list of 1451. Here she was assessed on £4; she would at this time have been a widow for fifteen years. For comparison, in that year Agnes, the widow of judge William Paston, was assessed on £40, while Elizabeth Clere, another widow and a major benefactor to Cambridge's Gonville Hall, was said to have been worth £45. On the other hand, four of the city's twenty aldermen had incomes of only £2.[7]

"RECLUSE SOCIETY" OR "DEVOUT SOCIETY"?

The circles in which Margaret Purdans moved can be seen more clearly if we look at an earlier Norwich will, one which mentions Purdans herself. Seventeen years before, in 1464, the Norwich hermit Richard Ferneys who seems to have been a central figure in the city's life, had died. His friendship with Margaret Purdans is recalled by his legacy to her of an image of Christ painted on cloth. Ferneys had lived as a hermit for over twenty years; in 1429 he had been left £40 by a former Norwich mayor to make a pilgrimage to Rome and to Jerusalem. Based on Ferneys' several bequests to other hermits and anchorites Norman Tanner has posited "a kind of 'recluse society' similar . . . to the clerical society of the city."[8] While Ferneys' will includes three bequests to other male anchorites, in fact the female legatees in the will are twice as numerous. Because of the will's seven bequests to lay women, we might speak instead of Norwich's "devout society" comprised of hermits, anchorites of both sexes, laywomen, and sometimes clerks.

What Margaret Purdans' will demonstrates, in fact, is the complex interpenetration of such a society with the larger secular one. Comparison of Ferneys' will with Purdans', seventeen years later, shows that they shared a common set of friends and acquaintances. Five beneficiaries in Ferneys' will are mentioned also in hers. Notably, the institutions which receive gifts from both testators are female ones: Carrow, the only nunnery in Norwich, and Norman's hospital with its community of "whole" and "half" sisters, women who lived in community or who retired at night to private homes.

Three women were central enough in the lives of both Ferneys and Purdans to have been recalled by name in their wills. To Julian Lampett, the well-known anchoress of Carrow, the hermit gave 12d and a pair of sheets, while Margaret, in a deleted bequest, left her the much larger sum of 20s. The second woman mentioned in both wills Ferneys calls "Basilie de parochia Sancti Gregorii"; he left her a cloak and sixpence. From Margaret, who calls her "Basilie Payn," she received a veil and 3s 4d, while her daughter was given 12d. I have been unable to discover anything more about her.

The third woman whom both Ferneys and Purdans remembered, Christine Veyl, Ferneys calls "custodi mee." Tanner translates "my guardian" and suggests that, together with "my boy" she was the hermit's servant. He left her a number of domestic items: a pair of sheets, an oil jar, a little spoon, and 6s 8d. From Margaret she received a round pax with images of the Resurrection and of the three Marys, plus 3s 4d. This image, which recalls women's presence at the central manifestation of Christ's divinity, was carved on a tablet kissed by the priest and people before communion in a symbolic statement of unity (Figure 6). Christine Veyl was still alive in 1484–85, when she was living at Carrow and paying 6s 8d yearly for a tenement in the monastery precinct. The account roll for this year also shows that she bought ale brewed by the priory brewer on four occasions and paid for this supplement a total of 5s 8d.[9]

We can trace Christine Veyl still further and in doing so, can enlarge the Ferneys circle. Another of the hermit's bequests was made to Katherine Moryell, Christine Veyl's sister. Later under the name of Katherine Kerre, this woman too, like Margaret Purdans, left several books (as mentioned above). Though all three women were remembered in the hermit's will, and though Purdans and Kerre were both substantial bookowners, the two women's wills show some intriguing differences, both religiously and intellectually.

Figure 6 Women at the tomb. At the crucifixion, the entombment, and the resurrection women participated in the central events of Christ's life. Margaret Purdans' pax showing images of the resurrection and the three Marys was part of this visual tradition. Illumination by the Fastolf Master, from a book of hours made 1420–25 for Sir William Porter. New York, Pierpont Morgan Library MS M. 105, f. 114v.

THE FIRST WILL: KATHERINE KERRE

In 1497 Kerre left "to Dame Johan Blakeney ye book of seint kateryn yt she hath of me, a peyer bedys Aumbyr *with* gylt paternosters / yt wer ye Ankeres of Carrowe [probably Julian Lampett's], a gold rynge yt towched our lordys grave as it is seid. [a relic from Ferneys' pilgrimage to Jerusalem?] And iii s iiij d to dele [distribute] for me."[10] St. Catherine of Alexandria's late-medieval popularity is reflected in the survival of four versions of her prose legend, scattered over twenty-four manuscripts,[11] and Katherine Kerre's book may have been a life of this saint. In the 1440s the East Anglian poets Osbern Bokenham and John Capgrave each produced a verse life. A manuscript of Capgrave's poem (London, British Library Arundel 396) is associated with the female Augustinian house of Campsey, Suffolk; it carries the name of Domina Katerina Babynton, subprioress in 1492. Alternatively the book might have focused on St. Catherine of Siena – might even have been a copy of de Worde's *c.* 1492 edition titled "the lyf of saint katherin of senis" (*STC* 24766). Whichever saint was meant, both these East Anglian bookowners, Katherine Kerre and Katherine Babynton, were her namesakes.

The book of St. Katherine which Kerre loaned her friend had passed from one elderly widow to another. Though only a yeoman's daughter, Dame Joan Blakeney had made a particularly good match. She had married John Blakeney, a royal servant who became clerk of the signet and served in at least three parliaments.[12] He had been dead since 1471; his widow survived until 1503. Her will exists both in draft and in fair copy: in the former she calls herself "woesse" [vowess], but in the latter "wedowe," reflecting the difference between idiomatic and more formal usage. She commends her soul to God, the Virgin, St. John Baptist, and St. Dominic, asks burial at the Norfolk Blackfriars, and leaves bequests to three friars. Her private chapel's chalice, two vestments, altarcloths, and mass book witness to her piety. She was the sister of Sir Roger Townshend, a Norfolk sergeant-at-law and justice of the common pleas, who both represented the Paston family and lent money to John Paston II.[13] Like his sister, he was a bookowner. An inventory taken after Townshend's death in 1494/95 lists over forty books including an Alexander romance, a Latin text of Pope Gregory's *Regula Pastoralis*,

74

and two printed books of Latin sermons, as well as a life of Christ and a life of St. Blaise.[14]

A second book bequest in Kerre's will also represents a loan. To the anchoress of St. Julian's church, Conisford, perhaps Elizabeth Scott, Katherine Kerre bequeathed 6s 8d, a fox-furred gown, "and ye boke yt she hath of me." The two book loans Kerre made, one to a vowed woman in secular life, the other to an anchoress, illustrate the easy passage of books between women. Kerre's loan to the anchoress, like Purdans' book gifts to nuns' houses, also suggests the extent to which secular women's freer access to books may have influenced religious women's reading.

Kerre's will reveals, besides these female friendships, her strong bond with her sister Christine. The two first appeared together in Ferneys' 1464 will where both were remembered, Christine in a special way. They were reunited thirty years later in Katherine's 1497 document which makes her sister Christine both executor and legatee, stipulating, "And yf she comyth to nede I wull she [be] holpyn *with* my good*es* whyll she levyth."

THE SECOND WILL: MARGARET PURDANS

The hermit Richard Ferneys' and the widow Margaret Purdans' wills are separated in time by nearly two decades. Nonetheless Purdans' will illustrates the continuance of connections forged first among this hermit's circle. The widow's will, however, differs in substantial ways from the hermit's. Though both she and Ferneys left bequests to recluse Julian Lampett, Ferneys, in addition, gave money to three male hermits. By contrast, Margaret Purdans made bequests to four reclused women: Katherine Foster at Norwich's Blackfriars; Elizabeth Scott at the church of St. Julian; an unnamed woman at Norwich's Bishopsgate; and Joan, recluse at London's Bishopsgate. In addition, she remembered each sister of Norman's hospital and specified that Sister Alice Dawe should receive a veil and mantle, as well as 6s 8d.[15]

The will's emphatic focus on women is continued in a remarkable series of bequests to female houses. Of the eleven East Anglian nunneries, Purdans' will includes eight; all received money and three received books. She was particularly generous, of course, to the nearest, Carrow, which was given 13s 4d to be divided equally among the nuns, plus 6s 8d for repair of their church and house. (This distinction between individual gifts and institutional ones is frequently found in bequests to religious houses.) In addition Joan Elys, a nun there and probably the daughter of Purdans' old friends Thomas and Margaret Elys, received 3 s 4 d, while the house was given "unum librum anglicanum."[16]

Blackborough, a Norfolk Benedictine house, likewise received 6s 8 d to be divided equally, while its prioress Alice [Erle] received 3 s 4 d.[17] I have not been able to identify Dame Margaret Orungar, who was given 20d and a pair of jet beads. The following bequest of 20d to Dame Margaret Norwich probably went to a nun who is listed in Bishop Goldwell's 1492 visitation of Campsey (not in 1514 list). (It may be that, like Joan Elys, Margaret Norwich was the relative of a Norwich mayor, in this case William Norwich.)

Crabhouse, an Augustinian convent, was given 6s 8d to be distributed and 6s 8d for repair of their church and house, while Dame Audrey [Wulmer] the prioress was willed 3 s 4 d.[18] Institutional bequests were made to three Suffolk women's houses: 10s to Redlingfield; 6s 8d to Bungay; 6s 8d to Flixton. Thetford (Norfolk) received 6s 8d, and a further 6s 8d for repair of their house, plus a book called in English St. Bridget.[19] A larger sum, like Carrow's, was designated for Bruisyard: 13s 4d plus 6s 8d for repair of their house. It seems that Margaret Purdans had already given or lent the book called *Le doctrine of the herte* to Bruisyard nun Margaret Yaxley, since the house was now granted it when the nun should die (and she herself was bequeathed 6s 8d).

Though they were not related by blood, this woman might be considered a member of Margaret Purdans' extended family. The widow had two children: a son William and a daughter Alice who died May 5, 1474, before her mother's will was written.[20] She had married, as his second wife, Richard Yaxley, of whom Margaret Purdans speaks affectionately. The nun to whom she gave *Le doctrine of the herte*, Margaret Yaxley, was Richard's sister.[21]

This text, addressed to women living under rule, survives in four fifteenth-century manuscripts.[22] One of these, Durham Cosin v.iii.24, *c.* 1460, has been identified as "copied in East Anglia by more than one East Anglian hand," and more recently, as from Suffolk (where Bruisyard is located).[23] Further research will be needed to determine whether the Durham manuscript might be Margaret Purdans' gift book.[24]

According to the *Doctrine*'s editor this work does not deal with advanced levels of the spiritual life, but instead might be called an "ascetical treatise for the ordinary nun." Examination of conscience and confession are stressed, rather than reception of the eucharist, and moderation is everywhere recommended, along with reading, prayer, and meditation.[25] Margaret Purdans' ownership of it demonstrates its adaptability to lay life, and the contemporary interpenetration of female lay and religious worlds is illustrated by Purdans' gift of this book to a nun. The spiritual assistance represented by her gifts of books finds its parallel in the financial support which she offered these often struggling houses. The Purdans' will puts the resources of intelligence and wealth at the service of what in some cases might have been poorer and less advantaged women: her maidservants, for instance. She remembered women from her own social level as well. As we have seen, two of the six nuns to whom she made bequests were probably the daughters of old friends in Norwich governing circles: Joan Elys and Margaret Norwich. Two more were prioresses of their houses, hence perhaps more likely to have been of Margaret Purdans' own age: Alice Erle of Blackborough and Audrey Wulmer of Crabhouse. Although, of course, personal affinities must have played a part in these friendships, several may be traced, as well, to her husband's office. These connections between women thus recognize and reinforce a civic elite's ties with each other, through both its male and female members.

The focus in the will on the needs of women seems a conscious one. Margaret's concern for her household, which resembles Margery de Nerford's and indeed that of a great many well-off widows, is shown by her bequests to each servant of a pair of blankets, a pair of sheets, a bedcover, and a flat basin. With her servant, spinster Alice Catelyn, however, she may have had the same intimate relation as did Margery de Nerford with Christine Ypstans, since she provided for Alice a life interest in a little tenement in her messuage in the parish of St. Peter Mancroft.[26]

The several book bequests made to religious women had at least one secular counterpart. To Alice Barley she left "a book called Hilton." Two crossed-out bequests following this one, to Master William and Master John Barley, suggest that Alice may have been the sister[27] of these two Cambridge fellows of Gonville Hall, the former a lawyer, the latter master of the college for twenty years from 1483 to 1504.[28] (The hall had been closely connected with Norwich since its founding by William Bateman [*c.* 1298–1355], the son of a Norwich bailiff.) John Barley was, in addition, rector of St. Michael Coslany, Norwich, whose advowson belonged to Gonville Hall. Since he is said to have "built the parsonage house [of St. Michael's] from the ground . . . and glazed the windows," the surviving stained glass illustrating the labors of the months was probably Barley's commission (1502–04).[29] A recent historian of the college calls him a "Norfolk man devoted to Norwich."[30] Both the mastership and the Norwich pastoral post, however, would come after Margaret Purdans' death. She knew Barley rather as Cambridge fellow, doctor of theology, and, between 1459 and 1481, pluralist holder of several Norfolk cures and rector of St. Mary Ax, London.

Besides the Barleys, other clerics find a place in the Purdans' will. They are Norwich men, except for two. Like the Barleys, these two were fellows of a Cambridge college; their lives seem to have been lived entirely in Cambridge or London. Both were fellows of Pembroke, an institution which has recently been called both "a rising collegiate star" in the fifteenth century and "a college of marked intellectual conservatism in the late medieval period."[31] Both men were doctors of theology with similar academic careers, though separated in age by about forty-five years. To the younger, Richard Cokerham, who had been junior proctor of the university in 1473/74, Margaret Purdans left a bowl with a cover which the elder man, Hugh Damlett, had given her in his 1476 will.[32]

Damlett had been junior proctor himself in 1431/32, and after his fellowship became master of Pembroke in 1447. In the same year he assumed the rectorship of St. Peter Cornhill in London where he died in 1476, five years before Purdans' will. It may have been at his initiative that the parish library was established,[33] since he was himself a substantial bookowner. Emden lists seventeen texts which he willed to various institutions including Syon. He left money to Syon, Sheen, and the London Charterhouse, in addition to the nuns of Stratford, Haliwell, and the minoresses.[34] His intellectual reputation, in Norfolk at least, is illustrated by the consultative role assigned him in the large bequest made by another Norfolk man, Hugh atte Fenne, who in 1476 left 100 marks for repair of books at Cambridge.[35] That his theological opinions were conservative is indicated by his resistance to Reginald

Pecock's ideas.[36] It has recently been suggested that Damlett's pastoral interests, particularly his espousal of preaching, lay at the heart of his opposition to Pecock. Within this pastoral context Damlett and his friends have been called "enthusiasts for the cure of souls."[37] Such a relationship of spiritual advisement may have existed between Damlett and Margaret Purdans, but certainly there was a strongly personal attachment as well. After the many book bequests with which his will opens, the gift to her comes third in his list of personal legacies and its tone is intimate: "For a remembrance, my maplewood bowl from which I am accustomed to drink."[38] (The suggestion that she may have known Damlett in his London pastorate is strengthened by the presence of another London bequest in her will, to Joan, the anchoress of London's Bishopsgate.)

The second, younger, Cambridge fellow who was remembered in Margaret Purdans's will, Richard Cokerham, had been a protégé of Damlett, to judge by the latter's will. Damlett had left him not only five books, but a gown with furlined hood and a set of blue bed hangings decorated with ostrich feathers. The friendship between the older man and the younger must have been known to Margaret Purdans, who understood that Cokerham, as a protégé of Damlett, would be pleased to receive a memento of him. Thus Damlett's wooden bowl passed from one clerical owner to another, mediated by a female hand.

The Purdans will includes at least one more treasured item inherited, like Damlett's bowl, from a deceased friend. To her son-in-law Richard Yaxley whom she calls "my beloved son" the widow left her little psalter, once Master Richard Poringland's (d. 1471–75). He, too, was a Cambridge fellow (Peterhouse), a doctor of divinity, and in 1427, soon after the foundation of London's Whittington College, Poringland had become its third master. Since his will had left one mark each to the London Charterhouse, to Syon, and to Sheen, and since he was named executor by the devout hermit Richard Ferneys, Norman Tanner speculated that Poringland might have been, like his predecessor Richard Caistre the saintly vicar of St. Stephen's church, Norwich, an "unusual man of radical views." His brass, which shows him naked in his shroud, confirms the suggestion of a particularly intense piety.[39]

Tanner has suggested, in fact, that the priests of St. Stephen's might have comprised "a succession of radical vicars."[40] At the opening of the fifteenth century Richard Caistre advised Margery Kempe and, after his death in 1420, his tomb became a site for pilgrimage.[41] Margaret Purdans might just have known him, since her husband was elected mayor for his first term in 1420, though we do not know the year they married. With Richard Poringland, however, Caistre's successor in 1442, her involvement is certain. She and Poringland both appear in Richard Ferneys' will and, as we have seen, she left Poringland's psalter to her son-in-law. Their shared views are expressed in their common bequests to Sheen and Syon. (Caistre, too, had left money to the London Charterhouse, Sheen and Syon, and a later vicar of St. Stephen's, Geoffrey Champneis, who died in 1472, bequeathed to the first two.) Her sympathies both with the hermit Ferneys and with Poringland may suggest that Margaret Purdans was drawn to the more intense forms of the spiritual life.

In fact the tie with Syon is found at least once more in the Purdans' circle. Her will named four executors: her son, her son-in-law, and two clerics, John Eston and John Steyke, the latter a remarkable bookowner.[42] Recorded at Cambridge as a questionist in 1468/69, his connection with Norwich, as Tanner observes, seems to have lasted only during the four years when he was rector of St. Laurence, between 1480 and 1484. Most likely Margaret Purdans met him then, a year or two before the end of her life. After her death, he held just one more parochial post, at Brundall, Norfolk (1483–89). From that time until his death in 1513 he lived as a monk of Syon, leaving the community about seventy-five books, including titles in medicine, geometry, "a full . . . set of scientific works, particularly the Arab astronomers," Aquinas, patristics, and, for the first time at Syon, some texts by English mystical writers: an unspecified work by Hilton and the exposition on lessons for the dead by Rolle.[43] It would be natural to conclude that Margaret Purdans found in him an intellectual spirituality similar to her own – and that this shared perspective underlies Steyke's position as one of her executors.

SOCIAL AND SPIRITUAL DIFFERENCES

Here it may be useful to compare these two bookowning females' wills,[44] made sixteen years apart – Margaret Purdans' and Katherine Kerre's – in order to avoid a simple conflation of their similar positions. Both women came from approximately the same social level, since in the notes of probate Purdans is described as "generosa" and Kerre as "mulier nobilis et arma gerens," and the latter closes the will with her seal. Both bequeath books to female friends, lay and religious. But it is impossible to avoid the suspicion that Margaret Purdans was slightly more elevated socially and intellectually than Katherine Kerre, and, indeed, even that their spiritualities were different. (Though Ferneys left gifts to both, Purdans did not remember Kerre in her own will.)

First, the Purdans will contains more identifiable city and county names: James Hobart, for instance, Henry VII's attorney general and his wife Margaret, plus the Norwich mayors John Wellys, William Norfolk, and Thomas Elys (together with the wives of the last two). Second, both women have connections with Cambridge academics. Purdans mentions the Barley brothers, Poringland, Steyke, Damlett, and Cokerham, while Kerre names Edmund Stubbe and Roger Framingham, both doctors of theology, and Thomas Drentall and John Fyske, both masters.[45] But Purdans' friends include many notable bookowners, while Kerre's connections seem, in the absence of such strong bookishness, less intellectual, perhaps more pastoral. Third, Purdans leaves money to Syon and Sheen, Kerre does not, preferring bequests to the four orders of friars in Norwich and to four named friars, while Purdans gives only to the friars minor and friars mendicant, and names just one friar as a beneficiary.[46] (Purdans' will is in fact less clerical, naming only nine men, while Kerre names thirteen: four Cambridge graduates, four friars, five parish priests.) Such differences in taste, or posture, are the more interesting since the two women are initially found together as members of the same spiritual circle. Finally, it seeems possible that Purdans was a vowess, based on the appellation dame (*domina*) which prefixes her name in the 1451 taxation list. Though ten women are called widow, only Purdans and one other woman are called dame, and, since both are widows of Norwich city officials, not knights, both may have chosen this vocation. Kerre is not designated in this way.[47]

The will's compelling interest lies as much in its catalogue of religious objects as in its list of books. In their lavish multiplicity these objects come to dominate the will and recall R. F. Green's characterization of "a widespread [medieval] sensitivity, far more dynamic than anything we are likely to encounter nowadays, to the potential importance of physical objects as carriers of meaning."[48] The Purdans will is particularly strong in painted cloths, a class of devotional object which survives very sparsely despite its frequent presence in wills and inventories.[49] Most often these cloths appear to be hangings, though occasionally the equivalent of a modern framed picture seems intended. To Alice, wife of Richard Herward, Purdans left a painted cloth for an altar with images of the virgin and saints Margaret and Katherine which, given its purpose, must have been fairly large. Margaret Hurry, "once my servant," received 3 s 4 d and a picture of Dorothy on cloth, while Margaret Smyth was willed an image of St. Giles painted on cloth (the patron saint of the Purdans' parish). To her clerical executors John Steyke and John Eston she gave respectively "the face of Veronica" on cloth and "le pyte steyned" (the Man of Sorrows). Either of these objects might be the "pannum deputatum cum ymagine Christi" which Ferneys had left her and which she might now be transmitting to another close friend. Other religious objects were willed too: Steyke received a tabernacle with the passion of Jesus Christ and Eston a double cross decorated with the crucifixion.[50] Besides Christine Veyl's round pax with the three Marys, mentioned above, Joan Sylvester was given a pax "cum le pyte."[51] Transmission of such sacred objects, like the gift of books, alludes to beliefs powerfully held and shared.

Margaret Purdans herself had been the recipient of such gifts. Their connective power – "inextricably enmeshed in the human lifeworld," to use Green's phrase[52] – is visible in the lovingly detailed description of her legacy which John Baret composed for his 1463 will. Baret, whose startling cadaver tomb survives, was a clerical employee of the monastery of Bury St. Edmunds: wealthy, a collector of objects, and connected in some unclear way with the poet John Lydgate, half of whose royal pension was paid to Baret.[53] To Margaret he left a crucifix which was in his white chamber and a pair of beads with gold pater nosters "and on eche syde of the pater noster a bede of coral, and the Aue maryes of colour aftir marbil with a knoppe, other wyse callyd a tufft, of blak sylke, and ther in a litel nowch of gold, with smal perle and stoonys besekyng the seid Dame Margarete to prey for me, and that she wil vowchesaf if hire doughter leve longere, than she to have the said bedys after hire dissees."[54] Sadly, Margaret Purdans' daughter Alice died before she did, but Purdans' will left to her granddaughter Elizabeth a pair of coral beads which were once Elizabeth's mother's – perhaps the beads Baret had given Margaret Purdans twenty years earlier.[55]

Finally, the most revealing of the gifts Baret left the widow was a "doubyl ryng departyd of gold" set with a ruby and a turquoise and having "a scripture wrety*n* with inne, for a rememberaunce of oold love vertuously set at alle tymes to the plesur of God." Baret's gift was probably a gimmel ring (from *gemellus*, twin), a two-part, separable ring ("departyd") exchanged by lovers. Whether it was a two-part ring, or simply a two-stone one, its form announces what was probably a mutual attachment.[56]

Loved by the connoisseur Baret, remembered by the hermit Ferneys, linked to the ardent Poringland and the pastoral Damlett, Margaret Purdans in her turn passed to others the valued tokens of these attachments. The will shows us an attractive figure whose manifold connections form the outlines of two worlds: a male clerical and learned culture in which she occcupied a place, and a female culture running parallel to it, to which she also belonged.

The various members of this academically rooted male world, this assembly of literate, bookowning men, in Margaret Purdans' will are joined by a female presence. The male friends remembered in her will are remarkably similar to the connections made by another Norwich woman, the anchoress Katherine Manne, fifty years later. In each case it is Cambridge doctors of theology, fellows, and masters of colleges, who are involved in spiritual and intellectual exchange with Norwich laywomen. At least sometimes these relations seem to transcend the merely pastoral and to be based on an identity of vision: Purdans and Poringland perhaps; Manne and Thomas Bilney certainly.

The female culture from which the will springs is even more noteworthy. Margaret Purdans' Norwich offers the only English examples of laywomen living in community, examples which have been recently supplemented.[57] These references to Norwich women dedicated to chastity and dwelling together describe just one of many forms in which women's life, secular and religious, created itself there. The Purdans will, for instance, in a reference not noted elsewhere, leaves 8d each to "two women friends dwelling in the parish of St. Andrew, once servants of Rose Trewlove." Such forms reveal themselves in Margaret Purdans' concern for women's religious houses and hospital sisters, her friendship with individual nuns, anchoresses, and laywomen, and her loyalty to her woman servant. These female connections, with their shared spiritual and intellectual interests, must have encompassed both relations of equality and those of instruction. Purdans' and Kerre's wills allow us to glimpse this milieu and its mechanisms of exchange – its books.

4

Orthodoxy: The Fettyplace sisters at Syon

In the Fettyplace sisters we are presented with three able and intellectually acute gentry women whose lives display a range of dispositions. Dorothy and Susan were first married, then widowed; subsequently the former entered religious life and the latter chose the vowess vocation, while a third sister Eleanor remained celibate as a nun. All three were connected with Syon Abbey and consequently were marked by its intellectual scope and its religious orthodoxy. At the Dissolution their personal commitment to this orthodoxy was demonstrated as Eleanor and perhaps Dorothy became part of Syon's various attempts to continue the traditional monastic forms.

Founded in 1415 by Henry V, and the only Bridgettine house in England, Syon represented an ardent and apostolic spirituality. Rigorous, intellectual, deeply engaged with the definition of religious life, the foundation just outside London was a beacon to spiritual aspirants and was responsible for the dissemination of much late medieval spiritual writing. Its regular sponsorship of printing imitated a continental model unmatched by any other English house.

The Fettyplace sisters' intellectual interests found a suitable focus in their lives at Syon. These involvements are traceable in Susan's bequest of money for a school, in the four books which carry Eleanor's signature, and in Dorothy's provision for book purchases. Part of a wealthy, well-connected, literate family, they were influenced by the activities and interests of both male and female members of that family. Susan would perhaps not have endowed a school, for instance, were it not for the existence of the more ambitious foundation initiated by her uncle William; and, in fact, when the three women are remembered, it is principally through their mention in the work of their famous stepbrother, Sir Thomas Elyot.

Nevertheless the spiritual and intellectual connections between women which these lives present are strongly visible. Religiously, for instance, Susan's choice of the vowess vocation followed the example of her grandmother Alice. Intellectually, Dorothy entrusted the procurement of her books to her sister Susan. Personally, Eleanor's bond with another sister Elizabeth was witnessed by the inscription of the latter's death date in Eleanor's breviary. To a substantial extent, these connections between women were made in intellectual terms: through reading and book ownership.

THE VOWED LIFE, A FAMILY TRADITION

The Fettyplaces owned land in Berkshire from the thirteenth until the eighteenth century, when the male line ceased.[1] The sisters were the daughters of Elizabeth Beselles and Richard Fettyplace, who died late in 1510 or early in 1511. Since his will mentions marriage portions only for his daughters Dorothy and Eleanor, it is likely that Susan's marriage to John Kyngeston took place before her father's death.[2] Kyngeston died early in their married life, in 1514 when he was only 23. The marriage was childless and Susan lived at Syon thereafter, though the varying amounts entered for board in the monastic accounts indicate that her presence there was not continuous. She appears in the accounts, however, from 1514 to 1537 with some breaks, a residence which is registered by the mention of "Lady Kyngeston's chamber" in a post-Dissolution inventory.[3] Both Susan and her grandmother Dame Alice Beselles were identified in the latter's will[4] as vowesses, that is as women vowed to chastity, usually after a husband's death. This choice was recognized in an episcopal ceremony which conferred the mantle and ring, but the woman remained formally lay, free to arrange financial matters, to travel, even to litigate. Some vowesses continued their previous patterns of life while others, like Susan Kyngeston and Alice Beselles, attached themselves to communities of religious women.

Dame Alice Beselles is first recorded in the Syon cellaress' foreign accounts in 1520–21 where she is called "My lady kyngeston her Grauntdame." Her stay in this year was temporary, but she returned in

1523–24 and continued in the accounts for two subsequent years, accompanied by two servants.[5] The matriarch of a huge clan of Beselles, Fettyplaces, and Yates and the widow of William Beselles,[6] she calls herself "vowess" in her spring 1526 will and asks burial either with her husband at Oxford or at Syon. The vowess' freedom to come and go is shown in the will's provision of alternative places for burial depending, in Alice Beselles' case, on whether she died at her manor of Beselles Leigh, Berkshire, or at Syon. She is one of seven women whom the catalogue of Syon's brothers' library records as book donors: her gift, a folio edition of Italian lexicographer Ambrogio Calepino's Latin dictionary (perhaps the first edition of 1502), was clearly an expensive one.[7]

The heir of Alice and William Beselles was their daughter Elizabeth, the wife of Richard Fettyplace. After Richard's death Elizabeth married a second time, to Sir Richard Elyot, perhaps about 1512. The jurist, who was king's sergeant-at-law to Henry VII and VIII and Justice of Assize on the Western Circuit, was the father of Sir Thomas Elyot.[8] The family historian, J. Renton Dunlop, believes that Elizabeth was, like her mother Alice, a Syon vowess, based on Alice's will reference to Elizabeth as "Dame," but no other evidence survives.

SIR THOMAS ELYOT'S *SWETE AND DEUOUTE SERMON OF MORTALITIE*

When Elyot wrote the preface to his 1534 translation of this sermon by St. Cyprian, he and his Fettyplace stepsisters had thus known each other for over twenty years. Speaking to Susan, Elyot alludes to Cyprian's sermon,

> which I haue dedycate and sente vnto you for a token: that ye shall perceyue, that I doo not forgeat you: and that I doo vnfaynedly loue you, not onelye for our allyaunce, but also moche more for your perseuerance in vertu & warkes of true faith, praieng you to communicate it with our two susters religiouse Dorothe & Alianour, and to ioyne in your praiers to god for me.[9]

In producing a *contemptus mundi* text addressed to a religious woman, Elyot was writing within a recognized tradition. Earlier in the century, about 1510, Thomas More had published his translation of the *Life* of

Pico della Mirandola, together with several of Pico's short works and letters. More's work was dedicated to Joyce Leigh, a London minoress, as a New Year's gift. (More tells her she will find nothing more profitable for "purchasing of patience in aduersite" (*Complete works*, 1, 52/4-9)). Closer in time to Elyot's translation of St. Cyprian, perhaps a few months after it appeared, John Fisher was writing in the Tower his *Spiritual Consolation*, a *memento mori* dedicated to his own half-sister Elizabeth White, a Dominican nun of Dartford.[10]

Elyot's intention in translating Cyprian's work, an exhortation to steadfastness in troubles, has been variously interpreted: as alluding to Thomas More's tribulations (he was imprisoned in May 1534 while Elyot's sermon was published sometime between July 1 and the end of the year); as echoing More's own writings on Christian fortitude; as offering consolation for the difficult times brought on by the king's treatment of the religious orders.[11] Though Susan, its recipient, has been identified as Elyot's stepsister, until Pearl Hogrefe's biography of Elyot was published her affiliation with Syon had not been noticed, and she had been wrongly called a nun.[12]

Another recent set of events may also have been in Elyot's mind as he translated St. Cyprian. The controversies regarding Elizabeth Barton, the Nun of Kent, had been much in the public eye during the six months to a year before his book was published.[13] Her revelations strongly advised the king against his contemplated second marriage. Syon had been collectively quite interested in the Nun – Thomas More had met with her there more than once – although not univocally supportive. Female connections, however, had been at work in the matter. The abbess of Syon, Agnes Jordan, was close to the marchioness of Exeter whose husband's descent made him a prime claimnant to the throne, and the abbess had sent the Nun to the marchioness with at least an implicit recommendation. (The latter's frantically exculpatory letters to the king and Cromwell survive.)[14] It was perhaps natural that the foundation should see the Nun's warnings as part of a female prophetic tradition within which their own founder St. Bridget spoke and wrote; she had herself foretold the death of King Magnus of Sweden.[15]

The Nun had been arrested in September 1533; in November and December, with a group of supporters, she had made a public confession first at St. Paul's and then at Canterbury Cathedral. A parliamentary bill of attainder was passed in March 1534 and she and her adherents were executed on April 20 – only a few months before Elyot's book was published, sometime after July 1, 1534.

For Elyot, the affair of the Nun struck close to home. In fall 1533 Elizabeth Barton's supporters had been compelled to give the names of the persons to whom they had communicated her revelations. Susan Kyngeston's name appears in two lists.[16] She was told about the Nun's prophecies both by Hugh Rich, head of the Observant Friars' house at Richmond, and by Henry Gold, a secular priest who had been the Cambridge pupil of Richard Reynolds, the Syon monk who refused to acknowledge Henry's headship of the English Church. Both Rich and Gold died with the Nun. Some of the persons on these two lists were questioned and it is not impossible that Susan Kyngeston herself was interrogated.[17]

Cyprian's tract reminds the reader that the events of this life ("the toyes of fortune, or the crankes of the world," as Elyot calls them) are trivial, and powerfully argues for the exclusive happiness of the next. Cyprian says, in Elyot's translation: "And yet doeste thou delyte to tarye longe here amonge the swordes of people malycious, whan rather thou shuldest couayte and desire (dethe settynge the forwarde) to haste the towarde Christe" (B5). Again: "Lette vs accompte Paradise to be our very countray . . . There doothe abyde and looke for vs a greate numbre of our deere frendes, our Auncetours, our fathers and mothers, our bretherne and children. A plentuouse and great multitude, whiche nowe be sure of theyr immortalytie, and yet do care for our suretie, do desyre to haue vs in theyr company. To come to beholde & imbrace them, lorde god what a ioye and comforte shall it be bothe to them and to vs" (E2). Cyprian's words allude in a general way to the death of friends, but the recent deaths of Barton, Rich, and Gold may be recollected with particular poignancy given the way Elyot situates the occasion of Cyprian's sermon, "in the tyme whan there was continuall persecution" (A2^v). We cannot, of course, know the degree to which Susan Kyngeston supported the perspective of opposition which Elizabeth Barton offered; nevertheless the Nun's death only a few months earlier, together with that of the men Kyngeston had known, perhaps effected by the "swordes of people malycious," must have made St. Cyprian's strictures on the absolute futility of earthly life peculiarly telling.

SUSAN KYNGESTON, VOWESS

It is, in fact, the combination of her lay state with her position at Syon which may account for the privileged status which five family wills accord her. Beginning with her husband's brief 1514 document which says simply, "the ordre and forther Disposition of this I committ to my Wyff Susan Kyngeston," the picture of an unusually competent woman emerges from these wills. In 1523 Susan's uncle Sir Thomas Fettyplace left £400 to be held in trust for his daughter Katherine "by my nece Dame Susan Kyngeston at Syon." In the same year her sister Dorothy's will, made when entering Syon, left £46 13s. 4d. to be disposed as Dorothy specified by her sister Susan Kyngeston, and the care with which both women took this charge is indicated by reference to two indentures, one between Dorothy and her lawyer Thomas Englefield, and a second between Englefield and Susan. Three years later, in 1526, Susan was made executor of her grandmother Dame Alice Beselles' will, and in addition, with two others was named to hold in trust for Susan's nephew a large bequest of plate and household stuff. (The three were to judge whether the nephew, when he reached the age of twenty-four, was "towardly and thriving" or likely to misuse the stuff, in which case the bequest was to be postponed until the legatee turned thirty.) Finally, she was one of the witnesses to her uncle William's will of 1529.[18] Her early commitment to a strongly religious vocation is thus coupled with a notably high degree of secular involvement.

These several family responsibilities, in fact, are alluded to in Susan's own will[19] when she found it necessary to stipulate that if her executors should "be in trouble" for any reason concerning her various executorships for others, they must take what monies were needed to defend themselves. She here echoes her grandmother Alice's will, which attempted to shield Susan against the difficulties of an executor's position by specifying that if Susan were "troubilled and besid . . . she to haue of this forsaid substaunce to discharge hir self withall."

Two elements in Susan Kyngeston's will are striking. First, the document testifies to the assurance with which a number of legal matters, including a family lawsuit, were handled by the testator. Though she employed legal counsel, her grasp of her financial affairs was a secure one, and she was evidently accustomed to supervise these affairs personally.

To support a common pleas judgment favorable to her interests (which she cites by its date), for instance, she alludes to an Act of Parliament dated February 4, 1536 – the Statute of Uses which had, in effect, declared previous trusts and family land settlements invalid.

Second, her interest in education was demonstrated by the assignment of 80 marks, something over £50, from the sum the court had granted her to the foundation of a school. Her executors were to find a virtuous priest "to teche pore childern" in Shalston, Buckinghamshire, for twenty years at a salary of 4 marks per year.[20] In this bequest, which apparently was never implemented, both the educational emphasis of Syon where Susan Kyngeston lived for about a quarter century and a familial tradition of educational patronage may be observed.

Fifteen years earlier, in 1526, Susan's uncle William Fettyplace had established a perpetual chantry for himself and various members of his family, among them Susan and her brother John Fettyplace the elder. The chantry included both an almshouse for three poor men and a school whose elements were carefully specified. Historian of education A. F. Leach points out that Childrey School's curriculum represents perhaps the earliest example of instruction specified in English, then "Latin if required," and perhaps also the earliest combination of elementary and secondary schooling, that is, of reading and grammar.[21] Equally interesting is the charter's stress on the school's indirect educational mission, not only to the scholars themselves "but for all other families and persons where they [the scholars] resided, in order that they might instruct those who were ignorant in the premises."[22]

The Syon community was expelled from its monastery on November 25, 1539, according to Wriothesley's chronicle. Susan Kyngeston's absence from the cellaress's acounts after 1537 perhaps means that she left Syon before the Dissolution. In any case she died less than a year after the break, on September 23, 1540, at Shalston, Buckinghamshire, the home of her sister Anne Fettyplace and Anne's husband Edward Purefoy.

Her brass in the church there, where she is buried, is the second of two monuments to her: on it she is described as "vowes," and shown in mantle, veil, and wimple, with a ring on her right hand. (Figure 7, engraved in Lipscomb's *Buckinghamshire*, does not show the ring.) Dunlop says, "The artist has attempted a likeness – the broad face with the

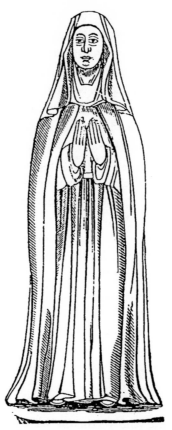

Here lyethe buryed Dame Susan Kynge=
stone, vowes, the eldyst daught' of Rychard
Ffetyplace of Est shytford in the Countye
of berk' Esquier decessyd & late the Wyfe
of John Kyngeston of Chelrey in the said
Countye of berk' Esquier also decessyd the
whyche said dame Susan dyed the xxiij day of
Septemb' in the yere of our Lord God a
M°ccccxl on whose sowle and all crysten
soull' jhu have m'cy amen.

Figure 7 Susan Kyngeston's vowess brass at Shalston (Bucks.). The engraving
omits her ring of profession. George Lipscomb, *The History and Antiquities of
the County of Buckingham*, 4 vols. (London, 1847), III, p. 75.

Figure 8 Monument to Sir George Fettyplace (d. 1743) by James Annis, Swinbrook church (Oxon.) A family resemblance to Susan Fettyplace Kyngeston can be observed in the broad face and dimpled chin. Royal Commission on the Historical Monuments of England AA 56/7037.

prominent dimpled chin is found again in the portrait bust of Sir George Fettyplace" who died in 1743, the last male Fettyplace (Figure 8). Her brass in Childrey parish church, Berkshire, prepared earlier at the death of her husband John Kyngeston (but without her death date) shows her with him, as wife rather than as vowed widow.[23]

ELEANOR FETTYPLACE'S BOOKS

Susan's younger sister Eleanor Fettyplace chose to join the Syon community as a nun. In his will made October 9, 1520, and proved May 26, 1522, her stepfather Sir Richard Elyot says:

> Item I will that my doughter in lawe [i.e. stepdaughter] Elynour, doughter of Richard Fetiplace, Esquier, have after hir marriage celebrate fourty poundes to hir exhibition [support] yerely iii li vi s viii d [or] till she be professed in religion. And at suche tyme as she shalbe professed to the said xl li as moche as shalbe necessary in bokes or apparell to that entent.[24]

Eleanor's profession date is unknown, but in view of Elyot's will it must be after 1520.[25] The £40 which he left her is close to the £46 13 s 4d which about the same time in 1523 her sister Dorothy earmarked for herself on entering Syon, and, although Elyot specifies that the money is "till she be professed," perhaps some such amount was thought to approximate a retired lifetime's allowance for non-necessities. A portion of her stepfather's bequest probably subsidized the four books which bear Eleanor's name: a psalter, a contemporary printed devotional work, a printed missal, and a breviary.

The psalter which she signed dates from the end of the fifteenth century. Though it now wears a mid-nineteenth-century binding, stains from its original pink leather are visible.[26] In addition she owned Richard Whitford's 1532 *Pype . . . of Perfection*, a defense of the religious life written by a contemporary at Syon. Her signature "Elynor ffetyplace" is written on the last leaf.[27]

Her two remaining books are connected with this nun's life after the Dissolution. Although a group of Syon monks and nuns went abroad to Flanders, seven small groups remained in England, many maintaining the monastic observance at their relatives' homes. Eleanor was part of one such community, as was her niece Elizabeth Yate: this group was housed at the manor of Buckland (Berks.), the home of Susan and Eleanor's sister Mary Fettyplace Yate and her husband James.

In a folio Sarum missal printed at Paris by G. Merlin in 1555 a hand-written slip now pasted on the inside front cover reads: "Of your charyte pray for the sowle of dame Elyzabethe ffetyplace, some tyme relygious in Amesburye / & also for me Elynor ffetyplace her suster / relygious in Syon, at whose charges thys boke was bought & geven to thys churche of Bocklond / anno domini 1556" (see Erler, "Three Tudor Women"). The name of Elizabeth Fettyplace is found in the pension list of Amesbury, a Benedictine house in Wiltshire, where she is recorded as receiving £5 annually. She and Eleanor, "my Susters," are each bequeathed 20s in the 1543 will of James Yate: hence it may be that Elizabeth was also part of the group at Buckland.[28]

J. R. Fletcher observed that on Queen Elizabeth's accession Eleanor probably got back the missal which she had given to the Buckland parish church, since the missal accompanied Syon abroad when the community fled again in 1559, after the queen's dissolution of the restored houses. When G. J. Aungier wrote his 1840 history of Syon, the missal was in Lisbon, owned by the Reverend Joseph Ilsley, vice-president of the English college there. It subsequently passed through the hands of Daniel Rock (1799–1871), canon of Southwark and collector of me-dieval service books (the volume has his bookplate), then of Fletcher himself, to the Southwark Diocesan Archives.[29]

Eleanor commemorated her sister Elizabeth a second time, in her own breviary and psalter where the obit of Elizabeth Fettyplace is found in the calendar at May 21 with the date 1556(?). Commenting on this Bridgettine breviary, A. Jefferies Collins says, "We are fortunate still to possess the books from which those two [Eleanor Fettyplace and her niece Elizabeth Yate] seem to have sung their daily Office in banishment" – that is, Eleanor's breviary and Elizabeth's office book, the books from which the two prayed at Buckland after the Dissolu-tion. Eleanor's breviary had been used by Syon nuns for about a century before she owned it. Its calendar carries the obit of Sir William Bo[ ] who died on September 14, 1432 (as in Syon Abbey MS 2, a related book of hours). The name is cropped, but the 1428 list of Syon mem-bers in Bishop of London William Grey's register (1426–31) shows the name of Anna Bowys. Since she is third from the end, hence relatively junior, she may be the nun whose Syon profession is registered in the breviary's calendar on October 12, 1427. The breviary has been dated *c.* 1420, around the first years of Syon's existence. Eleanor Fettyplace was thus the last in a chain of Syon owners stretching back to the time of the monastery's founding. In the breviary's pages the members of Anna Bowys' family and Eleanor Fettyplace's, a century and a quarter apart, together comprise part of the community of souls for which Syon interceded.[30]

Eleanor Fettyplace and Elizabeth Yate were part of the re-enclosed group when Syon was restored under Mary in 1557, but the restoration lasted only briefly. Eleanor died on July 15, 1565, according to the Syon *Martyrology.* Fletcher says her death occurred abroad "during the time Syon occupied the unhealthy, disused Franciscan house at Zurich Zee."[31] Perhaps she did not take the breviary abroad, since in 1613, about fifty years after her death, during the year he was Senior Bursar, Eleanor's book was presented to the Bodleian by a fellow of Brasenose, Thomas Manwaring, later a Doctor of Divinity.[32]

DOROTHY FETTYPLACE CODRYNGTON'S BOOKS

The third Fettyplace sister Dorothy was, like Susan, a widow, though unlike Susan she became a Syon nun rather than a vowess after her husband's death. Her decision is recorded on her husband's brass at Appleton (Berks.), which states that John Goodryngton died on December 31, 1518, and that "Dorathe his wyfe . . . after his dethe toke relyagon in ye monastary of Syon." That the widow was Dorothy Fettyplace is shown by a chancery suit brought by Dorothy's mother and stepfather, Sir Richard Elyot and Elizabeth his wife, against Christopher Codryngton, Esquire. It charges that Codryngton refused to complete the marriage settlement agreed upon because his son John, the bridegroom, had since died (PRO CI /405/29). Dorothy Fettyplace was probably married for only a year or less, since the marriage contract, made in October 1517, stipulated that Dorothy and John should wed before Ascension Day next, or May 13, 1518.[33]

On April 24, 1523 Dorothy made her will, as the community mandated before profession. It reveals both the Syon rule's expectation of book ownership at entrance[34] and a degree of personal interest in reading as well. "Imprimis I will there be bestowed vpon A song booke / and other Inglisshe book*es* for my self suche as my Suster Kyngeston will apointe the sum of iij li."[35] Presumably the first clause refers to the plain-song book necessary for divine office. The £3 may have been intended simply to supply additional service books needed immediately upon entrance, or it may have purchased English books later on, for private reading. In 1526 Dorothy's grandmother, Alice Beselles, left the same amount for a memorial stone should she die at Syon; hence it is clear that three pounds represents a considerable sum. Dorothy Codryngton's name is written in a copy of a devotional tract published twelve years after her will was made, the *Tree & xij frutes of the holy goost* (October 29, 1535), and it may be that this is one of the English books which Susan Kyngeston bought for her sister with the money she had reserved at Syon entrance.[36]

The *Tree*'s editor has pointed out, in fact, that it is probably Dorothy Codryngton's hand which has annotated the Ampleforth Abbey printed copy of *Tree*. The emendations she made have two purposes: to correct the print using a manuscript probably owned by Syon, BL Additional 24192 which had been the printed edition's copytext, and, at the same time, to restore faded or imperfect readings in the manuscript, using the print. Such textual comparison was not unusual at Syon. In a second print of *Tree*, one owned by Syon nun Margaret Windsor, at six points a reading from Additional 24192 has been entered. A third copy of *Tree*, now at the Folger Library, has likewise been annotated to bring it into accord with this manuscript.[37] Such emendation was the traditional practice of monastic scribes; what is perhaps unusual is Syon's continuing use of this manuscript practice in combination with the new technique of printing.

Dorothy Codryngton's will was proved on February 16, 1531, with Susan Kyngeston as one of its two executors. She appears in the Syon pension list of 1539 and the Marian pension list *c.* 1554. Based on these payments, Fletcher states that she was one of the group of religious housed at Buckland with James Yate. Like many of the Syon groups after the Dissolution (and presumably like those of other religious houses as well), the Buckland establishment was strongly familial. Mary Fettyplace Yate and her husband James would have sheltered Mary's Fettyplace sisters Eleanor and Dorothy from Syon, perhaps Elizabeth from Amesbury, as well as the Yates' own daughter Elizabeth. Buckland seems to have continued as a religious community for almost twenty years, from 1539 until the Marian re-establishment in 1557. The Syon *Martyrology* records Dorothy's death on April 26, 1586.[38] She apparently lived to an advanced age: if she had been sixteen at her marriage in 1518, her age at death would have been 84.

A POLITICS OF PATIENCE

The religious and cultural shifts of the 1530s are mirrored, somewhat differently, in the vernacular reading of these sisters. Though the *Pype of Perfection* (1532) may appear a purely devotional text, Jan Rhodes points out that its defense of traditional religious life was conceived by Whitford as a reply to Lutheran attacks.[39]

The *Sermon of Mortalitie* had even more immediate resonances. The execution of the Nun of Kent and of the several religious who were known to the community must have caused not only Susan Kyngeston but the entire house both sorrow and anxiety. They were under siege throughout 1534. In January of that year, pressured by John Stokesley, bishop of London, Syon had signed a document acknowledging the king's marriage to Anne Boleyn but had been urged to a more conclusive acceptance, which the brethren refused. In May, the month after the Nun's execution, they were visited by Rowland Lee and Thomas Bedyll, Cromwell's agents, to urge that they take the Oath of Succession, and throughout the spring and summer the clergy of the London religious houses, colleges, and parishes were sworn, almost without exception.[40] Elyot's book may have appeared at any time between its July 1 preface and the end of 1534. Dedicated to his stepsister and contemporary, the vowess Susan, and remembering his younger stepsisters the nuns Elizabeth and Dorothy, Elyot's work includes these women in the religious politics of the mid-1530s. Indeed their involvement in those realities was far from indirect. Though Syon's Richard Reynolds was not arrested and executed until a year later, in April and May of 1535, for the Fettyplace sisters at Syon the transcendence of fear and sadness which Elyot's gift advised may have been, in 1534, a counsel of perfection.

The books which surface so frequently in these family networks[41] serve several functions. They express personal connection: though them a shared past is recalled and acknowledged, as in Eleanor's purchase of the missal in her sister's memory. They demonstrate shared intellectual interests, as in Dorothy's confident assignment of her book acquisition to Susan. They invoke values held in common: Eleanor's recitation with her niece Elizabeth Yate of divine office from the books they shared in their manor-house community. Men as well as women are participants here: Elyot's open declaration to Susan that "I doo vnfaynedly loue you" recalls their connection, and his gift of the sermon on patience, whatever its political intentions, is posited on a common view of the world. Especially valuable, however, are the glimpses we are afforded of female intellectual and spiritual exchange, supported by the ownership and reading of books.

5

Heterodoxy: Anchoress Katherine Manne and Abbess Elizabeth Throckmorton

Recent work on Lollardy has offered a full and often moving account of women's part in a religious resistance which was supported at every turn by book ownership and reading.[1] Indeed the nature of women's role in this movement and the way in which they read has seemed one of the most intriguing aspects of Lollardy. By contrast in the following histories, though the reading itself is sometimes challenging in content, the readers – one probably lay, one religious – are closely linked with the institutional church: the anchoress of the Norwich Dominican friary, Katherine Manne, and the abbess of a Cambridgeshire house of Poor Clares, Elizabeth Throckmorton. The point of both accounts might seem to be the extremely fluid nature of religious positions in the late 1520s. More important, however, is the way these narratives allow us to see the mechanisms of intellectual exchange, and the way they reveal the presence of women as intellectual participants in the tense debates just before the break with Rome.

THE MARTYR AND HIS PUPIL

John Foxe first recorded the connection between the Cambridge reformer Thomas Bilney and a Norwich anchoress, but it was Rotha Mary Clay's discovery of Katherine Manne's life after the Dissolution which allowed her to be named. Norman Tanner's more recent addition of a 1530 Norwich testamentary bequest to "Katherynne Manne, the anchores at the Blacke Freires" has made this identification more certain.[2]

Foxe's two mentions of the unnamed anchoress position her centrally in Bilney's last months, during his capture and trial. Bilney, whose activity had made him a leading figure in Cambridge reforming circles, was licensed to preach in Ely diocese in July 1525 and did so until some time in 1526, when Wolsey made him swear not to preach Lutheran opinion. With Thomas Arthur, he resumed preaching throughout East Anglia in the summer of 1527. Katherine Manne is perhaps more likely to have heard him at this time, rather than earlier.

Bilney and Arthur were tried and compelled to recant in December 1527, and the former was imprisoned in the Tower for about a year, returning to Cambridge in 1529.[3] Foxe records his depression, so severe that his friends feared for him until a dramatic reversal sometime in 1531, when Bilney announced that "he would go to Jerusalem, alluding belike to the words and example of Christ in the gospel, going up to Jerusalem, what time he was appointed to suffer his passion." He

> immediately departed to Norfolk, and there preached first privily in households, to confirm the brethren and sisters, and also to confirm the anchoress, whom he had converted to Christ. Then preached he openly in the fields . . . And so, setting forward on his journey to the celestial Jerusalem, he departed from thence to the anchoress in Norwich, and there gave her a New Testament of Tyndale's trans-lation, and the *Obedience of a Christian Man*; whereupon he was apprehended and carried to prison.[4]

Bilney's statement at the stake, recorded by mayor of Norwich Edward Rede, attempted to preserve Katherine Manne from suspicion of heresy:[5]

> And where as that the lady Ankeres of the blak freres is put in grete trouble and surmysed that she shuld be an heretike and that I shuld teche & instructe her with heresyes as well by bookes as otherwise. Good cristen people here I take my deth upon it that I doo knowe her but for a full good & vertuous woman. I beseeche god to preserue her in her goodnes. And I know non heresy in her nor I neuer taught her heresy. I wold god there were many more so good lyvyng in vertue as she is both men & women.[6]

The role of books is emphasized by both these accounts. Bilney must have given Manne the first edition of *Obedience*, printed in Antwerp October 2, 1528 (*STC* 24445) and the first or second edition of the New Testament, either the 1525 partial edition (quires A–K) printed in Cologne (*STC* 2823) or the first complete edition which appeared at Worms *circa* 1526 (*STC* 2824). If, as it seems, she did not read these books until 1531, they were by this time formally prohibited, appearing at the head of the list of forbidden books proclaimed on June 22, 1530.[7]

Circulation of imported reforming books in East Anglia was widespread, as Norfolk bishop Richard Nix complained in 1530.[8] One of the best-known distributors of such books was Robert Necton, a Norwich man and brother to the city's sheriff Thomas Necton. Foxe describes the sheriff as "Bilney's special good friend."[9] Robert Necton's 1528 statement shows that he had sold books in Norfolk, Suffolk, Essex, and London, and indeed that he had, while staying at his brother's house in Norwich, been reported to Bishop Nix for possession of the New Testament. Three years later, in 1531, Robert Bayfield, a former Benedictine monk of Bury St. Edmund's, confessed to distributing books in Norfolk.[10] Whether or not these two were Bilney's suppliers, their activity in East Anglia demonstrates that the books Bilney gave Katherine Manne were among many such circulating there.

THE ANCHORESS' ADVISORS

The issues raised by Bilney's life and death continued to preoccupy Katherine Manne. Four years after his execution a letter was addressed to her by Dan John Bouge, then a Carthusian monk of Axholme in Lincolnshire.[11] Dated 1535, it must have been written after the execution of Axholme prior Augustine Weber on May 4, of John Fisher on June 22, and of Thomas More on July 6, since it constitutes, in part, a valedictory for all three. The Act of Supremacy's consequences had now been made painfully immediate, not only by the London executions but by the proclamation of June 9, 1535, ordering the clergy everywhere to preach and declare the king's "title, dignity and style of supreme head in earth immediately under God."[12] The Act of Supremacy, in fact, raises again the ecclesiological questions which the anchoress' earlier reading had presented. Tyndale's *Obedience* asked: what is the nature of the church and the relation of members to head? The Act of Supremacy puts these same theological questions again, in a political context. For a second time we see Katherine Manne engaged with these issues.

Bouge's letter is couched as a response to what must have been a verbal message, since, though he thanks the anchoress for her token, he wishes for even "a lyttyll byll of iij lynnys scribblyd with your owyn hand." In advising the anchoress "how to ordyr your selfe in this tyme of this gret scisme," Bouge invokes two principles: the first is "Credo in sanctam ecclesiam catholicam." Edward Rede's account of Bilney's death asserts that he repeated "Credo ecclesiam catholicam sondry tymes"[13] – words whose ambiguity may be considered a refuge, as both Bouge and Bilney certainly intended them to be.

The reformers' invisible community united by faith in Christ's saving work here confronts the powerful entity invoked in the second piece of advice which Bouge gave Katherine Manne: "Honor thy father and thy mother." Bouge's description of the church as the maternal principle would certainly agree with Thomas More's description of a benevolent but firmly institutional reality: "she whych engendreth vs to god & which both with mylke and strenger mete must fede vs & foster vs up / & none other nuryce is ther by whom we can be truely & faythfully brought vp."[14]

Manne must thus adhere both to the church her mother and to the "discrete and tawt fathyrs" whom Bouge recommends, "*Master* Doctor Boknam and *Master Doctor* Warner my good frendes and Mastyres," both of whom are identifiable from their Cambridge and Norwich connections.

William Buckenham was a Cambridge graduate (B.A. 1482–83; M.A. 1486; B.D. 1502; D.D. 1506–07), a fellow of Gonville Hall, and its master from 1514 to 1536.[15] The Hall had presented its master as rector of St. Michael Coslany in Norwich since 1464, and Buckenham served in this capacity from 1514 to 1540, dying at Norwich in that year, aged 81.[16] He was resident in Norwich part of the time, and, like his predecessors who likewise served both Cambridge and Norwich, he improved the Norwich property. "Buckenham 'bought a little piece of ground' to enlarge the yard 'where standeth the coop for capons and the privy and made the wall.' " The homeliness of these details contrasts with his intellectual and antiquarian interests. He had been executor to the notable scholar and physician John Argentein, and he compiled the Black Parchment Book which preserves copies of the university's medieval records. In 1535 he signed the Act of Supremacy in his capacity as master of Gonville Hall. Christopher Brooke calls him "a remark-able link between two worlds," that is, medieval Cambridge and the reformed or humanist university.[17]

William Warner's Cambridge career indicates that he was slightly younger than Buckenham (B.A. ?1497–98; M.A. 1501; B.D. 1508–09; D.D. 1512–13). He, too, was a fellow of Gonville Hall (1499–1517) and from 1515 to 1545 he was rector of Winterton, Norfolk.[18] He had been close to Bilney who, at his execution, chose Warner "as his old acquain-tance to be with him for his ghostly comfort," according to Foxe. When Bilney bade Warner, in farewell, to "feed your flock, feed your flock, that when the Lord cometh, he may find you so doing," Warner spake but few words for weeping."[19] Warner may thus have felt a particular responsibility for Manne whom Bilney defended in his last address. On the other hand, perhaps Bouge chose Warner as the anchoress' advisor because of their common friendship with the martyr.

Like Buckenham and Warner, Bouge was a Cambridge graduate, and in his letter recalls his friendship both with them and with John Fisher and Thomas More. He and Fisher "were batchelures of arte to gythyr and mastres of arte to gythyr and bothe off on day" (thus, respectively, in 1487 and 1491). The service he mentions at More's parish might have been, Emden suggests, at St. Stephen Walbrook.[20] Other facts about him are few.[21] How he knew Katherine Manne we have no idea (Norwich had no Charterhouse), unless the John Bowche recorded as a member of the St. George Tombland parish staff in 1492 might be identified as the letter writer.[22] Bouge's letter to Manne, however, provides an example of the kind of spiritual advising which male religious had always offered to devout women in the ordinary course of events. It is extraordinary only because, in the mid-1530s, the spiritual had become so inescapably the political.

In the period between her first contact with Bilney and the reformer's death, Katherine Manne received economic support at the highest level of Norwich's urban economy. Robert Jannys, who left her a lifetime interest in a tenement, was in doing so providing the anchoress with permanent maintenance. Though his 1530 will attempted a compre-hensive twenty-year plan of support for all anchorites in Norwich, at that time six in number,[23] Manne is the only one named. Jannys, a grocer, was alderman and twice mayor of Norwich (1517 and 1524) and one of the richest provincial merchants in England (in 1523 he was assessed on £1,100).[24] His bequest (witnessed, incidentally, by William Buckenham) prevents us from regarding Manne as either religiously or culturally marginal. Similarly, although her 1548 civic pension of 20s yearly, discovered by Clay, might be viewed merely as an exchange for relinquishing her rights to the Blackfriars anchoress' house, her 1550 civic license[25] formally acknowledges Manne's status as *femme sole*. It offers her economic independence: the ability to maintain a business, sue and be sued for debt, train apprentices.[26] Thus both before and after this period of religious change, she was supported by her city's mercantile elite – first by Norwich's mayor and later by its governing body. Such anchoritic patronage, which partakes of a long tradition, probably has more to do with the city's acknowledgement of its collective identity than with endorsement of a particular religious conviction.[27]

Intellectually, too, she moved at an elevated level, served by a variety of advisors. This relation too, like her economic patronage, can be seen in traditional terms: anchorites have often been the recipients of spiritual direction from distinguished guides. Her mentors included Bouge, the Carthusian monk, former schoolmate of Fisher and pastor of More, whose counsel was religiously conservative; Warner and Buckenham, the Cambridge doctors of theology who, despite their differences, might be grouped as moderates; and most centrally, she was taught by Bilney. Assessment of her own position, in view of these diverse influences, is impossible – the more so when we realize how successfully Bilney, her first instructor, has himself eluded a verdict (he has recently been called a "celebrated prevaricator.")[28] Davis' characterization of him as an evangelical is perhaps the most satisfactory assessment of Bilney's faith in Christ and in Scripture, his belief in preaching, and the irenic attitude movingly demonstrated by his death.[29]

Such positions, however, represented a temporary stage before the events of 1534. As Manne's 1535 inquiry shows, the political situation had by that time posed new difficulties. Whether Bilney's positions should have been considered formally heretical appears open to doubt, and to speak of Manne as Bilney's disciple in heresy is perhaps unjust to both. In her reincorporation, economic and quotidian at least, into her

Norwich community perhaps she is closer to Warner, Bilney's chosen friend who accompanied him to the stake but died in 1545 as rector of his Norfolk parish.

Partly her life conforms to a familiar medieval pattern: an anchoress living in a city where anchoritism had been historically recognized, and guided at least partly by the local clergy, here a distinguished group due to the proximity of the university. (Tanner judges that 25 out of 60 Norwich rectors and vicars between 1500 and 1532 were university graduates.)[30] Regional influence might be thought particularly strong in Katherine Manne's life, as in Margaret Purdans'. The degree to which each of these women, living about fifty years apart, was able to obtain spiritual counsel and support from male Cambridge (and London) contemporaries seems notable. In Norwich, the lively exchange between male and female devout persons whether lay or religious, the high number of parishes, the strong local identity, the influence of continental religious developments, seems to have produced an atmosphere especially stimulating to religious life, from which both Katherine Manne and Margaret Purdans benefited and which they might be said to represent. Her East Anglian origins may underlie Katherine Manne's identification as one of the few female respondents to the 1520s and 1530s nexus of theological and political issues – issues which are focused in the book which Bilney gave her, the *Obedience of a Christian Man*.

THE ABBESS, THE CONTINENTAL SCHOLAR, AND THE ENGLISH REFORMER

At almost the same time as Thomas Bilney gave Tyndale's *Obedience* to Katherine Manne, another woman was asking for a different work of Tyndale's, his translation of Erasmus' *Enchiridion*. In the 1528 interrogation of Humphrey Monmouth, the prominent London merchant described his support of William Tyndale, both as a member of his household and after Tyndale left England. Monmouth says, "the foresaid Sir William left me an English book, called *Enchiridion*. The which book the Abbes of Dennye desyred yt of me, and I sent yt to her."[31]

Perhaps the reason Monmouth's account has been so frequently quoted is that Elizabeth Throckmorton's intention here is so enigmatic. What was her interest in the *Enchiridion*? Although the book quickly became an international best seller after its 1503 publication in Latin, and was translated into Czech, German, Dutch, and Spanish by 1525, no English edition survives until 1533. The *Enchiridion* repudiates the greed and corruption of the established church and calls for a reformed monasticism and a Christianity governed not by rule but by charity. Ceremonies, pilgrimages, relics, are condemned, and Christ is offered as the seeker's only model. The appeal of such a rigorist position both inside and outside the church, is clear; its danger lay in "the subsumption of religion within a lay Christian humanism. . . . It is not difficult to see that [this] could lead to Protestant practices."[32]

In the 1520s other religious women were reading similar texts. The controversial *Image of Love*, sixty copies of which its printer sent to Syon in 1525, was a work which, like Erasmus', inveighed against external forms (in this case images) and which emphasized scripture's centrality.[33] Prayer, fasting, observances, were unimportant in comparison with interior dispositions; nevertheless it cautioned "we maye not leue of [leave off] the honourable and deuoute customes and holy ordynaunces of the chyrch" (E 3 v).

Its author John Ryckes was, like Elizabeth Throckmorton, a Franciscan, and a member of the Greenwich community to which the abbess' nephew William Peyto belonged. Written as a New Year's gift for a community of nuns, probably Syon, the *Image of Love* represents a moderate reforming position which nonetheless produced a strong response from bishop of London Cuthbert Tunstall.[34] It seems that Ryckes himself thought his views on reform of church practices and of religious life would find an appropriate forum for discussion amongst this community of religious. *Image of Love* and Erasmus' *Enchiridion* both speak, for the most part, from inside the institutional church, and it is in this context that Elizabeth Throckmorton's search for Erasmus' book should be viewed. The abbess' request identifies her as one of the first readers of Erasmus' work in English (before 1528). Like Tyndale its English translator, she may have been compelled by its call for a spirituality which would, as Erasmus says, pass beyond the flesh of external ceremonies to the living spirit. Her attempt to obtain this "model of true Christianity" as its title describes it, might best be understood as a wish to share in the period's re-examination of spiritual life and observances.

Other nuns may have read Erasmus' work as well. The 1554 inventory of William Pownsett, steward of Barking, headed "Certayne book*es* yn the Abbey of Barkynge" lists an "enchiridion milit*is* christ.' "[35] David Bell calls this a Latin edition of Erasmus' text, but since the English editions bore the Latin title, it might also have been an English version. Whether the books in Pownsett's list were his own or the abbey's remains uncertain. Laywomen too were part of Erasmus' English audience. On July 8, 1536, Richard Hore sent Honor Lisle a book which he called "the buckler to defend us from all troubles of mind and the sword where-with we overcome our spiritual enemies." This might have been either of the first two English editions of the *Enchiridion*: November 15, 1533 (*STC* 10479) or February 12, 1534 (*STC* 10480). Hore was a chaplain of Cranmer's and had met Lady Lisle when he preached at Calais in 1535 and 1536. Though his orientation was doubtless a reforming one, Honor Lisle's was deeply traditional.[36]

Abbess Throckmorton's desire for Erasmus' book in English might have been a natural consequence of her abbey's other contacts with the continental scholar, made about this time. In autumn 1525 Erasmus' former student Thomas Grey prevailed upon his teacher to send a greeting to Denny, where Grey's two sisters were nuns. The convent responded with a gift which was stolen en route to Erasmus. He in turn composed for them an *Epistola consolatoria in adversus*, printed 1528.[37] Knowles suggests that Erasmus might even have visited the abbey, when in 1513 to escape the plague in Cambridge he stayed with his friend William Gonnell at Landbeach, a mile away.[38]

In examining the abbess' desire for the *Enchiridion*, these suggestions have focused on Erasmus. But perhaps the focus instead should be Tyndale, the work's translator. The case of William Tracy of Gloucestershire was a cause célèbre of the 1530s. Tracy's 1530 reforming testament refused to leave money for masses and prayers, relying instead on faith in Christ's saving work. As a result his body was exhumed and burned. The will itself was published in 1535, along with theological commentary by John Frith and by Tyndale, who made it clear that he had known Tracy for a long time: "a learned man and better seen in the works of St. Austin twenty years before he died [i.e. since about 1510] than ever I knew doctor in England."[39] 1510 was the year in which Tyndale left his native Gloucestershire for Oxford, so perhaps the very young

Tyndale knew Tracy. In 1521 Tyndale returned to Gloucestershire, where he spent two years as tutor to the children of Sir John and Lady Walsh at Old Sodbury, and at this time he may have renewed his Gloucestershire aquaintance with Tracy. It was during these two years that he worked on his English translation of the *Enchiridion*, finished by the time he left for London in summer 1523.[40] Unsuccessful at obtaining service with Cuthbert Tunstall, Tyndale lived with Humphrey Monmouth until May 1524, when he took ship for Germany leaving with Monmouth, as the merchant testified, his *Enchiridion* translation.

When Abbess Throckmorton asked Monmouth for a copy sometime after this date, how did she know that a translation had been made and that Monmouth had it? The key may be the woman who was both William Tracy's wife and the abbess' sister, Margaret Throckmorton Tracy.[41] Through her the abbess may have heard about the reforming work of the continental scholar with whom she was already, albeit distantly, familiar – now recently Englished by a Gloucestershire connection of her sister and brother-in-law.

THE ABBESS AS CLIENT

The abbess' name may more tentatively be connected with a second devotional text, the *Directory of conscience, a profytable treatise for suche that be tymorous or ferfull in conscyence* written by William Bonde, a monk of Syon. Though the subject of scrupulosity may seem a narrowly pious one, its connection with problems of doubt and with questions of the correctness and validity of individual moral judgment made it a political topic as well in these decades. Susan Brigden points out that "it was through just such a crisis in faith [that is, an attack of scrupulosity], that Luther discovered his theology of grace."[42]

The treatise exists in two versions: the earlier one is described in its preface as written for "one of the Systres of Syon," Bonde's own house, and was published in 1527. After the author's 1532 death a second edition appeared around 1534 in two issues. One of these is directed to a devout but general audience ("those that obsarves and kepes the preceptes . . . of Iesu crist" rather than "spouses of cryste"), while the other's title page declares it is sent to a religious woman of Denny at the instance of a spiritual friend, who supervised the work and divided it into twenty chapters.[43]

Bonde's somewhat testy preface, which must have been written between 1527 and 1532, appears only in the version intended for the nun of Denny. "Youre charite mouyth me to wryte vnto you thoughe vnaquaynted / bycause ye haue sent to vs many & diuers tokens vndeseruyd on oure parte. I require you for the loue of our lorde that ye do no more so." Pointing out that worldly pleasures may constitute a hindrance to spiritual growth Bonde concedes, however, that historically "temporall tokens" have been exchanged between holy persons as expressions of love "wherin they be vnyed & knyte in oure lorde god that sendyth or receyueth suche tokens" (f. 2).

Since Elizabeth Throckmorton was abbess of Denny from at least 1512[44] (and perhaps earlier) it is unlikely that the gifts, either to Erasmus or to Bonde, could have been sent without her knowledge, if not her active initiative. The items sent slightly earlier to Erasmus might suggest that Bonde's tokens came not only from the same house but from the same hand.

In her edition of the *Directory*, Bridget Cusack points out that the responsibility which Bonde apparently felt toward Denny might stem from his position as a fellow of Pembroke College, Cambridge since Pembroke and Denny shared a common founder, Mary de Saint Pol, whose fourteenth-century draft statutes for the college require its fellows to serve as confessors to her nuns of Denny and to assist them generally. Presumably, then, the male spiritual friend who, as Bonde says in the preface, "so instantly mouyed me [to write the nun of Denny] that I can not conuiently denye his godly & deuoute request" might be the Syon monk and fellow of Pembroke John Fewterer, confessor general from 1523 to 1536.[45]

Perhaps the intellectual stimulus provided by this Syon connection has something to do with Denny's reputation as what A. I. Doyle has called a "center of vernacular devotion; for which the sole extant copy of [Osbern] Bokenham's *Legends [of Holy Women]* was possibly made, and other English writings in the early sixteenth century."[46] Two books from Denny's library survive.[47] The first is a copy of the northern homilies, an English verse rendering of the Sunday gospels with accompanying sermons (CUL Additional MS 8335). The second, which bears Elizabeth Throckmorton's name, is a late fifteenth-century manuscript of William of Nassington's poem on the Lord's Prayer, *Speculum Vitae* (Oxford,

Bodleian MS Hatton 18). Vincent Gillespie points out that this work was probably composed for oral performance and hence that the interest shown in it by religious might be due to its suitability for communal reading aloud; he calls it "the nearest thing to a vernacular *summa*."[48] The French book, *La ymage de notre dame* which Margery de Nerford left to Denny in 1417 (chapter 2) and the unnamed French book which the abbess of Denny was willed in 1448 by Agnes Stapilton,[49] may be representative of other French books which the house held earlier.

THE THROCKMORTON FAMILY

Denny was dissolved in 1539 (see Figure 9) when its last abbess retired with two or three nuns to Coughton, the family manor in Warwickshire. According to the eighteenth-century antiquary William Cole, there they

Figure 9 Dole gate from Denny Abbey (Camb.) carved with Abbess Elizabeth Throckmorton's name, from Coughton Court, the Throckmorton seat. Reproduced by permission of Mrs. Clare McLaren-Throckmorton, Coughton Court, Alcester, War.

"lived a *Conventual Life*, & in *their proper Habits, hardly ever appearing* in the *Family, & never* when *Company* was there; but *prescribed* to *themselves* the *Rules of their Order* as far as it was *possible* for them *to do* in *their present Situation* where their *Whole Employ* was *Attendance* in the *Oratory*, & *Work* at *their Needle*."[50] The nuns accompanying Elizabeth Throckmorton have so far remained anonymous, but the will of her brother Sir Robert leaves 20s apiece to "myne suster Dame Elisabeth abbas of Denny and my ij Doughtours Dame Margaret and Joyes." The same "Margaret, a nunne," appears in the Throckmorton pedigree though Joyce does not. Equally likely to have retired to Coughton is "Joanna monialis apud Dennie," daughter of John Peyto and granddaughter of Goditha Throckmorton Peyto, Abbess Elizabeth's sister.[51] The truncated community at Coughton may thus have comprised a family group of aunt, one or two nieces, and a great-niece, plus a woman servant whose identity we know because in 1543 the abbess' niece Elizabeth Englefield died and left the substantial bequest of 40s to Katheryn Tanner, "servant to my aunt Elizabeth Throckmerton late Abbess of Denny." A brass plate in Coughton church commemorates the abbess' death on January 13, 1547.[52]

Elizabeth Throckmorton's family background might be judged particularly literate and devout – a phrase used by W. A Pantin to describe the owner of the narrow parchment scroll containing a daily religious regimen which he discovered among the Throckmorton muniments.[53] The unusual record it provides of early fifteenth-century lay spirituality has been much noticed: Pantin speculated that its owner might have been Thomas Throckmorton (d. 1414) or John Throckmorton (d. 1445). The latter, a lawyer, courtier, soldier, M.P., and retainer and executor of Richard Beauchamp, earl of Warwick, was sub-treasurer of England, and is depicted on his memorial brass in armor with his wife Eleanor in widow's garb.[54]

The family tradition of piety is witnessed slightly later by the letter of fraternity issued in 1478 from the Grande Chartreuse to Elizabeth Throckmorton's mother, Margaret Olney Throckmorton, together with Robert Olney esquire, either Margaret's father or brother. Notice of its arrival, in the form of a letter to Margaret from her father, survives in the Coughton muniments.[55] Also among the family papers is a late fifteenth-century religious miscellany which contains among other texts a version of the "Treatise of Meekness" addressed to a woman rather than a man, and which bears the name "Elyzbeth" on its last folio. Edward Wilson points out that its date of acquisition by the Throckmortons is not known, but alludes to Abbess Elizabeth and to her sister-in-law Elizabeth Baynham, second wife of Sir Robert Throckmorton, in glossing the marginal name.[56]

The family focus on things spiritual is visible in the lives, male and female, of Elizabeth Throckmorton's generation as well. If we assume that Margaret Throckmorton Tracy shared her husband's reforming beliefs, nevertheless other siblings appear more orthodox. The heir to Coughton, Elizabeth's brother Sir Robert Throckmorton, belonged to an Augustinian confraternity and died at Rome while on pilgrimage. The 1518 will of this soldier and courtier displays particular and knowledgeable preferences in matters both liturgical and aesthetic. Throckmorton's chantry priest, for example, is to celebrate on Sunday mass of the Trinity, on Wednesday requiem mass, on Friday Jesus mass "except those Dayes afore reherssed fall vppon Doble ffeastis dayes." Five statues, richly painted and gilded, are assigned by subject and position to Coughton church, and the decorative program of the windows is likewise specified. The will's dramatic codicil, made by the dying Throckmorton in Rome, attempts to arrange his party's safe return to England and a Roman burial for himself.[57] Another brother, William, was a doctor of civil and canon law, a master in chancery, servant to Wolsey, and last warden but one of the collegiate church of Shottesbrook, Berks., where his effigy remains in the chancel (d. 1535).[58] Elizabeth's sister Margery's religious devotion is illustrated by her assumption of the vow of perpetual chastity on the death of her husband, Richard Middlemore of Egbaston, Warwickshire.[59]

Perhaps most interesting of the abbess' sisters and brothers, however, is Goditha Throckmorton, wife of Edward Peyto, and owner of the religious collection known as the Worcestershire Miscellany (London, BL Additional MS 37787). Written after 1388 in the Cistercian abbey of Bordesley northeast of Worcester, its English material includes a form of confession, the remnant of a verse Stations of Rome (a guidebook), a verse debate between the body and soul, two songs of love-longing, and a number of short religious lyrics.[60] The unexpected death of Goditha's husband at age thirty, in 1488, resulted in various legal claims on behalf of his widow and eldest son John Peyto, then aged nine and in ward to his uncle Sir Robert Throckmorton. Dower claims to the Warwickshire manors of Chesterton and (partially) Wolfhamcote and the avowson of Barton-on-the-Heath preserve Goditha's name,[61] and brasses of her husband and herself in Fladbury church, long the Throckmortons' parish, were engraved by Dugdale.[62] The best-known of Goditha's children was her son William Peyto, head of the Greenwich Observant Friars and a conservative in religion. Preaching before Henry VIII at Easter 1532 he warned the king that if he married Anne Boleyn, the dogs would lick his blood as they had done with Ahab.[63]

The Peyto–Throckmorton family connection visible here[64] is further illustrated by Goditha Peyto's donation inscription in the Worcestershire miscellany: "Iste lyber pertinet ad me mi lady Peyto. Amen yt est yta fyat amen so be heyte . . . by the gefte of d[ame] Goodyth Peyto thy booke Goody Throkmarton." The second Goditha's identity is uncertain: she was probably the child of the older Goditha's brother John or Richard, hence her niece.

These Throckmorton sisters illustrate in a particularly clear way the characteristic notes of late medieval devotion (Goditha Throckmorton Peyto's handwritten prayers at the end of her manuscript, two with the refrain "hail mary") and, at the same time, its openness to a renewed and purified spirituality (Elizabeth Throckmorton's request for the *Enchiridion*.) This spirituality was supported by the ownership and transmission of books, between women as well as men. Viewed in this light Elizabeth Throckmorton's active search for fresh vernacular treatments of theological and devotional subjects may be attributed not only to her personal interests and to her position as head of a religious house, but to her place in a late-medieval gentry family. The Throckmortons provided both models of such spiritual and intellectual concerns and a network of contacts through which to pursue them.

Like Katherine Manne's, Elizabeth Throckmorton's membership in these readers' networks manifested itself partly under a traditional guise. The request for spiritual direction which Manne presented to Bilney and later to Bouge, and which (probably) Throckmorton made both to her unknown spiritual friend at Syon and to Bonde, had distinguished precedents. Vowed or reclused women had always sought such counsel. It may be, in fact, the conventional and recognized nature of this relationship between spiritual mentor and protégée which allowed these two women to be part of the book-based controversies of the period. Katherine Manne and Elizabeth Throckmorton shared the vision of a purified church which seemed graspable to many in these years. For both women, an informed and intense spirituality made their participation in such intellectual exchange eminently natural.

6

Women owners of religious incunabula: the physical evidence

In the female reading which has been presented so far, manuscripts have gradually given way to printed editions. At this point, we might ask whether the coming of print made any substantial change in such reading. Between Caxton's first English printing in 1476 and the end of the century, a period of twenty-four years provides a manageable, limited, span of time in which to look at women's ownership of the first printed devotional books. We are accustomed, of course, to the claim that printing both increased the audience for reading and widened it. But to what extent were women part of that growing crowd of readers? Currently we have little sense of what difference printing might have made for female access to literacy. And, indeed, before this large question can be answered more specific ones appear and need to be attempted. Can early printed texts preferred by women be identified? Even more centrally, who were the women who owned the first printed books?

These women are not entirely unknown: their identities and to some extent the ways in which they read have interested many writers. So far, however, it has been difficult to form a clear idea of their significance from the pieces of information available. Perhaps a systematic approach to the surviving witnesses, to the books themselves, would be useful. If all the remaining copies from a particular early edition were examined, tabulation of their provenance, where the volumes revealed this, might supply a sense of what books were preferred by women and even what proportion of the surviving copies were owned by women. Such a search might also suggest whether or not a degree of continuity existed between women's reading before and after the coming of print. To some extent as well, the marks in these books – female ownership signatures and gift inscriptions – would illuminate the ways in which women used these volumes. As a result, the culture of women's reading in the quarter century just after English printing began might emerge somewhat more clearly.

Printing before 1500 was, of course, strongly religious in subject. Of the editions which appeared from 1476 to 1499, a recent count has estimated that 17 percent were liturgical and 21 percent were vernacular religious works (the largest subject category).[1] In producing so many English devotional books, the early printers were accurately reflecting private reading's overwhelming spiritual emphasis, a focus which transcended class, gender, and state in life. From these widely read books, eight incunable titles (eleven editions) were selected for examination; approximately 105 copies survive from these editions. To these were added all the extant largely complete copies of incunable Sarum books of hours: fifteen editions, about thirty-six copies, for a database of 141 books (see Appendix III). Of these 141 surviving incunabula (devotional texts and primers) 111 have been seen or reported on for signs of ownership, about 79 percent.[2]

A little over half of the women whose names are found in the first English printed books were nuns while ownership of the remaining books is divided between aristocrats and gentry women.[3] The number of nuns' books is only a bit higher than laywomen's (14 vs. 11), and perhaps the difference is not substantial enough to be significant. Nonetheless, it is slightly surprising, given the universality with which religious rules forbade private property. Several explanations might be suggested. By the last quarter of the fifteenth century the currency of discretionary income for religious has been acknowledged. For male houses, at least, wages were frequent rather than exceptional and some female houses, too, participated in this system.[4]

Late medieval wills illustrate another source of money for religious – the remembrance gifts for prayers directed both to individuals and to their houses. In 1498, for instance, Katherin Kerre of Norwich left to the prioress of Carrow 12d, to Dame Secyly Ryall 6s 8d, Dame Mary White 3s 4d, Dame Anne Martyn 6s 8d, and to every other nun of the house 3s 4d. In a culture which elevated reading's role in spiritual development, religious may sometimes have used such monetary gifts to buy books or have them written. In fact we know what contemporaries paid for some of the printed books actually owned by religious women and hence are able to assess the possibility of nuns' purchase. One of the incunabula discussed in this chapter, for instance, the *Scale of Perfection*, in 1505 and 1507 fetched the moderate price of 2s 8d. In 1504 *Vitas Patrum*, a thick folio, cost 5 s.[5] A bequest such as Kathryn Kerre's generous 6s 8d would have allowed an individual nun to acquire more than one of these early editions.

Certainly, too, some of the books which bear religious women's names were purchases made by their house. In particular, sixteenth-century names may be found in the remnants of institutional collections scattered at the Dissolution. Katherine Efflyn's *Vitas Patrum* (1495) might have belonged first to Dartford, and Susan Purefeye's *Speculum Vite Christi* (1490) might have been Syon's. If so, it appears that at least some women's houses had been prompt in acquiring the new printed books.

If this examination offers some idea of what women owned the first English printed books, it also reveals some preferred texts. The physical evidence in these pages shows that two books in particular often found their way to a female readership partly courtly and partly religious. The first of these is de Worde's edition of the Sarum primer; the second is Walter Hilton's *Scale of Perfection*. Both were printed in 1494.

DE WORDE'S 1494 PRIMER AND OTHER INCUNABLE BOOKS OF HOURS

This primer was produced at the request of Margaret Beaufort, as its colophon states.[6] Four more-or-less complete copies exist, plus the calendar from another copy. Of these five, four have been owned by women.

The Lambeth Palace copy has associations both with the Bridgettine community of Syon and with Margaret Beaufort. It contains, loose, an early engraving of St. Katherine of Sweden, the daughter of the Bridgettine foundress. The card's inscription shows its printing was commissioned by Dendermonde, a Bridgettine house in Flanders which provided shelter for Syon émigrée nuns at the Dissolution. The Lambeth copy's binding, made about 1494, constitutes the earliest use in London of a stamped panel; the book is traditionally said to have been bound for Margaret Beaufort.[7] Slighter evidence associates the Bodleian copy of this primer also with Syon, since it bears the parchment fore-edge tabs which have been considered characteristic of Syon's library.[8] The calendar only from this primer survives as the first item of a British Library collection-volume in which the name of a nun, Dame Margaret Necollson, appears. She may have belonged either to the community of Elstow, Bedfordshire, or to that of Wotton, Yorkshire.[9] A third copy has a strongly familial history. Between 1494 and her death in 1503 Mable, Lady Dacre, gave this new book to her nephew Thomas Parr (b. 1478), whose signature the book carries. Susan James believes it was used subsequently in his own children's schoolroom, on the basis of its "scrawls and ink-blots." After Thomas died, his widow Maud Parr gave the book to Thomas' brother Sir William Parr, probably as a memento of his brother. She had her children, including the future queen Katherine Parr, write polite gift messages to their uncle in what had by now – perhaps about 1520 – became a family heirloom.[10]

Women's signatures might be expected to surface in other Sarum *horae* as well, since books of hours were both the most widely produced and the most widely owned of all devotional reading, by both men and women.[11] Early printed primers' rate of disappearance, however, is high. Of the twenty-nine surviving primer editions printed before 1500, half (fourteen) exist only in fragments of a few leaves or even a single leaf, fragments in which it is unusual to discover ownership. From the remaining fifteen editions, thirty-six largely complete copies are listed by *STC*. Of the thirty I have seen, seven have been written in by women.

The first example is anonymous: in a Parisian primer of 1495 someone has written "I whas & ys & eu*er* schell be yowre awne true bed[e]women tyll I dee." The rest of these books carry female names and two of them were gifts from one woman to another. A unique Parisian primer of 1495 reads: "My nowne good nese I reqver you to remember me yor lovynge aunte marget grey." In another Parisian book from 1498 Elizabeth of York has written to an unknown woman, probably a member of her household: "Madam I pray yow Remember me in yowr god prayers yowr mastres Elysabeth R." Two more volumes simply register their owners' names. An English book of hours from 1497 has the inscription "Marg*ar*et Porter gentilwoma*n*" on c 3 v, while on later pages "Marg*ar*et" and "Porther" are written. A vellum primer printed May 16, 1498 at

Paris has been signed "Elysabethe Woodhowse"; the name is enclosed in a drawn scroll. Another copy from the same edition carries the rhyme: "good mesterys fenche I you requeer / to pray for me att my desyer / your asvryd kateryn roydon."[12]

The last of these female-owned books of hours is particularly unusual, since it constitutes one of a pair belonging to a single owner. Though the evidence of wills shows that women often possessed more than one book of hours,[13] it is rare for several of these books belonging to a single owner to survive. Just at the turn of the century, however, we find both a printed book of hours and a manuscript one which were owned by Anne Withypoll. Her husband Paul had a notable mercantile and political career; he traded in Italy, Spain, and the Netherlands, and was governor of the Merchant Adventurers as well as several times Member of Parliament for London. The Tudor humanist Thomas Lupset was her son Edmund's teacher and dedicated to his pupil his *Exhortation to Young Men*. Her daughter Elizabeth who died young at the age of twenty-six, was a precocious linguist, fluent in Italian, Spanish, and Latin.

Anne was married twice before she became Paul Withypoll's wife and her first two marriages are recorded in a Paris-printed primer of 1495, where she has written: "This booke is myne. Anne ffrevile alias Reede" (D 1). Her first husband, who died soon after their 1494 marriage, was William Freville of Little Shelford, Cambridgeshire. The date of her second marriage, to William Rede, a Boston merchant of the staple, is marked in the calendar of this book of hours: April 24 (no year). Her third marriage, to Paul Withypoll in January 1509 (i.e. 1510), is also noted in the calendar, as is their child's birth in February 1512 (i.e. 1513).[14]

Anne's other primer, the manuscript one, was written after the death of Queen Elizabeth in 1503. It contains a prayer for marital concord in which the name "Paulum" has been written over an erasure, and thus it seems likely that this book was made at the time of one of her earlier marriages, either to William Freville or William Rede, perhaps between 1503 and 1506. The inscription, however, must have been entered after her third marriage in 1510, since it reads: "Anne Withypoll oweth this boke."[15] In the three decades after printing's English introduction, other women besides Anne Withypoll doubtless owned both manuscript primers and the new printed versions. The record of her two books, however, acquired and annotated around the first decade of the sixteenth century, testifies to the simultaneous use of manuscript and printed books of hours which must have been fairly widespread as printing became naturalized. Along with their books of hours, during these years women also owned less liturgical devotional texts.

THE SCALE OF PERFECTION

Seventeen copies of the *Scale*'s first, 1494, edition are known;[16] of this number at least six belonged to women. Two copies were owned by female members of the Syon community. The first bears a note recording Katherine Palmer's gift of it to Anthony Bolney. This Syon nun had in 1539 taken a group from the dissolved community abroad, while in England Abbess Agnes Jordan rented a farmhouse called Southlands, near Denham, Buckinghamshire, for another group of Syon religious. Upon the abbess' death, January 30, 1546, Katherine Palmer returned to England to lead the remainder of the Denham group to the continent. (The 1546 move suggests that the English community could not continue without Abbess Jordan's generous pension of £200 annually.) It was in this year and probably on this visit to England that Palmer, now abbess of Syon, made the gift to Bolney, a Cluniac monk who had been sub-prior of Lewes abbey, Sussex, at the Dissolution.[17]

Another copy of the *Scale*, much noticed for its detailed annotation, passed through the hands of Sheen Carthusian James Grenehalgh to Syon nun Joan Sewell, probably as a gift on her profession day, April 28, 1500 (Rosenbach copy). Grenehalgh used a variety of manuscripts to emend the printed text, producing a copy whose readings had been meticulously reviewed. Michael Sargent points out that "a full third of Grenehalgh's 655 annotations" were in Latin; hence it seems likely that Joan Sewell was Latinate.[18]

Though the transmission of books between male and female religious was not unknown, this gift was profoundly unusual. Tracing Grenehalgh's annotations in other books, Sargent has suggested that the gift book with its wealth of notes (including a page of protective prayers) probably illustrates a singular attachment, to which Grenehalgh's eventual transfer from Shene to Hull Charterhouse may be attributed.

The instructive tenor of Grenehalgh's annotations has led to speculation that he was Sewell's spiritual director, although no other evidence exists. For instance near the volume's end (f. 135 v) Grenehalgh
has drawn a diagram which Sargent suggests may represent the plan
of "an idealized 'urbs refugii', with a fountain clearly visible in the
center (of a cloister?)," and with Joan Sewell's name also positioned
centrally, surrounded by "Sanctus Saluator" (Syon monastery's official
dedication), "Birgitta," "Maria," and "Sanctus Augustinus." Beneath
the diagram Grenehalgh has written, from the office for compline
(Ps. 90.5–7): "A timore nocturno A sagitta perambulante in die. A
negocio perambulante in tenebris. Ab incursu et demonio meridiano,
Sed cadent a latere tuo," and below that "Ad te autem JS non appropin-
quabit" (Figure 10).[19] ("From the terror of the night, from the arrow
that walks [sic] by day, from the business that walks in darkness, from
the assaults of the noonday devil, [though] they fall at your side – To
you, however, JS, it will not approach.") Eric Colledge points out that
the final line of the psalm refers to an angelic promise to St. Bridget,
one "famous among the English mystics of the early fifteenth century,"
that "impossibile est Diabolo appropinquare tibi."[20] Other protective
prayers are written above the diagram so that the whole page demonstrates not only Grenehalgh's familiarity with a particularly Bridgettine
piety, but also his concern for Sewell's spiritual well-being. The page
perhaps also reveals some personal element in that concern.

A copy of the *Scale* now at the Pierpont Morgan Library belonged
to a nun of St Ursula's, Louvain, whom Sargent identified: Dorothy
Clement, the child of Dr. John Clement and Margaret Giggs, Thomas
More's adopted daughter.[21] Since this couple were married around
1530, their daughter's book is unlikely to have been inscribed before
the 1550s. Three copies can be associated with women in secular life:
Margaret Beaufort and Elizabeth of York's gift of the *Scale* to their
gentlewoman Mary Roos is well known.[22] The owner of the St. John's
College Cambridge copy is less readily identifiable. It bears the single
word "Elizabeth" in a late fifteenth- or early sixteenth-century hand
below the title-page woodcut.[23] Finally at the bottom of a page in the
Folger copy is written "i prey for the rebel Jone stafforton" (q8). Thus
three surviving copies of the *Scale*'s 1494 edition belonged to nuns and
three were owned by laywomen.

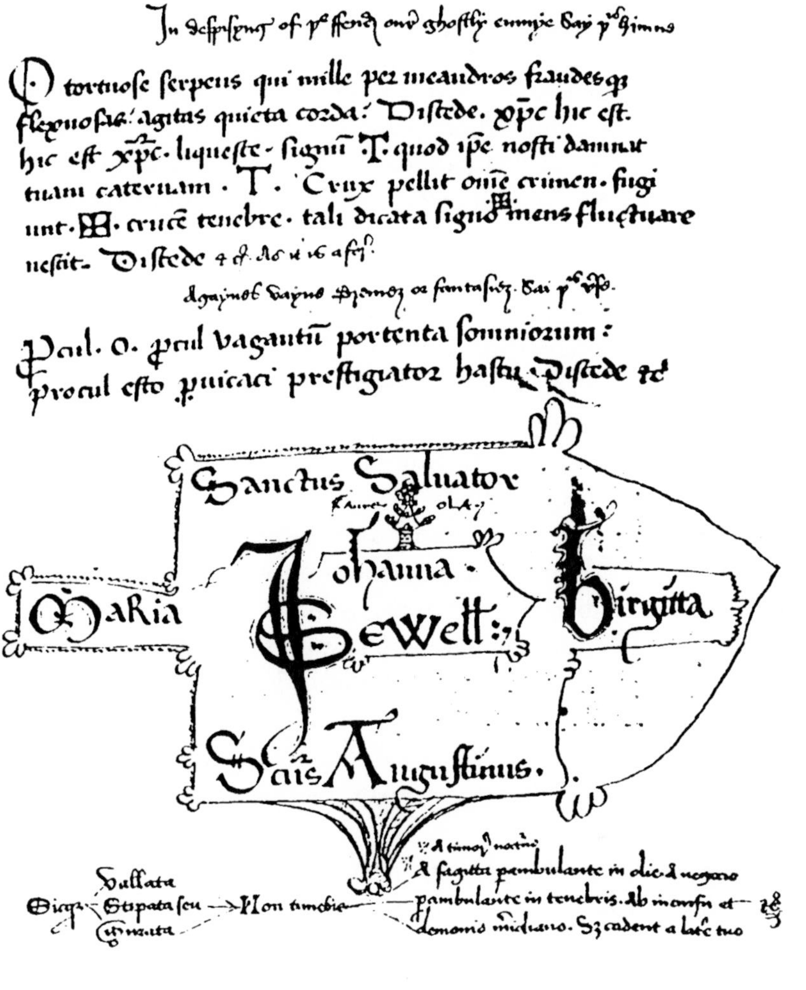

Figure 10 James Grenehalgh's gift to Joan Sewell. His annotations are found in the Rosenbach Foundation (Philadelphia) copy of Wynkyn de Worde's 1494 *Scale of Perfection* (STC 14042, f. 135 v).

Nicholas Love's translation of the pseudo-Bonaventuran *Speculum Vite Christi* appeared in four editions before 1500, testifying to the universal appeal of this gospel-based harmony of Christ's life. From these four incunable editions, eighteen more-or-less complete copies survive and two bear female names.[24] In a vellum copy of Caxton's second edition (1490), the fluent and graceful ownership signature of Susan Purefeye, a nun of Syon, appears on the bottom margin of the first leaf (a ii) and a contemporary hand, perhaps hers, has corrected the work throughout. De Ricci says that this British Library copy was "found by [William] Maskell [the nineteenth-century liturgist] in a Catholic Seminary of the West of England [and was] sold through him in 1864 to the BM."[25]

One of Syon's last vocations, Susan Purefeye entered the community in the years just preceding its dispersal. She was most likely the niece of Susan Kyngeston, a longtime Syon vowess who left Syon at the Dissolution to make her home with her sister and brother-in-law Anne and Edward Purefeye at Shalston, Buckinghamshire. There her vowess brass, one of only a handful of known examples, records Kyngeston's death in 1540. She had been born a Fettyplace and two of her sisters, Eleanor Fettyplace and Dorothy Fettyplace Codrington, were nuns of Syon. All three – Susan, Eleanor, and Dorothy – were aunts to Susan Purefeye.

Susan was probably the daughter of Anne and Edward Purefeye, since she was living at their home, Shalston, when she received her Syon pension of £6 in 1554. She seems to have entered the order about 1534 and died, according to the Syon *Martyrology*, in 1570.[26] Hence, like many of the women discussed here, she did not record her ownership until some time after the book's publication – in her case perhaps half a century later.

Another copy of Love's *Mirror*, from Pynson's 1494 edition, has an ownership signature which reads: "This Boke is myn Elizabeth Massey." Both the *Scale of Perfection* and Love's *Mirror* were devotional classics whose established reputation was being disseminated even more widely in the 1490s by printing. Margaret Beaufort's ownership of the *Scale*, described above, perhaps strengthens the possibility that the woman who owned the 1494 *Mirror* may have been a member of the Beaufort household. An Elizabeth Massey was one of the king's mother's gentle-women; in the 1507–08 household accounts she paid for various items given to almswomen and to poor folk. Margaret Beaufort's will remembered her with ten marks in money and ten marks in an annuity.[27]

THE CHASTISING OF GOD'S CHILDREN

A text composed for female religious between 1382 and 1408, *Chastising* showed from its beginnings strong evidence of women's ownership. In this connection two women's wills of the mid-fifteenth century have been often cited: Agnes Stapilton in 1448 and Mercy Ormesby in 1451 left manuscript copies of the *Chastising* to, respectively, the Cistercian nuns of Esholt near Leeds and the Benedictine nuns of Easebourne, Sussex.[28] These mid-century bequests offer one of the earliest points at which we are able to see clearly the confluence of secular and religious women's reading. In addition the wills suggest a significant role for the contributions of secular women to female institutional libraries, and hence they reaffirm laywomen's influence on nuns' reading.

Once in print, the *Chastising* continued to interest religious women. It appeared from de Worde's press in 1493. Nineteen copies can be listed,[29] though two are now lost and another is a fragment of two leaves. Of the remaining sixteen books, three contain paired female names; each was a gift from one nun to another within the same community. Edith Morepath (d. 1536) gave a copy to Katherine Palmer (d. 1576) (Syon); Mary Nevell (d. 1557 or 1558) to Awdry Dely (d. 1579) (Syon); Elizabeth Wyllowby to Catherine Symond (early sixteenth century) (Campsey).[30] These three examples in which *Chastising* was circulated within a particular house suggest that printing helped it to become a standard work, especially for religious women. In a fourth copy of the *Chastising* the name or names are lay: at the top center of the title page in two different italic hands of the sixteenth century is written "Elizabeth Alford" and "Elisabeth" (Folger copy).

VITAS PATRUM

Another work that continued to be popular with women was the *Vitas Patrum*, to give it Caxton's title. Caxton translated the lives of these desert saints, some of which were written by St. Jerome, from French; they were printed by de Worde in 1495. These biographies were a staple of monastic refectory reading, particularly since some manuscripts of the work contained excerpts from the *Collationes Patrum* and *De Institutis Coenobitarum* of John Cassian, an author recommended by St. Benedict to his monks (*RB* 42).[31] The *Vitas Patrum* seems always to have been considered particularly suitable reading for women as well, both lay and religious.[32] The aristocratic Elizabeth de Burgh hired a scribe to copy this work for her in 1324 at a cost of 8s, plus room and board. In 1399, a French manuscript including the work was bequeathed by Eleanor, duchess of Gloucester, to her daughter Isabel, a nun at the London minoresses. A French version is the first item in a manuscript miscellany which Sibyl de Felton, abbess of Barking, bought from the executors of Philippe de Coucy, the widow of the ninth Earl of Oxford, after 1411.[33] These instances show a common readership of secular aristocrats and religious women – the same audience as the one which owns incunabula about a century later. *STC* records 10+ copies of the *Vitas Patrum*; actually twenty-six copies may be located, though not all are truly incunabula.[34] Four of these copies witness to a mixed readership of religious and lay women. One of these, a copy owned by Bristol widow Joan Regent and inscribed by her friend Katherine Pole, has been described elsewhere.[35]

The Lambeth Palace copy of the first printed edition carries two women's inscriptions, along with several other names. The earlier presumably records a woman's gift to her spiritual director; it reads: "I pray you mastyr pray for me your gostly chyld that gaue thys booke Alyanor Verney" (last leaf of first gathering, aa 8v). Again, as in the case of Elizabeth Massey who wrote her name in Love's *Mirror*, we may be dealing with a gentlewoman at court. In Elizabeth of York's accounts for 1502–03 an Eleanor Verney appears ten times. Her £20 wage is one of the highest in the annual lists. Her husband Sir Ralph was the son of London mayor Ralph Verney (d. 1478) and was successively chamberlain to Princess Margaret and Princess Mary. Eleanor was Margaret Beaufort's niece; her mother Edith St. John Pole was the countess's half-sister. Eleanor was remembered in Lady Margaret's 1508 will with the large legacy of £20, the amount of her yearly salary in the household. In the will her bequest appears just after Lady Margaret's gift to her granddaughter Mary, "princess of Castile."[36]

Another ownership note in this volume may be that of a nun. "Thys bouke belongyth to martha fabyan" appears twice, on a 1 and xx 6 (recto of last leaf). A woman of that name joined the Benedictine community of Barking, Essex, between 1499 and 1527; she occurs in the pension lists of 1539, 1553, 1556, and 1559.[37] She may be related to the chronicler Robert Fabyan.[38]

A male and female religious, together with a third person called "Margaret, her relative" owned the Glasgow copy of *Vitas Patrum*. On the colophon leaf recto above Caxton's device is written in a contemporary display hand, "Dompnus Wyllm*us* Burton / Et alicia Burtun monica" and below the device, "Iste liber constat d*omi*ne Alicie burton. Et margarete cognate eius. Tuar*um* facta et desideria sint deo beneplacita: et sibi operis meritaria ad vita*m* eterna*m*." ("This book belongs to Dame Alice Burton and Margaret, her relative. May your deeds and desires please God and may your works merit eternal life.") The wording suggests a gift to the two women, religious and lay. Together these two also owned a manuscript containing the *Prick of Conscience* and Rolle's *Form of Living* (*olim* Beeleigh Abbey, Foyle MS). It is inscribed, "Iste liber constat domine Alicie Burton nec non et Margarete consobrine ejus."[39] These two women's joint ownership of books appears to have transcended whatever separation their states in life imposed.

The third copy of the *Vitas Patrum* in female hands also has the name of a nun, Katherine Efflyn of Dartford, Kent. Excluding the monastic officers, she was fourth in the 1539 seniority list at the Dissolution (hence clearly was not a young woman), and received a pension of 100s. Between 1539 and 1556 she was one of a group who rented a house at Sutton at Hone, two and a half miles from Dartford. Seven Dartford nuns, including Efflyn, successfully petitioned Philip and Mary to be restored to religious life in 1557. On the accession of Elizabeth, however, the restored houses were suppressed and in June 1559 a group of twelve from Dartford, of which Efflyn was part, fled to Belgium. At this time the youngest Dartford nun was fifty and three were eighty. That this copy of *Vitas Patrum* accompanied the aged Katherine Efflyn abroad is indicated by the volume's other inscriptions: "Shene" and "inglissen Cartusers," that is, the house called "Sheen Anglorum," the English male Carthusian foundation in Nieuport, near Bruges. Since the Dartford nuns moved to Bruges in 1568, it is likely that Efflyn died after that date and that her book then passed into other hands in Bruges.[40]

One more title survives which can demonstrate something of the way in which women used and circulated these early printed volumes. Ten copies exist of Caxton's 1484 *Royal Book*.[41] The British Library copy was shared by two gentry women whose devout and political families we have met in an earlier chapter. Goditha Throckmorton was one of a notable group of brothers and sisters which included Elizabeth Throckmorton, the last Franciscan abbess of Denny, and Margery Throckmorton Middlemore, who became a vowess after her husband's death. Goditha married Edward Peyto: among their children was William, head of the Greenwich Observant Franciscans and later a cardinal. She gave the manuscript known as the Worcestershire Miscellany (BL Additional MS 37787) to her namesake Goditha (or Goody) Throckmorton, perhaps the daughter of one of her brothers, John or Richard. In the manuscript she wrote: "by the gefte of d[ame] Goodyth Peyto thy boke Goody Throkmarton."

The hand which wrote this donation inscription is a distinctive one; it employs an idiosyncratic flourished final s with a tail slanting diagonally upward. It is the same hand which writes at the end of the first gathering of the *Royal Book*, a location frequently used for inscriptions: "Thys booke I leve to my Cossyn elzabeth ynglefald" (Figure 11). Though the donor does not give her name, the characteristic handwriting confirms her identity. The recipient is called "cousin," but the word often means simply a blood relative and it seems that, as she did with the Worcestershire Miscellany, Goditha Peyto was giving a book to one of her nieces.

Goditha's will, made on December 22, 1530, is very much a widow's document.[42] Central in its assortment of family and household is her chaplain, Sir Edmund Whelar, whose name occurs five times. To him she left "my Legent aurea," and to her "cousin" Mary Burdett, probably another niece,[43] "my Sawter booke." The will was witnessed by her son William Peyto, her maid Margaret Clayton, her priest Sir Edmund, and her niece Elizabeth's lawyer husband, Thomas Englefield. It was

Explicit

(a)

(b)

Figure 11 (a) Goditha Peyto's gift inscription, directed to Elizabeth Englefield and written, perhaps about 1530, in a copy of Caxton's [1488?] *Royal Book* (*STC* 21429, BL c.10.b.22 [a5 v]). (b) Elizabeth Englefield's probable gift inscription to her daughter-in-law, written in the same book perhaps thirteen years later [q8v].

Elizabeth to whom probate was granted, however, and her own will shows a degree of closeness between herself and her aunt Goditha.

Elizabeth Throckmorton Englefield was the daughter of Goditha's brother, the Throckmorton heir Sir Robert (d. 1518). She married Sir Thomas Englefield, who was sheriff of Oxfordshire and Berkshire in 1519, a sergeant-at-law by 1523, and joint master of the wards and a justice of the common pleas in 1526.[44] Probably the marriage took place by 1518, since her father's will, made in that year, does not mention her.[45] (Francis, her first son, was born in 1521/22).[46] The wording of Goditha Peyto's note to her, "I leve," suggests a deathbed bequest and we might assume she gave the *Royal Book* to Elizabeth in the year she died, 1530. Elizabeth's own will, made in 1543, mentions her aunt, and also another woman whom we have met earlier. To her second son John she left "all the plate which I bought of Dame Susan Kingston [the Syon vowess who had died in 1540] . . . And also all the plate which I had of Dame Gooddeth pewto . . . and also all the other parcells of my plate which I have lying together with the said plate before remembered in a basket."[47]

A second note is found on the verso of the *Royal Book*'s last leaf, in addition to Goditha Peyto's. Across the bottom a more facile and later hand has written, "Thys boke I gyve to my dowgh*ter* Englefelde." If it is Elizabeth Englefield who writes, the use of the surname indicates that the book was intended for her eldest son's wife, rather than for her own daughter Susan, unmarried in 1543 when she wrote. Catherine Fettyplace married Francis Englefield between his father's death in 1537[48] and his mother's will-making in 1543. Francis subsequently had a distinguished career under Mary, but after her death from 1559 until 1596 he lived abroad, a supporter of the old religion and of resistance to Elizabeth.[49] The family interest in books is emphasized by Alan Coates' recent demonstration of Francis Englefield's central role, after the Dissolution, in the preservation and dissemination of the major monastic collection from his region, that of Reading Abbey.[50]

Thus the *Royal Book* changed hands twice, descending in the female line of two closely related gentry families from aunt to niece about 1530 (the Throckmortons) and then from mother-in-law to daughter-in-law approximately thirteen years later (the Englefields). About fifty years after its publication, the parting gift which aunt left to niece, the book in which the older woman wrote the prayers of her personal use, had come to constitute a family keepsake – one whose transmission we may see in several ways as peculiarly female.

This single copy of the *Royal Book* provides a powerful contrast with a group of books mentioned in Elizabeth Englefield's will – books which passed exclusively through male ownership and which were identified with a male tradition. To her sons Francis and John Englefield went all the "books of Scripture, Law and other which were their late father's deceased to be between them equally divided by the oversight of my executors" within a month after their mother's death. The vehicle for the *Royal Book*'s transmission, on the other hand, was not the public statement which a will constitutes, but a private message, passed from hand to hand, hidden within the covers of a book. In addition the substantial size of the legal/scriptural collection, and its consequent cultural recognition as valuable, sets it apart from the humble, single book which Elizabeth Englefield bequeathed. The contrast, both between the size of male and female holdings and their transmission in, respectively, public or private ways, could hardly be more clearly illustrated than by Elizabeth Englefield's will, on the one hand, and her gift, on the other. Scarcity in numbers and privacy in transmission – the realities of women's book ownership – underlie the difficulties of tracing this tradition.

This aunt and niece, Goditha Peyto and Elizabeth Englefield, belonged to the same world of family connections as did Syon vowess and nun Susan Kyngeston and Susan Purefeye, another aunt and niece. Elizabeth's purchase of Susan Kyngeston's plate demonstrates this; so does Susan Kyngeston's employment of Elizabeth's husband Thomas Englefield as her man of law. In the fifteenth and sixteenth centuries, the Fettyplace–Throckmorton–Englefield connection produced a wealth of marriages and of land transactions.[51] These women were

Figure 12 Mary and Martha, representatives of the contemplative and active lives. A woodcut from the copy of Caxton's [1488?] *Royal Book* owned by Goditha Peyto and Elizabeth Englefield (*STC* 21429, BL C. 10.b.22, q8).

members of gentry families prominent in their regions – Berkshire, Buckinghamshire, Oxfordshire, Warwickshire – whose royal servants and able lawyers and judges were responsible for their members' advancement and reputation over several generations.

The spiritual writings these women owned – the Worcestershire Miscellany, the *Speculum Vite Christi*, and the *Royal Book* – originated in different periods, and though to some extent a lay spirituality was developing, the monastic ideal was still powerful. Some degree of tension must have continued to be felt. Women's interest in Mary's life is indicated by the extreme popularity of the various New Testament Marys, understood in the Middle Ages as embodied in Mary Magdalen: contemplative, preacher, miracleworker, visionary, anchorite and *imitatrix Christi*. Both in its public aspect and its hidden one, this life contrasted with the faithful daily service of Martha's. Mary and Martha, in fact, can be seen as versions of the religious and the lay state, positioned side by side in the woodcut of the two sisters with which the *Royal Book* accompanies its discussion of the two vocations (Figure 12). (We might note that a chapter from St. Bridget's *Revelations* on the active and contemplative life [*Rev. 6.65*] was copied separately in at least five manuscripts, three of them associated with women.[52]) The *Royal Book* which Elizabeth Englefield bequeathed to her daughter-in-law was at about the same time being read by a Franciscan nun of Bruisyard.[53] Its text says that the contemplative soul will "put al other thynges in forgetyng" (q8v), but in her own preparations for death Englefield was as much Martha as Mary. She specified that at her burial seven poor men should receive shirts and black gowns, seven poor women petticoats and smocks, "which I intend God willing to leave in readiness for them."[54]

CONCLUSION

The identification here of women book owners previously unknown makes its contribution to a more complex definition of readership. Further work will certainly uncover more female names and will describe with more richness of detail the circumstances under which women's reading took place.[55] The texts which these women preferred, as well as books of hours, include the extremely popular *Scale of Perfection* and *Vitas Patrum* and the slightly less popular *Chastising*; Nicholas Love makes a less strong showing. Other incunabula register a lower number of female owners. At least two of the ten extant copies of the *Royal Book* have female names. Similarly, the *Book of Divers Ghostly Matters*, which survives in five copies, has women's names only in one. The *Life of St. Katherine* has eight copies with one female signature, and the four copies of St. Bernard's *Meditations* have none.

The two most popular texts for women represent two different instructive traditions. *Vitas Patrum* was a centuries-old product of monastic spirituality. *Scale*, from the late fourteenth century, represented newer attempts to broaden the audience for spiritual instruction. These two texts' relative popularity now at the end of the fifteenth century must be regarded merely as suggestive, since the survival of early printed books is so largely inflected by chance. Nevertheless both had been strongly popular in manuscript versions, and this survey of female incunabulum ownership points to women's unchanged involvement with some of the devotional writings which they had owned and lent in the years before printing.[56] It is hardly necessary to observe that this interest is not exclusively a female one: the role of male Carthusians and of Franciscan friars, for instance, in disseminating such texts is well known. Still, many of the surviving incunabula which bear women's names witness to continuity within a women's devotional tradition.

The female audience for early English printing had been developed in the fifteenth century – nuns and aristocrats with an admixture of gentry. It seems clear that the early printers' choice of texts to publish often relied on and acknowledged this audience. Female book ownership did not register a substantial presence lower on the social scale, however, until over a century after printing's introduction, when Frances Wolfreston, a Midland squire's wife, assembled her notable collection of English vernacular books (1607–77).[57]

These incunabula continue a tradition of books as tokens exchanged between women. Besides gifts from mother to daughter (Joan to Agnes Regent) and from aunt to niece (Goditha Peyto to Elizabeth Englefield), the early printed editions testify again to the same kind of exchanges visible in the manuscript period: to nuns' friendship inside religious community (Mary Nevell and Awdry Dely), to laywomen's mutual affection in retirement (Joan Regent and Katherine Pole), and to female connection spanning religious and secular life (Alice and Margaret Burton).

Epilogue

One goal of this work has been the recovery of quantifiable information about women's devotional books. So, for instance, chapter 1 analyzes the record of books left to women's religious houses over a century and a half (1349–1501) and in doing so is able to trace the change in nuns' book ownership from volumes whose primary purpose was support of the liturgy, to volumes intended primarily for non-liturgical use. This change was not confined to female readers, but the evidence offered here from female sources confirms more widely registered trends. This book thus uses bibliography to make some suggestions about the history of reading and of spirituality.

Chapter 6 offers another example of quantifiable work. It attempts to discover whether printing's genesis in England changed the female audience for devotional books, or how it did so. When about 80 per cent of the surviving copies of certain titles printed before 1500 were examined, indications of female reading preference were visible in the signatures of women written on these pages. Working from the total number of surviving copies, we can tell what proportion of these books give evidence of female ownership, and thus speak with a degree of surety about female reading taste.

Recovery of numerical information, then, has had some part in characterizing female book ownership. Equally important, however, has been the investigation of women's reading practices. Through glimpses of women reading and reflecting, often together with other women, this study has attempted to understand what these practices meant to the readers whose lives are here presented. Thus, for instance, the examination of ownership inscriptions has at one point provided a taxonomy of the occasions on which nuns gave and received books.

Such circulation of books within women's houses demonstrates women's use of the same practices as monastic men. More largely, however, these nuns' exchanges can be located as part of new patterns of acquisition and circulation of books, discernable from the middle of the fifteenth century. The "common profit" manuscripts which specify that a particular book was to pass successively from owner to owner constitute the best-known examples of such plans, but recent work has identified parallel arrangements for passage of books among members of other groups: parish priests or Oxford scholars, for instance. Such formal channels, often described in wills, find a less structured counterpart in the more informal exchanges between religious women illustrated here.

It may be, in fact, that it is the change from liturgical to devotional reading alluded to above which actually *produces* such schemes for book circulation. The developing mechanisms of transmission described in this book and elsewhere might thus be regarded as the visible signs of a new interest in personal reading, an interest which antedates the coming of printing. Printing would then, on its arrival in England, merely take advantage of such recent growth in transmission networks. Rather than generating fresh interest in private reading, the new technology might better be recognized as accelerating existing interest. Indeed, Caxton's entrepreneurship might be considered a response to his recognition of such widespread interest in reading, and to the presence of structures of exchange which themselves stimulated reading, both on the Continent and in England.

In this way the reading practices described here may offer a basis for warrantable larger speculation. As women's book exchange constitutes one element among many in developing arrangements for book transmission, so several female narratives presented here allow us to ask how women readers were inserted into public discourse. Perhaps not surprisingly given the primarily religious nature of these books, the contested nature of women's reading is frequently visible. So the story of Susan Kyngeston's brush with a treason trial (chapter 4) has its origins in the book dedicated to her, and Katherine Manne's reading reveals her participation in the theological and political struggles of the 1520s and 1530s (chapter 5). Similarly, if indeed Margery de Nerford did own a Wycliffite glossed psalter, we might find in her a complex combination of heterodox sympathy and institutional loyalty (chapter 2). All these women must be counted as sharing in contemporary intellectual controversies, which regularly took a religious form.

Their reading suggests a common female concern. One of the ways in which anxiety about justice, about entitlement and deprivation, manifests in traditional religious culture is in speculation about the nature of the Church – speculation which can be found in the texts which all three women read. In the early sixteenth century the issues of institutional wealth and power, the claims of a visible church versus a body of believers, were addressed by Tyndale in his *Obedience of a Christian Man*, which Katherine Manne owned. Likewise Erasmus' call for a purified church found a reader in Elizabeth Throckmorton, just as the *Image of Love*'s author similarly appealed to the nuns of Syon. Earlier, the same critique is found in the *English Psalter* which may have been Margery de Nerford's. Several of these female readers, then, appear to have been drawn towards versions of the spiritual life in which institutional religion assumed a more vital shape.

Significantly, all the women in this book were close to men whose positions in religious controversy were a matter of public record – as was their book ownership. The closeness of female bookowners to men with similar interests – sometimes as members of the same family – recurs in these records. The shared books of William de Bergh and Margery de Nerford, together with their shared staff and recreation and interest in St. Christopher's, suggest a kind of intimacy conventionally imagined as marital. Margaret Purdans' plethora of women friends is remarkable, yet Hugh Damlett may have influenced her as well – in a conservative direction, as Richard Poringland in a radical one, while Katherine Manne was similarly connected to a number of clerics whose positions were not univocal. In the early sixteenth century the Fettyplace sisters came from a family whose women (and whose men as well) had owned books for generations. These relationships imply that female book ownership was strongly dependent on membership in a community of readers, a community which could take many forms: natal family, interest group, religious institution. In a family like the Fettyplaces, or in a self-selected devout coterie like those found in fifteenth-century Norwich, transmission of valued books was a marker both of shared interests and of group membership. Such transmission occurred in religious women's houses as well, when the goods of a predecessor were passed to a younger generation. In both secular and religious groupings, then, the book served as marker of an affiliation with others, of an identity more inclusive and more complex than the personal.

In allowing women such a focus and centrality we have consistently implied the presence of a definably female reading culture. Some female reading practices may be identical to male customs: the development of book circulation among friends within a religious community, for instance. About other practices it is difficult to judge. Historically it has seemed that female lay and religious lives tended to turn towards one another; the evidence is the multiplicity of episcopal injunctions attempting to separate them. Whether in the fifteenth century all of religious life should be seen as moving gradually toward the world, or whether female life was particularly eager to breach such barriers, at this point seems unclear. Thus it is difficult, in the present state of our knowledge, to say for instance that laywomen's habit of making book gifts to women's religious houses, which this study has often noticed, is more frequent than similar male generosity.

Some book practices, however, do seem to have been particularly endorsed by women. The written requests for others' prayers so frequently found in books of hours are not exclusively female, but they are heavily so, and it appears that in these volumes women found a vehicle particularly suited for registering their ties, both temporal and spiritual. The similarity of female texts of formation, with their emphases on routine, on seclusion, on self-abnegation, likewise suggests a common spirituality for lay and religious women, bolstered by a common set of texts. A female attention to movement between states in life often seems discernable, movement which could span the vocations of religious and laywomen. These loans and gifts of devotional books among widows, anchoresses, nuns and vowesses allow us to infer relationships of mentoring and tutelage as well as those of equality, of intellectual and spiritual exchange, between women. And, lest female reading should be viewed too univocally, the juxtaposed wills of Margaret Purdans and Katherine Kerre provide an opportunity to differentiate the reading tastes and the reading circles of two contemporaries (chapter 3).

Finally, the study of women's book ownership has provided an indirect way of tracing what is hard to recover directly: the narrative of women's connection, even their friendship. Letters between women are scarce; their interior lives are notoriously obscure; but books' silent witness to women's ties can sometimes reveal what is elsewhere elided.

APPENDIX I

Surviving religious women's books not listed in Ker–Watson or Bell

Bulkeley, Anne

London, British Library MS Harley 494, a book of private prayers, has the following inscription on f. 1v: "*domi*ne Anne Bulkeley attinet liber iste" and the name is repeated on f. 2r in decorative lettering. A woman of this name was fourteenth in the Amesbury pension list of 1539 (Dugdale, *Monasticon*, II, 340) and appears again in the list of 1555–56 (*Monasticon* II, 334n). Rhodes pointed out ("Devotion," II, p. 12) that an excerpt from William Bonde's 1526 *Pylgrimage of Perfection* (*STC* 3277) was copied into this manuscript, as was the anonymous *Dyurnall for Deuoute Soules* ([1532?] and later eds.)

Bodley MS e museo 23, a manuscript of "Auenture and Grace," a translation of the *Somme des Vices et des Vertues* made in 1451, bears the inscription: "Modo liber Thome kingswood ex dono Magistre Anne Bulkeley" (according to Doyle, "Survey," II, 271). *SC* reads "Ryngwood," dates the inscription *c.* 1500. Pächt and Alexander, 1051, mention its fifteenth-century Winchester binding. (A Joan Ryngwode was a nun of Amesbury in 1409 [Timmins, *Register*, p. 157] while a Dorothy Ringwood appears in Nunnaminster's 1539 pension list.)

Ownership by Joan or Alice Bukley, nuns of Syon, has been suggested (d. Sept. 29, 1532; d. Nov. 6, 1495), but, in addition to the discrepancy with regard to the dates and the difference in christian names, the surname is differently spelled.

AMESBURY

CANONSLEIGH

Oxford, Bodleian MS 9, written *c.* 1420–30, contains a psalter and a collection of prayers and poems, in Latin, French, and English. Because of "expressions on ff. 26, 87v, 121 point[ing] to a nun," including a commemoration of St. Etheldreda, the *SC* suggested an origin at Canonsleigh, the only English nunnery dedicated to her (II.i.84). Ker rejected this attribution (*MLGB*, 375), but subsequently the editor of Canonsleigh's cartulary pointed out the similarity in the names of Canonsleigh's grantee after the Dissolution (Sir John St. Leger in 1543) and the donor of this book to the Bodleian (John Leuger, 1620). (London, xxxi).

Efflyn, Katherine

The Cambridge University Library copy of De Worde's 1495 edition of *Vitas Patrum* (Inc.3.J.1.2.[3538]; *STC* 14507) bears the name of this nun of Dartford on the verso of the last leaf (twice). She appears fourth in the pension list of 1539, was part of the restored community in 1557, and emigrated in 1559 to the Low Countries. See the Dutch inscriptions in the book (ff. 1 and 2), and the inscriptions "Shene" and "Ingliss Cartusers" (f. 4), that is Sheen Anglorum, the English male Carthusian foundation in Nieuport, Flanders. She died abroad perhaps between 1568 and 1573. (Palmer, "Notes," 269–71; Lee *Nunneries*, pp. 119–31 and see chapter 6).

DERBY

John Rylands University Library French MS 6: folios 1–8 of this manuscript, and perhaps also its remaining folios 9–12, were once part of BL Egerton 2710, a thirteenth-century Anglo-Norman miscellany which bears a fifteenth-century gift inscription to Derby (Bell, *What Nuns Read*, p. 136). See Russell, "Fragment."

ELSTOW OR WOTTON

Necollson, Margaret

T. A. Birrell (1987) recognized the elements of this disassembled collection-volume in the British Library (c.20.c.20) as originally comprising one book and identified its owner's name as belonging to a nun of Elstow. Subsequently Carol Meale noted another woman of the same name at Wotton ("Miracles," 132n). The volume consisted of fifteen printed books published between 1494 and 1525 (?) (no. 7 should be dated 1521, not 1526).

LONDON MINORESSES

Wodward, Margaret

London, British Library MS Sloane 779 is a manuscript copy of Caxton's *Game and Play of the Chess* (1474; *STC* 4920) and *Cordiale* (1479; *STC* 5758). It is dated 1484. On f. 151v appears "Quod Dominus Grace" and below that a horizontal flourish. The scribe may be the Dominican friar Cornelius Grace, assigned by the master general on July 3, 1474 for study at Cambridge toward the degree of doctor of theology (Emden, *BRUC*, 266), although "Dominus" is usually applied to secular priests. Between the name and the flourish below it is written "& constast dane [sic] margaret" and below the flourish "Wodward." The hands and inks differ. In the London minoresses pension list of 1539 this woman was described as aged 52, hence born in 1487, suggesting the inscription cannot be earlier than the sixteenth century (*L&PH8*, xiv(i), no. 680).

ST. MARY WINCHESTER (NUNNAMINSTER)

Cambridge, Trinity College MS B.II.4 is an abbess' psalter, *c.* 1220–30, with two illuminations of an abbess and a nun (fos. 113 v, 130). Nigel Morgan describes the calendar as Augustinian of the London diocese, but with a few entries of Winchester saints; he mentions the high color grading for both St. Edburga feasts (her relics were at Nunnaminster), and discusses what the abbess' costume might reveal about provenance (*Early Gothic Manuscripts*, I, no. 51). A fourteenth-century note in French on f. 36v says the book was loaned by Dame Ida de Ralegh to Walter Hone, abbot of Newnham (Devon) during his life and then to Dame Johane de Roches of Nunnaminster. Coldicott points out (54, 66) that she may have been related to Bishop of Winchester Peter des Roches (1205–38). Hone was confirmed as abbot in 1338; Ida was the wife of Sir John de Ralegh of Beaudeport, Devon; she is mentioned in 1346.

SYON

Boeria, Magdalene

The John Rylands University Library copy of Syon monk John Fewterer's *Myrrour of Christes Passion* (*STC* 14553) has this Syon nun's name on the last leaf of the first gathering (+6v); the initials "m b" appear on the book's fore-edge. The book was printed December 12, 1534; Boeria died in June 1539 (*Martyrology*, f. 43).

Regent, Agnes

De Worde's 1495 edition of *Vitas Patrum* (JRUL 15441; *STC* 14507) has the inscription above the colophon: "Liber do*mine* Agnet*es* Regent qua*m* saluet Ihe*s*us." Notes exchanged between her mother, Joan Regent, and her mother's friend Katherine Pole, survive in the book's margins. Joan Regent was a widow living at the Bristol hospital of St. Mark's or Gaunts; her 1509 will leaves plate and linen to her daughter Agnes, a nun of Syon (PRO Prob 11/25/16). Syon's accounts show boarding charges for Agnes Regent in 1504/5 (PRO sc 6/Hen 7/1730). She died in February 1524 (*Martyrology*, f. 26)

Spycer, Joan

What is probably a donation inscription, rather than an ownership one, is found in the British Library copy of Pynson's 1526 edition of Syon monk William Bonde's *Pylgrimage of Perfection*. On A6v, the last leaf of the first gathering, is written "of your charyte I pray you to pray for dame Iohan. Spycer in syon" (G 11740; *STC* 3277). She died on 1 December, sometime between 1526, the date of this edition, and the making of the 1539 pension list, but the Syon *Martyrology* does not record the year (f. 66).

Tresham, Clemence

A Sarum primer of 1533 (BL C.35.a.12; *STC* 15979) bears on its title page the name "Clemence tressham," a nun of Syon whose ownership of two other books has been noted (Watson, *Supplement*, 10). It is closely related to another book of hours (BL C.35.a.14; *STC* 15978) printed in 1532 and owned by Thomas Godfrey of Syon (see Erler, "Embellishments"). The daughter of John Tresham of Rushton (Northamptonshire) and the sister of Sir Thomas (d. 1559), Clemence Tresham was one of the two most junior members of the community in 1518 (Aungier, *History*, p. 82). Her Dissolution pension was collected by Richard Whitford, probably indicating that both were living, with two other Syon nuns, at the London house of the fourth Lord Mountjoy. She was re-enclosed under Mary but subsequently expelled under Elizabeth. Justinian Isham in 1717 noted that the parsonage house of St. Peter's, Rushton was "built for her when she retired from Syon." She died on September 6, 1567 (A. Butler). Bridges in 1791 described her full-length recumbent marble tomb figure, in black and white habit, destroyed in 1799 (*Northamptonshire* II, 72).

Syon: Ownership unknown

London, Lambeth Palace MS 72, the *Gilte Legend*, is given a Syon provenance in the index to Pickering and O'Mara on the basis of its two Syon-associated texts: (1) Simon Winter's *Life of St. Jerome* "substituted in the MS alone for the normal *Gilte Legende* life of Jerome," (*Index*, p. 8) although lacking its dedication to the Duchess of Clarence and its prologue; (2) a life of St. Barbara "inserted into the GL in this MS alone," (p. 10) having an original preface "which specifically mentions Augustine and Brigit, and therefore seems to have been written for Syon" (Görlach, *Legends*, p. 80, n. 119), although that preface is omitted in Lambeth 72.

London, Lambeth Palace MS 432 is a religious miscellany containing among other texts Syon monk Simon Wynter's *Life of St. Jerome* and a series of short extracts from St. Bridget's *Revelations*. Pezzini points out that in translating these the translator drew on Alphonse Pecha's *Celeste Viridiarum*. Use of such

Bridgettine source material indicates the ms was probably made at a Bridgettine house where it was readily available. Two additional texts in the manuscript raise the question of male Bridgettine ownership rather than female. Its fifteen unique Marian miracles are present in summary form which might suggest their use in sermons rather than in personal reflection. In addition the manuscript's "visitatio infirmorum" contains a series of questions regarding belief to be administered to the sick, suggesting a priestly role; but the "visitatio" contains no instructions for sacramental administration, and it is full of meditative material on death whose use might equally be general (as Pezzini suggests). See Pickering and O'Mara, *Index*, pp. 31–33; Pezzini "Meditacion," 280–95.

Longleat House, Marquess of Bath MS 14, Nicholas Love's *Mirror*, "has an added list of chapters to be read at collation . . . with an invocation of St. Bridget of Sweden, which points to the only English house of her order, Syon Abbey" (Doyle, "Study," pp. 169–70).

Oxford, Bodleian Holkham misc. 41, a mid-fifteenth-century manuscript, contains a unique sequence of prayers and meditations composed by a religious woman ("make me a good woman") for another woman in religion, titled "The Feitis and the Passion of Oure Lord Ihesu Crist," and also William Flete's *Consolatio Anime*. Its four-line lyric "Syke and sorowe depely" occurs in nine manuscripts, several associated with Syon. See Pollard, "Bodleian MS" and Barratt, *Women's Writing*, pp. 205–18.

WHERWELL

In the preface to his 1517 English translation of the *Rule of St. Benedict* for women, Bishop Richard Fox says that besides the printed copies (*STC* 1859) he provided his four Hampshire nunneries "aboue and besyde certayne bokes." Cambridge University Library MS Mm.3.13, which contains the *ordo* for female religious profession and a donation inscription to St. Mary Winchester, has long been recognized as one of these gifts. In addition Bodleian MS Barlow 11, a sister manuscript, represents Bishop Fox's gift to Wherwell. See Erler, "Manuscript Gifts."

UNIDENTIFIED HOUSE

Burton, Alice and Margaret her relative

These women's names are joined in two volumes. The first, a manuscript dated [1465?], contains the *Prick of Conscience*, followed by Rolle's *Form of Living*. "Iste liber constat domine Alicie Burton nec non et Margarete consobrine eius," Christie's Sale July 11, 2000, lot 77, *olim* Beeleigh Abbey, Maldon, Essex, Foyle

MS, f. iv^v (Lewis and McIntosh called the language Warwickshire, *Descriptive Guide*, p. 35, but the Christie's cataloguer, p. 232, attributed it to Worcestershire on the basis of a letter from Lewis).

The second, a copy of de Worde's 1495 edition of *Vitas Patrum* (*STC* 14507), is in the Hunterian Collection, Glasgow (BV 2.13). On the recto of the colophon leaf (CCCxlvii) above Caxton's device in a display hand is written: "Dompnus Wyllm*us* Burtun / Et alicia Burtun monica." Below the device: "Iste liber constat d*omi*ne Alicie burton. Et margarete cognate eius. Tuarum facta et desideria sint deo beneplacita: et sibi operis meritaria ad vitam eternam."

Cambridge University Library MS Additional 3042 is a collection of liturgical and devotional texts written for a woman, by divers hands, one of which is Stephen Dodesham's. A hymn to St. Etheldreda suggests Canonsleigh, the only English house dedicated to her, but spelling and language indicate, variously, eastern Lincolnshire, Norfolk, Leicestershire, or Northamptonshire. Since a form of confession alludes to St. Augustine, the house might be Augustinian, or perhaps Dartford or Syon. See Barratt, "Books for Nuns."

Cambridge University Library MS Kk.6.39 is described by Frere as a "psalter and private devotions of an English Benedictine of the fifteenth century, with a later appendix added by a nun" (*Bibliotheca*, II, 93). According to the Cambridge University Library catalogue, "ff. 150 to the end are written in a different hand and contain devotions to our lady, the cross, and various saints, and lastly to the Holy Spirit, ending with a litany" in which the final element is a prayer for "abbatissam et priorissam nostram" (III, 731). A. I. Doyle suggests that in the early to mid-fifteenth century the MS belonged to a monk of Winchester, judging by the saints mentioned (e.g. Ethelwold) and that in the second half of the century alterations from masculine to feminine forms (e.g. ff. 89, 101) and St. Mellor's name in the litany indicate it was owned by a nun, perhaps of Nunnaminster (private communication).

London, British Library MS Arundel 327, Osbern Bokenham's *Legendys of Hooly Wummen*, whose colophon says that the manuscript "was doon wrytyn i*n* Canebryge by hys sou*n* Frer*e* Thomas Burgh. The yere of our lord a thousand four hu*n*dryth seuy*n* & fourty Whose expence dreu threttys schyligys & yafe yt onto this holy place of nu*n*nys that þei shulde haue mynd on hym & of hys systyr Dame Betrice Burgh Of þe wych soulys ih*e*su haue mercy. Amen" (Serjeantson, p. 289). A. I. Doyle suggested that the house might have been Denny ("Books Connected," p. 286 n. 8).

London, British Library MS Cotton Vespasian D.xxvi, a collection of prayers and meditations of St. Anselm, together with other Latin prayers and hymns, from the second half of the twelfth century. It was modified for the use of an Augustinian canoness by substitution of feminine inflections and of Augustine's name for Benedict's. See Bestul "Collection."

Appendix I

Possibly

AMESBURY

Oxford, All Souls College MS 6 ("the Amesbury psalter"), *c.* 1250–60, has long been associated with this house. The case pro and con is most recently summarized by Watson, who concludes: "In spite of the absence of firm evidence an Amesbury connection of some kind seems probable" (*Medieval Manuscripts*, 14), and see N. Morgan *Early Gothic Manuscripts*, II, no. 101.

BARKING

London, British Library MS Harley 100, a psalter and book of hours, was attributed to Barking by C. E. Wright (*Fontes Harleiana*) since in the calendar at October 11 is added "in die sancte ethelburge de Berkyng." The litany, f. 145, lists saints Etheldreda, Mildreda, Wythburga, Sexburga, Radegundis, but not St. Ethelburga or London saints.

BRUISYARD

Wentworth, Jane

Cambridge, Gonville and Caius MS 124/61, a fifteenth-century English translation of Deguilleville's *Pelerinage de l'Ame*, has at the end, "This boke longis to dame Jane Wentworth" (f. 129v). McGerr has proposed two lay candidates, one from Yorkshire, the other from Suffolk (*Pilgrimage*, p. lxxiv). There was also a Bruisyard nun of this name: Thomasine Hopton left her 10 marks in 1497 (PCC 18 Horne Prob 11 /11 /151-52) and she is recorded as receiving her pension in 1555 (Baskerville, "Married Clergy and Pensioned Religious," 219).

DENNY

London, Lambeth Palace MS 3597, formerly the Coughton Court manuscript, a religious miscellany. Its provenance – the Throckmorton manor of Coughton Court, Warwickshire, to which Denny's last abbess, Elizabeth Throckmorton, retired at the Dissolution – argues for Denny ownership. In addition, another manuscript firmly attributed to Denny, Oxford, Bodleian Hatton 18, bears a Latin inscription which witnesses to Abbess Throckmorton's ownership "teste Thoma Gylberd in eodem monasterio olim manenti" (Bell, *What Nuns Read,* 134). Lambeth 3597 bears the name "Robt Gilberd," suggesting that it too, like Hatton 18, originated at Denny (E. Wilson, "Manuscript," 298).

Pickering and O'Mara point out that this ms shares eight items with London, MS Harley 4012, Lady Anne Harling's manuscript. They date the hand of Lambeth 3597 1450–75, while Harley 4012 has been dated *c.* 1460. E. Wilson

believes they were independently derived. The possibility of a connection between Denny and Lady Anne Harling is hinted at, however, by a begging letter
in 1461 or 1462 from Joan Keteryche, Abbess of Denny, to John Paston as
executor of Sir John Fastolf, which may indicate that the abbess knew Fastolf;
Lady Anne Harling had been Fastolf's ward (E. Wilson, "Manuscript,"299 and
302, for a suggestion from Davis, *Paston Letters*, that the hand of Harley 4012
resembles that of one of Fastolf's scribes who wrote in 1455 and 1456).

Oxford, Bodleian Gough Liturg. 9 (18335), a book of hours written in the first
half of the fifteenth century, contains the obit of Margaret Pympe "abbatisse," at
January 8, 1484. She does not occur in the *VCH Kent* list of Malling's abbesses
(there is a gap from 1469 to 1484), but is mentioned as prioress of Malling in
a 1475 will (PCC 10 Wattys), along with her sister Alice Pympe, a nun there.
Margaret probably became abbess between 1475 and her death. (Alice Pympe
was prioress by May 1484; see Prob 11/8/26). Other Kent names in the calendar
(Rykhill; Bruyn) suggest a Malling connection but, since the other obits appear
to be mostly laypersons, this book of hours might also have been owned by a
secular.

Oxford, Bodleian MS Auct.D.4.3. (4052), *c.* 1300, which the *SC* calls "a Gallican
Psalter for private use . . . Owned in the late 15th cent. by Rose Tressham, who
has inserted at fol. 6v the following advice to readers: 'Lerne to kepe your
books fayre & ockapy them well & use to clasp them whan you have done,'
[a motto used by Thomas Betson, monk of Syon, e.g. in his *A ryght profytable
treatyse*, 1500, *STC* 1978, whose last line is "Lerne to kepe your bokes clene
&c."]. In the 16th cent. 'Oliverus Yate me possidet'. Then 'liber Eduardi Yate
Somatochristiani ex dono . . . Eduardi Yate de Buckland armigeri consanguinei
sui, 7 Julii 1601." Pächt and Alexander (*Illuminated Manuscripts*, 1, no. 289)
identify Rose as the daughter of Sir Thomas Tressham "saec.xv.ex." Since he
died in 1471, Rose Tresham's ownership would probably have come in the last
quarter of the fifteenth century. She might be the aunt of Syon nun Clemence
Tresham (see above); Rose's name does not appear in the Syon *Martyrology*.
Though Clemence Tresham was not one of Syon's post-dissolution community
at Buckland, the home of the Yate family, the presence of two Yate inscriptions
also suggests a Syon provenance for this book.

APPENDIX II

Multiple book ownership by religious women

The information here has been tabulated from Ker (*MLBG*), Watson (*Supplement*), and Bell (*What Nuns Read*) to show multiple ownership. All the women listed are sixteenth-century, except for Sibyl de Felton. When the inscription was not readily available in Bell, I have provided it.

Brainthwaite, Alice. Dartford

Book of hours, fifteenth century, Taunton, Somerset County Record Office DD/SAS c/1193/68. Ker and Piper *MMBL* IV, 489. Ker, p. 57. Bell, pp. 133–34.
Prickyng of Love, Hilton (?), and *Mixed Life c.* 1400. London, BL Harley 2254. Ker, p. 57. Bell, p. 131.

Burton, Alice, and Margaret her cousin. Unknown house

Prick of Conscience and Rolle's *Form of Living*. Christie's Sale July 11, 2000, lot 77, *olim* Beeleigh Abbey, Maldon, Essex, Foyle MS. "Iste liber constat domine Alicie Burton nec non et Margarete consobrine eius," f. iv^v. Lewis and McIntosh, *Descriptive Guide*, p. 35.
Vitas Patrum, de Worde 1495 (*STC* 14507). Hunterian Lib BV.2.13. "Dompnus Wyllmus Burtun / Et alicia Burtun monica." [Caxton device] "Iste liber constat domine Alicie burton. Et margarete cognate eius. Tuarum facta et desideria sint deo beneplacita: et sibi operis meritaria ad vitam eternam," f. cccxlvii.

Colvylle, Anne. Syon

A miscellany including *Cursor Mundi* and *Parliament of Fowles*, 1459. Oxford, Bodl. Laud misc 416. Ker, p. 186. Bell, p. 195.
Hilton's *Eight Chapters*; *A Treatise of the Discretion of Spirits*. London, BL Harley 993, fifteenth century, a "common profit" ms. Ker, p. 185. Bell, p. 190.

de Felton, Sibyl. Barking

Ordinale, fifteenth century, Oxford, University College MS 169. Ker, p. 6. Bell, p. 115.

Nicholas Love's *Mirror of the Life of Christ*, fifteenth century, Christie's sale July 11, 2000, lot 72, *olim* Beeleigh Abbey, Maldon, Essex, Foyle MS. Ker, p. 6. Bell, p. 107.

Vies des saints Pères, late thirteenth–early fourteenth centuries, Paris, Bibliothèque National. Fr. 1038. Ker, p. 6. Bell, p. 115.

Gospel book, tenth–eleventh centuries, Oxford, Bodl. MS 155. Her name in it, according to Doyle, "Survey," p. 240, note 5. Ker, p. 6. Bell, p. 111.

Clensyng of Mannes Sowle, fourteenth century, Oxford, Bodl. 923. "Anno domini 1401," Bazire and Colledge, *Chastising*, p. 36. Ker, p. 6. Bell, p. 111.

Fettyplace, Eleanor. Syon

Psalter, fifteenth century, Brussels, Bibl. Royale IV. 481. Watson, p. 64. Bell, pp. 176–77.

Breviary, fifteenth century, Oxford, Bodl. Auct. D.4.7. Elizabeth Fettyplace's obit in calendar. Ker, p. 186. Bell, p. 194.

Pype of Perfection, 1532 (*STC* 25421). Oxford, Bodl. 4°w.2.Th.Seld. Ker, p. 186. Bell, p. 196.

Missal, Paris 1556 (*STC* 16217). Southwark, diocesan archives no. 72.

Palmer, Katherine. Syon

Chastising of Gods Children, 1493 (*STC* 5065). Cambridge, Sidney Sussex College BB.2.14. Ker, p. 185. Bell, pp. 182–83.

Scale of Perfection, 1494 (*STC* 14042). CUL Inc.3.J.1.2. 3534. Bell, p. 183.

Opera omnia, Johann Tauler, Cologne, 1548. Syon Abbey, now University of Exeter. Info Dr. Ann Hutchison to Bell, p. 183.

Slyght, Dorothy. Syon

Disci mori, fifteenth century, Oxford, Jesus College 39. Ker, p. 186. Bell, pp. 196–97.

Processional, fifteenth century, Syon Abbey 1. Ker, p. 187. Bell, p. 199.

Throckmorton, Elizabeth. Denny

Northern Homilies, fifteenth century, CUL ADD. MS 8335. Watson, p. 15. Bell, p. 134.

William of Nassington, *Speculum vitae*, fifteenth century, Oxford, Bodl. Hatton MS 18. Ker, p. 57. Bell, pp. 134–35.

Tresham, Clemence. Syon

Book of hours, 1534 (*STC* 15979). London, BL C.35.a.12. Her name on tp. Erler, "Embellishments."

Sawter of Mercy, xv–xvi c. Durham UL, Cosin V.v.12. Watson, p. 64. Bell, p. 184.

Thomas à Kempis, *Opera*, Paris 1523. A. I. Doyle. Watson, p. 64. Bell, p. 185.

Wylby, Elizabeth. Campsey

Chastising of Gods Children, 1493 (*STC* 5065). Untraced. Ker, p. 28. Bell, p. 125.
Scale of Perfection, Books I and II; Suso's *Seven Points*, Cambridge, Corpus Christi College 268, fifteenth century. Ker, p. 28. Bell, p. 123.

Windsor, Margaret. Syon

Boccaccio, *De Casibus Virorum Illustrium*, Lyons, 1483. New York, PML 600. Ker, p. 186. Bell, p. 192.
Psalter, fifteenth century, Oakly Park, Earl of Plymouth. Ker, p. 186. Bell, p. 193.
Tree & xij frutes of the holy ghoost, 1534–35 (*STC* 13608). Cambridge, Trinity College 0.7.12. Ker, p. 185. Bell, p. 183.

Surviving copies of various incunabula
in female ownership

Following *STC*'s distinction between imperfect copies and fragments, in the list below I have included only more-or-less complete copies, not fragments. I have included lost copies where information on these was available.

		STC copies	plus	*seen/ have info*	*not seen*
A: Devotional Works					
STC 1917	Meditations, St Bernard 1499	4	O	3:L,CUL(2)	I:HD
STC 3259-62	Speculum Vite Christi 1484,-90, -94(2)	15 +	3	14:3259 C 3260,L(2),L², C,G²,M,LC, PML	4:3260 NLW; 3262 O⁷,Cant, StevensCox
	names in 3260:L, 3262:L			3261 L,M 3262 L,C,C⁴	
STC 3305	Book of divers ghostly matters 1491 names in PML	5	O	5:L,C,DUR,M, PML	O
STC 5065	Chastising of God's Children 1493	9 +	9	17:L,C(2),G²,M, LINC,COPRL,L⁴, C⁶,C¹⁷,GottUL, HarlCat; F,HN, IND, PML(2)	I:Leeds
	names in C¹⁷, GottUL,F				

STC 14042	*Scale of Perfection* 1494	10 +	6	14:L,C,G^2,M, LINC,F,HN,Y, PML,ROS, C^4, C^5,Mellon, CopRL	2:L^{44}, Perryville
	names in C,F,Y, PML,ROS,C^5				
STC 14507	*Vitas Patrum* 1495	10 +	16	16:L(2),O(2),L^2, C^4,G^2,Black, M NY,F,Y,PML Mellon,HN,LC	10:CUL(3), DUR,LINC, St,C^2,Ill, IN,Gordan
	names in L^2,G^2,O,C,M				
STC 21429	*Royal Book* 1488?	9	I	5:L,M.PML, LC,F	5:C(2),CB, HD, HN
	names in L				
STC 24766	*Life of St. Katherine* 1492?	8	O	7:L(2),C,M,F, Mellon,CopRL	I:WN
	names in L				
		total: 105		*seen*: 81	*not seen*: 24

B: Primers

STC 15867	PML	I
STC 15869	O^a	I
STC 15875	L^2, O, C(2)	4
STC 15876	L	I
STC 15879	L	I
STC 15880	L,O	2
STC 15881	L	I
STC 15881.3	O	I
STC 15881.5	L,^{a} Paris^a	2
STC 15885	L,O,C,M,F,PML	6
STC 15886	O	I
STC 15887	L,L^2,O(2),C,C^2,PML	6
STC 15888	C,C^2,M, HN^a	4
STC 15889	M,St^a,F,PML	4
STC 15890	D^a	I
	total 36	*seen*: 30	*not seen*: 6

Surviving copies of devotional incunables and incunable primers: 141. Seen: 111. Not seen: 30.

a = not seen

Notes

PROLOGUE

1 According to English common law, wives could not will, though widows and single-women could. R. H. Helmholz concludes that "by the middle of the fifteenth century, wills of married women had become rarities in England." "Married Women's Wills in Later Medieval England," in Sue Sheridan Walker (ed.), *Wife and Widow in Medieval England* (Ann Arbor, 1993), 165–82, ref. p. 170.

2 N. R. Ker (ed.), *Medieval Libraries of Great Britain: A List of Surviving Books*, 2nd edn (London, 1964); Andrew G. Watson, *Supplement to the Second Edition* (London, 1987) (hereafter *Supplement*); David N. Bell, *What Nuns Read: Books and Libraries in Medieval English Nunneries* (Kalamazoo, Mich., 1995).

3 Susan H. Cavanaugh, "A Study of Books Privately Owned in England: 1300–1450," Ph.D. thesis, University of Pennsylvania, 1980.

4 The central work on this topic has been done by Carol Meale. See her survey, " '. . . alle the Bokes that I Haue of Latyn, Englisch, and Frensch': Laywomen and their Books in Late Medieval England," in C. M. Meale (ed.), *Women and Literature in Britain 1150–1500* (Cambridge University Press, 1993), pp. 128–58.

5 Robyn White, "Early Print and Purgatory: the Shaping of an Henrician Ideology," Ph.D. thesis, Australian National University (1994), "Appendix 1: *STC* Books Published 1475–1499."

6 *The New Interpreter's Bible. Vol. III* (Nashville, 1999), p. 978.

7 Richard Beadle, "Medieval Texts and Their Transmission, 1350–1500: Some Geographical Criteria," in M. Laing and K. Williamson (eds.), *Speaking in Our Tongues: Proceedings of a Colloquium on Medieval Dialectology and Related Disciplines* (Cambridge, 1994), 69–91, ref. p. 74.

8 Recent work on this topic appears in a collection edited by Susan Frye and Karen Robertson, *Maids and Mistresses, Cousins and Queens: Women's Alliances in Early Modern England* (Oxford, 1999).

9 A. I. Doyle, "A Survey of the Origins and Circulation of Theological Writings in English in the 14th, 15th and Early 16th Centuries with Special Consideration of the Part of the Clergy Therein," Ph.D. thesis, University of Cambridge (1954), pp. 294–97.

INTRODUCTION: DINAH'S STORY

1 Joyce M. Horn (ed.), *The Register of Robert Hallum, Bishop of Salisbury 1407–17*, Canterbury and York Society 72 (Torquay, 1982), p. 121.

2 *The Jerusalem Bible: Reader's Edition* (New York, 1966) translates "to visit." The Vulgate has "ut videret mulieres regionis illius." Robert Alter's recent translation from the Hebrew renders this phrase "went out to go seeing among the daughters of the land." He observes: "the sense of the verb in context may be something like "to make the acquaintance of" or "travel around among," though he rejects "to visit." *Genesis*, translation and commentary Robert Alter (New York, 1996), p. 189.

3 M. B. Salu, trans., *The Ancrene Riwle* (London, 1955), pp. 22–4. Blake Leyerle, "John Chrysostom on the Gaze," *Journal of Early Christian Studies* 1 (1993), 159–74. Elizabeth Robertson, *Early English Devotional Prose and the Female Audience* (Knoxville, Tenn., 1990), pp. 50–52, points out that the *Wisse* author's discussion of Dinah is based on St. Bernard's *De Gradibus Humilitatis et Superbiae*.

4 C. C. Mierow, trans., *The Letters of St. Jerome* in *Ancient Christian Writers* 33 (Westminster, Md., 1963), Letter 22, vol. I, pp. 158–59. For Alcock: *STC* 286, B I. For an allegorical reading of Dinah's story, see Sidney J. H. Herrtage (ed.), *Early English Versions of the Gesta Romanorum*, EETS ES 33 (London, 1879), p. 70. Here Dinah "was in the hous *with* iacob her Fader . . . and so as long as we beth *with*in the boundes of the commaundements of god, we beth not in the lepre of synne."

5 For a survey of such commands before 1100, see Jane Tibbetts Schulenburg, "Strict Active Enclosure and Its Effects on the Female Monastic Experience (ca. 500–1100)," in John A. Nichols and Lillian Thomas Shank (eds.), *Distant Echoes: Medieval Religious Women* (Kalamazoo, Mich., 1984), I, pp. 51–86, ref. p. 53. She concludes that the legislation, reflecting "an atmosphere of fear, suspicion and distrust of women and their sexual weakness," was one factor in the decline in women's monasticism from the mid-eighth to the end of the eleventh century, and was partly responsible for the poverty of female houses. For women who left, see F. Donald Logan, *Runaway Religious in Medieval England c. 1240–1540* (Cambridge, 1996).

6 James A. Brundage and Elizabeth M. Makowski, "Enclosure of Nuns: The Decretal *Periculoso* and Its Commentators," *JMH* 20 (1994), 143–55, ref. p. 152.

7 Kaspar Elm, "Die Stellung der Frau in Ordenswesen, Semireligiosentum und Häresie zur Zeit der Heiligen Elisabeth," in *Sankt Elisabeth, Fürstin, Dienerin, Heilige* (Sigmaringen, 1981) and "Vita Regularis sine Regula: Bedeutung, Rechtsstellung und Selbstverständnis des Mittelalterlichen und frühneuzeitlichen Semireligiosentums" in F. Smahel (ed.), *Häresie und Vorzeitige Reformation im Spätmittelalter* (Munich, 1998), 239–73.

8 John van Engen, "Friar Johannes Nyder on Laypeople Living as Religious in the World," in F. J. Felten and N. Jaspert (eds.), *Vita Religiosa im Mittelalter: Festschrift für Kaspar Elm zum 70. Geburtstag* (Berlin, 1999), 583–615.

9 Textual rubrics which register a shift from an anchoritic or monastic readership to a more general one are not rare in the fifteenth century; see Vincent Gillespie, "'*Lukynge in haly bukes*: Lectio in Some Late Medieval Spiritual Miscellanies," *Analecta Cartusiana* 106 (1984), 1–27; and Gillespie, "Vernacular Books of Religion," in J. Griffiths and D. Pearsall (eds.), *Book Production and Publishing in Britain 1375–1475* (Cambridge, 1989), pp. 317–44. More interesting are texts whose ownership demonstrates crossover from an intended lay audience to a religious one. *Contemplations of the Drede and Love of God*, for instance, written 1375–1425, though it is addressed to "suche þat be nat knowing" was given by a nun of Swine to another at Nun Cotham and, in a second manuscript, was owned by a nun of Shaftesbury. Margaret Connolly (ed.), *Contemplations of the Drede and Love of God*, EETS 303 (Oxford, 1993), pp. xv–xvi.

10 Schulenburg, "Strict Active Enclosure," p. 51; see B. Dolhagaray, "Clôture," *Dictionnaire de théologie catholique*, 15 vols. (Paris, 1909–50), III, cols. 244–57.

11 Eileen Power, *Medieval English Nunneries c. 1275 to 1535* (Cambridge, 1922), pp. 345, 342.

12 Brundage and Makowski, "Enclosure," p. 152.

13 Elizabeth Makowski, *Canon Law and Cloistered Women: Periculoso and Its Commentators 1298–1545* (Washington, D.C., 1997), p. 40.

14 Barbara Harvey, *Living and Dying in England 1100–1540, The Monastic Experience* (Oxford, 1993), p. 210.

15 Ilana F. Silber, *Virtuosity, Charisma, and Social Order: A Comparative Sociological Study of Monasticism in Theravada Buddhism and Medieval Catholicism* (Cambridge, 1995), pp. 38–40, 43, 45.

16 Marilyn Oliva, *The Convent and the Community in Late Medieval England: Female Monasteries in the Diocese of Norwich, 1350–1540* (Woodbridge, 1998); Roberta Gilchrist, *Gender and Material Culture: the Archaeology of Religious Women* (London, 1994).

17 Nuns in London, Norfolk, and Kent witnessed and supervised lay wills, for instance. For London: Catherine Paxton, "The Nunneries of London and Its Environs in the Later Middle Ages," Ph.D. thesis, University of Oxford (1993), pp. 151–2; for Norfolk: Oliva, *Convent and Community*, p. 150; for Kent: Paul Lee, *Nunneries, Learning and Spirituality in Late Medieval English Society: The Dominican Priory of Dartford* (York, 2001), pp. 104–5. For the prioress of Dartford, Lee, *Nunneries*, p. 106.

18 Although Janet Burton points out that "the evidence of the wills suggests that a number of [nuns] remained a perceived part of a secular family." "Yorkshire Nunneries in the Middle Ages: Recruitment and Resources," in J. C. Appleby and P. Dalton (eds.), *Government, Religion and Society in Northern England 1000–1700* (Stroud, Glos., 1997), pp. 104–16, ref. p. 115.

19 A. Hamilton Thompson (ed.), *Visitations of Religious Houses in the Diocese of Lincoln*, 3 vols., Canterbury and York Society 17, 24, 33 (London, 1915, 1919, 1927), II, 4.

20 Power, *Nunneries*, p. 395.

21 Ibid., pp. 412, 414, 416. Lady Audeley paid 40s. in rent annually.

22 Lee, *Nunneries*, p. 19, n. 40.

23 Lillian J. Redstone, "Three Carrow Account Rolls," *Norfolk Archaeology* 29 (1946) 41–88, ref. p. 43.

24 Martha Carlin notes that at the minoresses' "a great mansion was built within the precinct in 1352 by Elizabeth de Burgh . . . a second such great house was in existence by 1538," "St Botolph Aldgate Gazeteer. Holy Trinity Minories," in Keene and Harding (eds.), *Historical Gazetteer of London . . .* (London, 1987).

The Duchess's request comes from *Calendar of Entries in the Papal Registers Relating to Great Britain and Ireland: Papal Letters*, 30 vols. (London, 1893–), 483–4. She was born Elizabeth Talbot, daughter of the Earl of Shrewsbury, and was the widow of John Mowbray, fourth duke of Norfolk (d. 1476) (*DNB* XIII, 1122). She figures prominently in the Paston letters; for instance c. 1472, the year she gave birth to her only child Anne, the duchess may have described John Paston II's remarks on her pregnancy as crude and awkward (Davis (ed.), *Paston Letters* I, 450). She perhaps was sympathetic to the Pastons in their struggle over Caister; see Colin Richmond, *The Paston Family in the Fifteenth Century: The First Phase* (Cambridge, 1990), p. 193. Her papal permission came just three months before her death in November 1506; see John Ashdown-Hill, "Norfolk Requiem: The Passing of the House of Mowbray," *The Ricardian* 12 (2001),

198–217. The 1504 will of the duchess's gentlewomen Elizabeth Brakkyngbury survives (PRO Prob 11 /14/163 v–164).

25 Norfolk Consistory Court, 104–108 Platfoote. Conflict over space could extend even to the toilets, as at Ankerwyke in 1441 when the question was raised of secular vs. religious womens' use of these facilities (Thompson, *Visitations*, II, 4).

26 PRO LR/14/813, dated March 24, 1492, one part of a two-part indenture.

27 John Tillotson, "Visitation and Reform of the Yorkshire Nunneries in the Fourteenth Century," *Northern History* 30 (1994), 1–21.

28 *John Hopton, A Fifteenth-Century Suffolk Gentleman* (Cambridge, 1981), pp. 220–21.

29 "Household Roll of Eleanor, Countess of Leicester, AD 1265," in Beriah Botfield (ed.), *Manners and Household Expenses of England in the Thirteenth and Fifteenth Centuries*, Roxburghe Club no. 57 (London, 1841), pp. 6–8, 18, 20, 31, 33, 34. Margaret Wade Labarge suggests a political context: "In some cases a friend, like the Prioress of Amesbury, sought a favour from the king, who was in the Earl's control, and the request was forwarded through Eleanor." "Eleanor de Montfort's Household Rolls," *History Today* 11 (1961), 490–500, ref. p. 497. For Amesbury's list of prioresses, see *VCH Wiltshire* III, 259, where Ida occurs in 1256 and 1273.

30 C. H. Hartshorne, "Illustrations of Domestic Manners during the Reign of Edward I," *JBAA* 18 (1862), 214, 217.

31 Jennifer C. Ward, *English Noblewomen in the Later Middle Ages* (New York, 1992), p. 78 and see her "English Noblewomen and the Local Community in the Later Middle Ages," in Diane Watt (ed.), *Medieval Women in Their Communities* (Cardiff, 1997), pp. 186–203.

32 C. D. Ross, "The Household Accounts of Elizabeth Berkeley, Countess of Warwick, 1420–21," *TBGAS* 70 (1951) 81–105, ref. p. 94. For Westwood, *VCH Worcester* II, 151.

33 *VCH Warwickshire* II, 68–9; C. Munro (ed.), *Letters of Queen Margaret of Anjou*, Camden Society no. 86 (London, 1863), pp. 163–64. For a recent summary of earlier MSS owned by English Fontevrault houses see Berenice M. Kerr, *Religious Life for Women c. 1100 – c. 1350, Fontevraud in England* (Oxford, 1999), pp. 125–28.

34 John Redgard (ed.), *Medieval Framlingham: Select Documents 1270–1524*, Suffolk Record Society 27 (Ipswich, 1985), pp. 86–128, refs. pp. 107, 117–18. For the prioress's name, *VCH Suffolk* II, 82. Can Prioress Katherine de Montacute be identified with the Katherine de Monte Acuto who fled Bungay ten years earlier in 1376 (Oliva, *Convent and Community*, p. 211 n., citing *CPR 1374–77*, p. 490) or Katherine Montague (Power, *Nunneries*, p. 442 n. citing PRO *Chancery Warrants*, Series F, file 1759)?

35 C. M. Woolgar, *Household Accounts from Medieval England*, 2 vols., Records of Social and Economic History n.s. 18 (Oxford, 1993), no. 24, p. 578, and see Colin Richmond, "Thomas Lord Morley (d. 1446) and the Morleys of Hingham," *Norfolk Archaeology* 39 (1942), 1–12, ref. p. 3. Lady Morley was the person Margaret Paston consulted on whether Christmas festivities should be held after the death of Sir John Fastolf in 1459 (Woolgar, *Household Accounts*, p. 574). Carrow's prioress was perhaps Mary Pygot, who had been elected in 1444 (*VCH Norfolk* II, 354; Oliva cites her as Margaret, *Convent and Community*, pp. 36, 78, 81, 97).

36 Summarized in Francis Blomefield, *An Essay Toward a Topographical History of the County of Norfolk*, 10 vols. (London, 1800–10), II, 430. For instance she was patroness of the priory of Aldeby, Norfolk, as heir to the founders (*VCH Norfolk* II, 328). The will is dated 1464 and was proved February 28, 1466 (NRO, Norwich Consistory Court, Register Jekkys, f. 50ff). Lady Morley was born in 1415.

37 Katherine de la Pole's period of rule (1433–73) is treated in E. A. Loftus and H. F. Chettle, *A History of Barking Abbey* (Barking, 1954), pp. 47–8. A 1422 order from the king's council forbids the abbess of Bruisyard to allow Katherine, then eleven, to make religious profession; though it says that her sisters Elizabeth and Isabel are dead, this would seem to be a mistake, at least in Isabel's case (*CCR 1419–22*, p. 247). See also *CIPM 1413–18*, p. 138.

38 N. H. Nicolas (ed.), *Privy Purse Expenses of Elizabeth of York* (London, 1830), p. 8; Frederick Madden (ed.), *Privy Purse Expenses of Princess Mary*, (London, 1831), p. 29.

39 Muriel St. Clare Byrne (ed.), *The Lisle Letters: An Abridgement* (Chicago, 1983), pp. 121–24, 242–43, 248–49.

40 Gilchrist, *Gender and Material Culture*, pp. 127, 189–91.

41 Jonathan Hughes, *Pastors and Visionaries: Religious and Secular Life in Late Medieval Yorkshire* (Woodbridge, Suffolk, 1988), p. 49.

42 For Norfolk nuns' socioeconomic level: Oliva, *Convent and Community*, pp. 54, 105–10; Barbara J. Harris, "A New Look at the Reformation: Aristocratic Women and Nunneries 1450–1540," *JBS* 3 (1993), 89–113. Oliva found that over nearly two centuries the diocese of Norfolk had 1% of aristocratic nuns and 10% of upper-gentry ones, while Harris estimated that during the latter half of this period, using aristocratic wills with no particular geographic distribution, 2.47% of aristocratic women belonged to religious orders (*Convent and Community*, p. 94).

43 Hughes, *Pastors*, p. 49. His reference to the Stapilton will should be *TE* II, 270–72.

44 Joan Newmarch's will is London, Guildhall MS 9171/5, f. 110. The Dartford book is London, BL MS Harley 2254; the minoresses' book is Cambridge, Trinity College MS B.14.15 (301).

45 William F. Pollard, "Bodleian MS Holkham Misc. 41: a Fifteenth-Century Bridgettine Manuscript and Prayer Cycle," *Birgittiana* 3 (1997), 43–53, ref. p. 47.

46 C. Horstmann, "Marienlegenden," *Anglia* 3 (1880), 320–25, ref. p. 324. The manuscript is London, Lambeth Palace 432 (see Appendix I: *Syon*).

47 Thompson, *Visitations* II, 46–52 for Catesby. The Tynggelden will is London, Guildhall MS 9171/9, ff. 149v–150.

48 Colin Richmond, "Elizabeth Clere: Friend of the Pastons," in Jocelyn Wogan-Browne et al. (eds.), *Medieval Women: Texts and Contexts in Late Medieval Britain: Essays for Felicity Riddy* (Turnhout, Belgium, 2000), p. 269.

49 For a fuller treatment of the vowed state see Erler, "English Vowed Women at the End of the Middle Ages," *Mediaeval Studies* 57 (1995), 155–203.

50 See chapter 4. Historians have frequently confused the categories of vowess and nun. To take just one instance, Stanford E. Lehmberg's biography *Sir Thomas Elyot, Tudor Humanist* (Austin, Tx., 1960) says of Elyot's half-sister vowess Susan Kyngeston that she "had become a nun after the untimely death of her husband . . . in 1514" (p. 128).

51 See Jocelyn Wogan-Browne, "Rerouting the Dower: The Anglo-Norman Life of St. Audrey by Marie (of Chatteris)," in J. Carpenter and S. B. MacLean (eds.), *Power of the Weak: Studies on Medieval Women* (Urbana, Ill., 1995), 27–56, ref. p. 39.

52 Power, *Nunneries*, p. 381.

53 Caroline M. Barron, "Introduction: The Widow's World," in Barron and Anne F. Sutton (eds.), *Medieval London Widows 1300–1500* (London and Rio Grande, 1994), p. xxii, note 25.

54 For remarriage estimates, which must have varied in times of economic hardship and for women with young children, see ibid., pp. xxiv–xxv.

55 Theodore Erbe (ed.), *Mirk's Festial: A Collection of Homilies by . . . John Mirk*, EETS es 96 (London, 1905), p. 214. For more on St. Anne see Kathleen Ashley and Pamela Sheingorn (eds.), *Interpreting Cultural Symbols: Saint Anne in Late Medieval Society* (Athens, Ga., 1990).

56 Osbern Bokenham, *Legendys of Hooly Wummen*, ed. Mary S. Serjeantson, EETS os 206 (London, 1938), p. 259. Catherine Lawless has recently shown the dependence of saints' cults on local variation in law and custom, using the example of St. Anne and Florentine attitudes to inheritance and widows' remarriage. See "'A Widow of God'? St. Anne and Representations of Widowhood in Fifteenth-Century Florence," in Christine Meek (ed.), *Women in Renaissance and Early Modern Europe* (Dublin, 2000), pp. 15–42.

57 Jocelyn Wogan-Browne, *Saints' Lives and Women's Literary Culture c. 1150–1300: Virginity and Its Authorizations* (Oxford, 2001), p. 212.

58 John Fletcher, "Slices from a Deep Cake: Dating Panel Paintings of St. Etheldreda from Ely," *Country Life* (March 28, 1974), 728–30; and Fletcher, "Four Scenes from the Life of St. Etheldreda," *Antiquaries Journal* 54 (1974), 287–89; Margaret Rickert, *Painting in Britain: The Middle Ages* (Baltimore, Md., 1954), pp. 180, 202.

59 Cavanaugh, "Study," p. 9.

60 Norman Tanner, *The Church in Late Medieval Norwich 1370–1532*, Pontifical Institute of Mediaeval Studies Studies and Texts 66 (Toronto, 1984), p. 111.

61 Jo Ann Hoeppner Moran, *The Growth of English Schooling 1340–1548: Learning, Literacy, and Laicization in the Pre-Reformation York Diocese* (Princeton, N.J., 1985), p. 205.

62 For a detailed examination of this process at work in the formation of the Vernon manuscript, Ralph Hanna III (ed.), *IMEP: Handlist XII: Smaller Bodleian Collections . . .* (Woodbridge, Suffolk, 1997), pp. xii–xv. See also Gillespie, "Vernacular Books of Religion."

63 P. S. Jolliffe, "Middle English Translations of the *De Exterioris et Interioris Hominis Compositione*," *Mediaeval Studies* 36 (1974), 259–77, ref. p. 275.

64 Marta Powell Harley (ed.), *The Myrour of Recluses: A Middle English Translation of Speculum Inclusarum* (Rutherford, N.J., 1995), xxviii–xxix.

65 Gillespie, "*Lukynge in haly bukes*," 4.

66 Joan Kirby (ed.), *The Plumpton Letters and Papers*. Camden 5th ser., vol. 8 (Cambridge, 1996), p. 24. Thomas Stapleton (ed.), *The Plumpton Correspondence*, Camden Society o.s. IV (London, 1839), p. xxxv, notes that George Plumpton had been ordained priest in 1418. At the time of the letter he was living in retirement at Bolton Abbey in Craven, having resigned his living, though retaining an annual pension of £10 (p. xxxvii).

67 Felicity Riddy, *Sir Thomas Malory* (Leiden, 1987), p. 10. The quotation concludes: "at least until the rise of the speculative trade in manuscript books in the fifteenth century." With the coming of printing it seems likely that the necessity for personal connection lessened, but probably not soon. In fact one important function for printed books may simply have been to provide more available exemplars for hand-copying, and thus to make access to the *manuscript* book easier.

68 [Nicholas Barker], "Provenance," *The Book Collector* 45 (1996), 157–70, ref. pp. 166–67.

69 Philippa Maddern, "'Best Trusted Friends': Concepts and Practices of Friendship among Fifteenth-Century Norfolk Gentry," in Nicholas Rogers, (ed.), *England in the Fifteenth Century, Proceedings of the 1992 Harlaxton Symposium* (Stamford, 1994), 100–17. See pp. 113–15 for discussion of why female friendship appears so seldom in the historical record.

70 Christine de Pizan, *The Book of the City of Ladies*, trans. Earl Jeffrey Richards (New York, 1982), II. 36.2.

I OWNERSHIP AND TRANSMISSION OF BOOKS: WOMEN'S RELIGIOUS COMMUNITIES

1 London, British Library MS Harley 2397. A. I. Doyle has identified Abbess Horwode's father as a London goldsmith with whom Robert Alderton (or Allerton) was associated in a document of 1431. Allerton was Clerk of the Kitchen to Henry V, Bachelor of Laws, prebendary of Lincoln, Ripon, Windsor, and Chichester, and rector of Amersham, Bucks. He died in 1437 and left 20s to Elizabeth Horwode and the same amount to the house. Doyle says: "She may have bought or commissioned the book shortly afterwards (though it does not appear to be of much before the middle of the century), the inscription only being later." He dates her period of office between 1455/56, the death of Abbess Christine St Nicholas, and 1481, when Joan Barton is recorded as abbess. "A Survey of the Origins and Circulation of Theological Writings in English in the 14th, 15th and Early 16th Centuries with Special Consideration of the Part of the Clergy Therein," Ph.D. thesis, University of Cambridge (1954), pp. 213–14.
2 Clive Burgess quoting Jacques Le Goff in "A Fond Thing Vainly Invented': An Essay on Purgatory and Pious Motive in Late Medieval England," in Susan Wright (ed.), *Parish, Church, and People* (Leicester, 1988), 56–84, ref. p. 67.
3 "There are signs of early 'pro anima' inscriptions in Balliol manuscripts: MSS 106, 112, 241, 317," N. R. Ker, "Oxford College Libraries before 1500," reprinted in Andrew G. Watson (ed.), *Books, Collectors and Libraries: Studies in the Medieval Heritage* (London and Rouncevert, 1985), 301–20, ref. p. 310. The terms of the exchange are exceptionally clear in a devotional miscellany whose owners bequeathed it to the Franciscans of Lichfield in 1486. Its inscription specifies that the book is given in return for thirty masses of St. Gregory with placebo, dirige, and penitential psalms, to be said for the souls of Alice, Joyce, and Alan. Toshiyuki Takamiya, "'On the Evils of Covetousness': An Unrecorded Middle English Poem," in Richard Beadle and A. J. Piper (eds.), *New Science Out of Old Books: Studies in Manuscripts and Early Printed Books in Honour of A. I. Doyle* (Aldershot, Hants., 1995), pp. 189–206, ref. p. 190.
4 David N. Bell, *What Nuns Read: Books and Libraries in Medieval English Nunneries* (Kalamazoo, Mich., 1995), pp. 139–40.
5 Wendy Scase, "Reginald Pecock, John Carpenter and John Colop's 'Common-Profit' Books: Aspects of Book Ownership and Circulation in Fifteenth-Century London," *Medium Ævum* 61 (1992), 261–74. In most cases the books bequeathed were to pass from hand to hand, each owner praying for the original donor. Male academic connections may be illustrated by a 1474 will in which "John Savage, chaplain and fellow of King's College Cambridge, left a breviary for the use of Master John Hogekyns. He was to give this and a psalter to Nicholas Burnham *alias* White, when he became a priest, who was to pray especially for John Savage's soul and the souls of Thomas Brown and John White. On his death he was to leave the breviary to another priest who was to do likewise for the term of his life, and he to another priest for his, on pain of excommunication." Virginia R. Bainbridge, *Gilds in the Medieval Countryside: Social and Religious Change in Cambridgeshire c. 1350–1558* (Woodbridge, Suffolk, 1996), p. 81, quoting KCC Ledger, Book I, f. 78. Both regional loyalty and academic connection are visible in a 1517 priest's bequest of his books to Oxford scholars "so that att their departing frome the universite

thayme remayne to other scolers of the seid diocese [York] and so frome scoler to scoler and tyme to tyme." Ida Darlington (ed.), *London Consistory Court Wills 1492–1547*, London Record Society 3 (1967), no. 77.

6 For a recent exploration of the complex subject of book survival see David McKitterick, "The Survival of Books," *The Book Collector* 43 (1994), 9–26, particularly pp. 17ff.

7 Josiah Cox Russell, "The Clerical Population of Medieval England," *Traditio* 2 (1944), Table 9, p. 212; p. 181.

8 David Knowles and R. Neville Hadcock, *Medieval Religious Houses: England and Wales* (London, 1953), p. 364.

9 Henry Ansgar Kelly, "A Neo-Revisionist look at Chaucer's Nuns," *Chaucer Review* 31 (1996), 115–32, ref. p. 116.

10 Power, *Nunneries*, p. 1.

11 Knowles and Hadcock, *Medieval Religious Houses*, p. 364.

12 John H. Tillotson, *Marrick Priory: A Nunnery in Late Medieval Yorkshire*, Borthwick Paper No. 75 (York, 1989), p. 2.

13 Ibid.

14 Knowles and Hadcock, *Medieval Religious Houses*, p. 210. Marilyn Oliva has noted a strong correlation between female size and wealth for the poorest and the richest East Anglian houses; the correlation is less strong for houses in the middle range. *Convent and the Community*, p. 41.

15 Power, *Nunneries*, p. 2.

16 Ibid., p. 241, summarizing W. H. Blaauw, "Episcopal Visitations of the Benedictine Nunnery of Easebourne," *Sussex Archaeological Collections* 9 (1857), 1–32. For Easebourne's connection with the local parish, Oliva, *Convent and Community*, p. 148. Easebourne's twenty-four books compare favorably with the list of eight service books which Archbishop of Canterbury Walter Reynolds (1313–27) had required for parish ownership: an antiphoner, gradual, lesson book, manual, missal, ordinal, psalter, and troper. F. M. Powicke and C. R. Cheyney (eds.), *Councils & Synods with Other Documents Relating to the English Church AD 1205–1313*, 2 vols. (Oxford, 1964), II, 1387–88.

17 *Rule of St. Benedict*, ch. 48, 15–16. For an overview of the ceremony in male Benedictine houses see Karl Christ, *The Handbook of Medieval Library History* (repr. edn, Metuchen, N.J. and London, 1984), pp. 16–18.

18 Titchfield (Hants.), a male Premonstratensian abbey, supplies one model for bookcase size. It had four bookcases which in 1400 contained 224 volumes, hence an average of a little over fifty-five books each, though of course volume dimensions and shelf sizes would vary. E. Maunde Thompson et al. (eds.), *New Palaeographical Society Facsimiles of Ancient Manuscripts*, 2 vols. (London, 1903–12), II, plate 18, no page.

19 J. B. L. Tolhurst (ed.), *The Ordinal and Customary of the Benedictine Nuns of Barking Abbey: University College, Oxford, MS 169*, 2 vols., Henry Bradshaw Society 65 and 66 (London, 1927–28), I, 67–8.

20 "The ordinal speaks of 'sinquante Dames' [50] in the time of Sibyl Felton (p. 360)," Winifrid M. Sturman, "Barking Abbey: A Study in its External and Internal Administration from the Conquest to the Dissolution," Ph.D. thesis, University of London (1961), p. 489.

21 Tolhurst, *Ordinal*, p. 374, reflecting the Rule, 48.17.

22 Betty Hill, "Some Problems in Washington, Library of Congress MS Faye-Bond 4," in J. Lachlan Mackenzie and Richard Todd (eds.), *In Other Words: Transcultural Studies in Philology, Translation, and Lexicology Presented to Hans Heinrich Meier* ... (Dordrecht,

Holland, 1989), pp. 35–44. The text I print is from Hill's transcription. Jeanne Krochalis discovered the text: "The Benedictine Rule for Nuns: Library of Congress, MS 4," *Manuscripta* 30 (1986), 21–34.

23 Hill believes that the bird is a swan (Krochalis suggested a crane). The prior of Hatfield Broad Oak from 1395 to *c.* 1416 was William Gulle, but the bird's long graceful neck means it cannot be a gull. See G. Alan Lowndes, "History of the Priory at Hatfield Regis Alias Hatfield Broad Oak," *TEAS* n.s. 2 (1884), 117–52, ref. pp. 143–5.

24 Ruth J. Dean and M. Domenica Legge note that in a mid-fifteenth-century French manuscript made for the nuns of St. Armand, Rouen (Vatican Regin. lat. 343), a text of the Rule is followed by a further version of the material from chapters 48 and 49 which deal with Lent and Lenten reading, as in MS Faye-Bond 4. Other manuscripts with textual complications around these chapters are BL Titus A.iv and Sens MS 44; see *The Rule of St. Benedict: A Norman Prose Version* (Oxford, 1964), Appendix, pp. 103–4.

25 Robert Jowett Whitwell, *EHR* 25 (1910), 121–23, gives the bookbinder's name incorrectly as Thomas Raille.

26 Canterbury Cathedral, Dean and Chapter MS, Register R, f. 115v.

27 Richard H. Rouse and Mary A. Rouse (eds.), *Registrum Angliae de Libris Doctorum et Auctorum Veterum*, Corpus of British Medieval Library Catalogues (London, 1991), p. 264.

28 Ker/Watson, *MLGB* and *Supplement*.

29 Thompson, *New Paleographical Society*, plate 17.

30 Bell, *What Nuns Read*, pp. 42–43.

31 Ibid., p. 38.

32 Ker, *MLGB*, p. xvi. The formula, in a fourteenth-century hand, appears in CUL Addl. 7220 (a thirteenth-century psalter); BL Additional 40675 (a fourteenth-century psalter); and BL Additional 70513 (a fourteenth-century collection of saints' lives labelled "de lire a mengier"). Bell, *What Nuns Read*, pp. 123–25.

33 For the Dartford manuscript, see John Scattergood, "Two Unrecorded Poems from Trinity College Dublin MS 490," *RES* 38 (1987), 46–9 (Bell, *What Nuns Read*, pp. 130–1). The Carrow manuscript is Baltimore, Walters Art Gallery MS 34; see Nigel Morgan, *Early Gothic Manuscripts 1250–85*, 2 vols. (London, 1988), II, 88–90 (Bell, *What Nuns Read*, pp. 126–7).

34 R. Sharpe, J. P. Carley, R. M. Thomson, and A. G. Watson (eds.), *English Benedictine Libraries: The Shorter Catalogues*, Corpus of British Medieval Library Catalogues vol. 4 (London, 1996), 644–46. Bell, *What Nuns Read*, is cautious about assigning these books to Wilton, see p. 213.

35 "The English Provincial Book Trade before Printing," in Peter Isaac, *Six Centuries of the Provincial Book Trade in Britain*, St. Paul's Bibliographies (Winchester, 1990), pp. 13–29, citing W. Oakeshott, "Winchester College Library before 1750," *The Library* 5th ser. 9 (1954), 1–16, ref. pp. 14–15.

36 Titles of nuns' books from Ker's and Watson's lists of monastic volumes (*MLGB* and *Supplement*) have recently been extracted and reprinted, with descriptions from the relevant catalogues, by Anne Clark Bartlett, *Male Authors, Female Readers: Representation and Subjectivity in Middle English Devotional Literature* (Ithaca, N.Y., 1995), pp. 149–71.

37 University textbooks donated by monks, which formed a surprisingly large component in male monastic libraries, were of course unavailable to female houses. See Barbara Dodwell, "The Monastic Community," in I. Atherton, E. Fernie, C. Harper-Bill, and H. Smith (eds.), *Norwich Cathedral, Church, City, and Diocese 1096–1996* (London and Rio Grande, 1996), pp. 231–54, ref. pp. 247–48.

38 Bell, *What Nuns Read*, p. 33.

39 Ibid., "Appendix: Cartularies and Related Documents," pp. 219–22, based on G. R. C. Davis, *Medieval Cartularies of Great Britain* (London, 1958). Twenty-one houses have surviving cartularies, making Janet Burton's total, "fewer than twenty," seem a little low; *Monastic and Religious Orders in Britain 1000–1300* (Cambridge, 1994), p. 85. (Aconbury, Blackborough, Buckland Minchin, Canonsleigh, Chatteris, Clerkenwell, Crabhouse, Flamstead, Godstow, Harrold, Lacock (2), Marham, Nun Cotham, Nunkeeling, Rowney, Shaftesbury (2), Stamford, Stixwould, Westwood, Wherwell, Wilton.)

40 Christopher de Hamel, *Syon Abbey: The Library of the Bridgettine Nuns and Their Peregrinations after the Reformation*, Roxburghe Club (Otley, 1991), pp. 114–24.

41 Bell, *What Nuns Read*, pp. 175–210.

42 Ibid.: Barking, pp. 107–20; Dartford, pp. 130–34; Shaftsbury, pp. 163–68; Amesbury, pp. 103–05; London minoresses, pp. 149–52; St. Mary Winchester, pp. 214–16; Campsey, pp. 122–26; Tarrant Keynston, pp. 210–11; Wherwell, pp. 212–13. The books in Appendix I have been added to the totals given by Bell. For Pownsett's book list see Patrick Carter, "Barking Abbey and the Library of William Pownsett: A Bibliographical Conundrum," *TCBS* 10 (1998), 263–71.

43 Serjeantson (ed.), *Legendys of Hooly Wummen by Osbern Bokenham*, p. 289.

44 A. I. Doyle, "Books Connected with the Vere Family and Barking Abbey," *TEAS* n.s. 25 (1958), p. 236, n. 8.

45 Power, *Nunneries*, p. 698. The references are conveniently gathered and reprinted in Bell, *What Nuns Read*, under the heading for each house: Brewood (one mass book in the church); Campsey (a mass book in the church); Castle Hedingham (two mass books, six books of parchment in the choir); Chesunt (ten books in the choir, one mass book in the dorter, a chest of evidences in the prioress' chamber); Flixton (divers books of their use in the choir); Higham/Lillechurch (a gospel book with silver and crystal cover); Kilbourne (two *Legenda Aurea*, one manuscript, one printed, in a chamber next to the church, two mass books, one written, one printed, four processionals, two legenda, two chests with divers books pertaining to the church, in the church); Langley (two mass books in the church); Marham (a mass book and six books in the church); Redlingfield (one antiphoner with a grail and four other books in the choir, a mass book in the church).

46 Mackenzie E. C. Walcott, "Inventories and Valuations of Religious Houses at the Time of the Dissolution," *Archaeologia* 43 (1871), 245.

47 Claire Cross, *The End of Medieval Monasticism in the East Riding of Yorkshire*, East Yorkshire Local History Society no. 47 (Beverley, 1993), pp. 27, 44. Kathleen Cooke mentions ex-nuns of "Elstow, Fosse, Bullington, and Kirklees living together," "The English Nuns and the Dissolution," in John Blair and Brian Golding (eds.), *The Cloister and the World: Essays in Medieval History in Honour of Barbara Harvey* (Oxford, 1996), 287–301, ref. p. 300, n. 32. For Norfolk former nuns, Marilyn Oliva and Roberta Gilchrist, *Religious Women in Medieval East Anglia: History and Archaeology c. 1100–1540*, Studies in East Anglian History 1 (Norwich, 1993), p. 71.

48 Throckmorton: *VCH Cambridgeshire* II, 301–02; Kyppax: Clare Cross and Noreen Vickers (eds.), *Monks, Friars and Nuns in Sixteenth-Century Yorkshire*, Yorkshire Archaeological Society 150 (Huddersfield, 1995), pp. 9–10; Dartford: Lee, *Nunneries*, pp. 119–20; Syon groups: J. R. Fletcher, "History of Syon Abbey 1539–1563," notebook, deposited at Exeter University Library; Barley: Sturman, "Barking Abbey," p. 447; Shelley: Diana K. Coldicott, *Hampshire Nunneries* (Chichester, Sussex, 1989), pp. 143–44.

At least two instances of male monastic attempts to save their houses' libraries may be mentioned. Robert Barker, clerk and vicar of Driffield (Yorks.) who died in 1581 owned about 150 books which probably came to him from an earlier Robert Barker, former prior of Byland Abbey. Claire Cross, "A Medieval Yorkshire Library," *Northern History* 25 (1989), 281–90. William Browne, prior at Monk Bretton (Yorks.), with three of his monks after the Dissolution actively worked to reassemble the monastic library and managed to gather about 150 books. Cross and Vickers, *Monks, Friars and Nuns*, pp. 9, 20–29, and see for Kirkstall, p. 146.

49 The twenty-nine book gifts to women's houses were culled from Bell, *What Nuns Read* and Susan H. Cavanaugh, "A Study of Books Privately Owned in England: 1300–1450," Ph.D. thesis, University of Pennsylvania (1980).

50 Bell, *What Nuns Read*, p. 148 (Cavanaugh, "Study," p. 857).

51 1374: Bell, *What Nuns Read*, p. 120 (Cavanaugh, "Study," pp. 103–4); 1376: Bell, *What Nuns Read*, p. 156 (Cavanaugh, "Study," pp. 540–1); 1391: Bell, *What Nuns Read*, p. 140 (Cavanaugh, "Study," p. 862); 1392: Bell, *What Nuns Read*, pp. 122–3 (Cavanaugh, "Study," p. 70); 1398: Bell, *What Nuns Read*, pp. 146–7.

52 The shift from psalters to primers in the mid-fifteenth century is confirmed by P. J. P. Goldberg's reading of 2,286 York wills. He notes nineteen psalters bequeathed in the first half of the century, only six in the second half. "Lay Book Ownership in Late Medieval York: The Evidence of Wills," *The Library* 6th ser. 16 (1994), 181–89.

53 In 1412 Elizabeth Darcy, widow of Lord Philip Darcy, left to Heynyngs chapel in the priory of St. Mary Heynyngs, Lincolnshire, "a great missal and her portiforium and great psalter to be chained there," Bell, *What Nuns Read*, p. 142 (Cavanaugh, "Study," p. 229).

54 Bell, *What Nuns Read*, p. 156 (Cavanaugh, "Study," pp. 828–9).

55 Bell, *What Nuns Read*, p. 153 (Cavanaugh, "Study," p. 129).

56 Bell, *What Nuns Read*, pp. 106, 135, 138, 157, 168 (Cavanaugh, "Study," pp. 815–6). Besides the five books she gave to nunneries, Stapilton left five more to friends and family. Her will illustrates substantial friendships with friars as well as nuns. It includes bequests to several of these men and asks for burial in the Dominican church at York with her husband Sir Brian. Her widow's clothing, veil, and *barbes* feature prominently in the bequests, though no record of a vow has been discovered. Ann K. Warren believes that vowess Margaret Stapilton who lived at Clementhorpe nunnery in the suburbs of York and died in 1466 was Agnes Stapilton's daughter-in-law. *Anchorites and Their Patrons in Medieval England* (Berkeley, Calif., 1985), pp. 214–16.

57 Bell, *What Nuns Read*, pp. 151–2 (Cavanaugh, "Study," pp. 110–11) where the reference to the Duchess of Gloucester's will is provided: J. Nichols (ed.), *A Collection of All the Wills . . . of the Kings and Queens of England* (London, 1780), p. 183.

58 Cavanaugh, "Study," p. 346 for Countess of Hereford's will.

59 For the Bohun manuscript group see Lucy Freeman Sandler, *Gothic Manuscripts 1285–1385*, A Survey of Manuscripts Illuminated in the British Isles, 2 vols. (London and Oxford, 1986), II, pp. 147–63 (nos. 133–41) and pp. 163–69 (related manuscripts nos. 142–45). Edinburgh, National Library of Scotland MS Advocates 18.6.5 (Sandler no. 142, pp. 163–65) is the hours and psalter commissioned by Eleanor de Bohun. And see further, M. R. James and E. G. Millar (eds.), *The Bohun Manuscripts*, Roxburghe Club, Oxford, 1936. Millar suggested that the Advocates manuscript might be the book willed to her daughter Joanna (d. 1400): "book with the psalter, primer, and other devotions, with two clasps of gold, enamelled with my arms, which book I have often used."

60 Thomas of Woodstock's will is excerpted in Cavanaugh, "Study," pp. 844–51.

61 Isabel of Gloucester's name occurs as abbess in 1421–22 (*VCH London* I, 519).

62 Bell, *What Nuns Read*, p. 151.

63 "Women connected with merchant families began to appear in transmissions of religious literature in the first quarter of the fifteenth century." Anne M. Dutton, "Passing the Book: Testamentary Transmission of Religious Literature to and by Women in England 1350–1500," in Lesley Smith and Jane H. M. Taylor (eds.), *Women, the Book and the Godly: Selected Proceedings of the St. Hilda's Conference 1993, Vol. I* (Cambridge, 1995), pp. 41–54, ref. p. 45.

64 1451: Easebourne, Bell, *What Nuns Read*, p. 136 (Cavanaugh, "Study," pp. 629–30).

65 1467: Hampole, Bell, *What Nuns Read*, p. 141.

66 1479; Nun Monkton, Bell, ibid., p. 157.

67 1481: Arden, Bell, ibid., p. 106; Bruisyard, Bell, ibid., pp. 121–22; Thetford, Bell, ibid., pp. 211–12.

68 1485–86: Nun Monkton, Bell, ibid., p. 157; Swine, Bell, ibid., p. 171.

69 1495: Syon, Bell, ibid., pp. 209–10.

70 1501: Bruisyard, Bell, ibid., p. 122. I have not included a *c.* 1470 bequest to Nun Appleton of a breviary and a York missal, since they were directed to the use of the testator's chantry priest (Bell, ibid., p. 156). In addition to the bequests listed by Bell Cavanaugh and, Marilyn Oliva has recently published the following: a new psalter to Isabella Virly, a nun of Flixton, 1473; all Elizabeth Fincham's books to be divided between her daughter Elizabeth and her fellow nuns at Shuldham and Elizabeth's brother Simon, PRO PCC Prob 11/22/33, no date given. Most interesting, as illustrating the exchange of reading between religious and seculars, is the bequest made by Reginald Rous of Dennington, Suffolk, to Campsey of "the three best French books which belong to me which they have in custody." He asks that they return a fourth book to his son. *Convent and Community*, p. 69.

71 Doyle, "Books Connected," pp. 222–43. In addition, Doyle suggested that BL Additional MS 10596 may have migrated from Dartford to Barking (p. 233).

72 V. M. O'Mara (ed.), *A Study and Edition of Selected Middle English Sermons*, Leeds Texts and Monographs n.s. 13 (Leeds, 1994), pp. 170–71.

73 The letter was exhibited at the Early Book Society conference, Durham, summer 1989.

74 Claire Breay (ed.), *The Cartulary of Chatteris Abbey* (Woodbridge, Suffolk, 1999), p. 3.

75 A. I. Doyle, "Book Production by the Monastic Orders in England (*c.* 1375–1530): Assessing the Evidence," in L. L. Brownrigg (ed.), *Medieval Book Production: Assessing the Evidence* (Los Altos Hills, 1990), pp. 1–19, ref. p. 14. Carthusian strictness in this regard contrasts with widespread general practice. In 1496 the prior of Sheen asked the general chapter, "If anyone wished to give an old book, or other thing, to a particular person for life, might a prior license the latter to receive it?" The answer was no. E. Margaret Thompson, *The Carthusian Order in England* (London, 1930), pp. 273–5.

76 Nigel Ramsay, "The Cathedral Archives and Library," in P. Collinson, N. Ramsay, and M. Sparks (eds.), *A History of Canterbury Cathedral* (Oxford, 1995), p. 371. He cites the practice at Durham: "Many other books were acquired by individual Durham monks and held by them as their personal property until death, when they either reverted to the common library or were distributed among the younger friends and colleagues of the owner." R. B. Dobson, *Durham Priory 1400–1450* (Cambridge, 1973), p. 373.

77 Sidney Sussex College MS Bb 2.14; Syon's *Martyrology*, f. 61v, 68. For examples of such transmission in French women's houses see Joan Naughton, "Books for a Dominican Nuns' Choir: Illustrated Liturgical Manuscripts at Saint-Louis de Poissy, *c.* 1330–1350," in M. M. Manion and B. J. Muir (eds.), *The Art of the Book, Its Place in Medieval Worship* (Exeter, 1998), pp. 67–110.

78 Taunton, Somerset County Record Office, DD/SAS C/1193/68; see Ker, *MMBL* IV, 488–89; Bell, *What Nuns Read*, p. 133; Lee, *Nunneries*, 199–205.

79 BL Cotton Appendix XIV, f. 56v, photographed in de Hamel, *Syon*, p. 95. Note slips for *MLGB* say that "xxx s x d" is written "on a binding leaf at the end" – probably the volume's cost. Syon's distinctive headdress with its five squares of red arranged in the same configuration provides another example of the use of this symbol.

80 JRUL 15416. Inc. 23.G.13. Lambeth 1530.3.

81 Yvonne Parrey, "'Devoted Disciples of Christ': Early Sixteenth-Century Religious Life in the Nunnery at Amesbury," *BIHR* 67 (1994), 240–48. Bell, *What Nuns Read*, p. 104.

82 Mary C. Erler, "Bishop Richard Fox's Manuscript Gifts to His Winchester Nuns: A Second Surviving Example," *JEH* 52 (2001), 1–4.

83 Oxford, Magdalen College MS lat.41 was probably bequeathed to Barking in the will which the countess made but which does not survive; see Michael Hicks, "The Last Days of Elizabeth, Countess of Oxford," *EHR* 103 (1988), 76–95. According to a deposition printed by Hicks she died about December 27, 1473, so the inscription records the transmission of the book to Barking either two months after her death (February 26, 1474) or four years later (1477). For her life, see Anne Crawford, "Victims of Attainder: The Howard and de Vere Women in the Late Fifteenth Century," *Reading Medieval Studies* 15 (1989), 59–74.

The Elizabeth de Vere who gave Oxford, Magdalen College lat. 41 to Barking was married to John de Vere, 12th earl of Oxford. It was her daughter-in-law, also Elizabeth de Vere (d. 1537), wife of the 13th earl, who owned MS Harley 1706, a manuscript probably first owned by Barking and later by the countess (Doyle, "Books Connected," passim.)

84 See Mary C. Erler, "Exchange of Books between Nuns and Laywomen: Three Surviving Examples," in Beadle and Piper (eds.), *New Science*, pp. 360–73, ref. p. 363–4. Agnes Ratcliffe's commission to veil: James Raine (ed.), *Testamenta Eboracensia*, 6 vols. (Durham, 1836–1902) (*TE*), III, 350.

85 *VCH Norfolk* II, 360. The cartulary is now NRO Hare 1 232XI, according to Oliva, *Convent and Community*, p. 120.

86 Agnes Scrope's brother John left two printed books, a Bible and a *Chronica Chronicarum*, to Easby, a Yorkshire Premonstratensian house less than ten miles from Marrick with which the Scropes had long been associated, *TE*, IV, 94–7.

87 Margaret M. Manion, Vera F. Vines, and Christopher de Hamel (eds.), *Medieval and Renaissance Manuscripts in New Zealand Collections* (Melbourne, 1989), p. 119.

88 For more information on Beatrice Cornburgh see Mary C. Erler, "Three Fifteenth-Century Vowesses," in Barron and Sutton, *Widows*, pp. 165–84, ref. pp. 167–71. Grace Centurio does not appear in A. F. C. Bourdillon, *The Order of Minoresses in England* (Manchester, 1926). For more on reading at the minoresses' see Julia Boffey, "Some London Women Readers and a Text of The Three Kings of Cologne," *The Ricardian* 10 (1996), 387–96.

89 BL G 11740, A6v; not in Ker–Watson, *MLGB* and *Supplement* or Bell, *What Nuns Read*. Joan Spycer died on December 1, sometime between 1526 and the making of the 1539 pension list, but the Syon *Martyrology* (f. 66) does not record the year.

90 Mary C. Erler, "The Abbess of Malling's Gift Manuscript (1520)," in Felicity Riddy (ed.), *Prestige, Authority, and Power in Late Medieval Manuscripts and Texts* (York, 2000), pp. 147–57.

91 Erler, "Exchange of Books," in Beadle and Piper (eds.), *New Science*, note 25. For a description with photographs: Christie's William Foyle sale, July 11, 2000, lot 72 (catalogue 1.218–20).

92 Sturman, "Barking Abbey," p. 285.

93 NYPL, Spencer Collection Eng.1519. Sister M. Denise, "The *Orchard of Syon*: An Introduction," *Traditio* 14 (1958), 269–93. *VCH Lancashire* v, 165–66; William Langton (ed.), *Visitation of Lancashire . . . 1533*, Chetham Society 98 (1896), pp. 59–63. F. R. Raines sums up Ashton's career: "[He] distinguished himself by his bravery and valour at Flodden, and by his piety and munificence in rebuilding the Church of Middleton. He added considerably to his paternal estate, retained the royal favour and his country's gratitude, avoided the pilgrimage of grace, embraced the reformed faith, and, dying in a good old age [about 68] escaped the persecutions of the next reign." *Examynytyons Towcheynge Cokeye More . . .* Chetham Society Miscellanies 2 (1855).

94 *VCH Worcestershire* III, 399.

2 THE LIBRARY OF A LONDON VOWESS: MARGERY DE NERFORD

I wrote briefly about Margery de Nerford in "Three Fifteenth-Century Vowesses," in Barron and Sutton (eds.), *Medieval London Widows* pp. 179–80, 182–83. Subsequently her life and books have been discussed by Margaret Aston and Colin Richmond in their introduction to *Lollardy and the Gentry in the Later Middle Ages* (Stroud, Glos. and New York, 1997), pp. 16–18.

1 Christine Weightman, *Margaret of York, Duchess of Burgundy 1446–1503* (New York, 1989), pp. 204 and following, based on the work of G. Dogaer and Muriel Hughes.

2 *Complete Peerage* (hereafter *CP*), ed. G.E.C., vol. 9 (London, 1936), p. 471. *Calendar of Close Rolls . . . 1374–1377* , p. 158 (hereafter *CCR*), September 25, 1375, which mentions her holdings of the manor of Wyset, Suffolk, and "divers other manors and lands" in Norfolk. This entry identifies her as "of full age," and married to John de Brewes. This information is confirmed by the inquisition post-mortem of Agnes Mautravers, Margery's father's second wife, on July 27, 1375. Here Margery is referred to as "wife of John Brewes" and aged "17 years and more."

3 *Calendar of Patent Rolls . . . 1374–1377*, p. 260 (hereafter *CPR*).

4 *CP* IX, pp. 471, 486. She is called Alice de Neville, baroness, by the London poll-tax collectors of 1379; Reginald R. Sharpe (ed.), *Letter Book H 1375–1399* (London, 1907), p. 131. Her first two marriages were to Thomas de Nerford (d. 1344), Margery's grandfather, and to Robert de Morley *le filz* (licence in 1346, *CPR 1345–48*, p. 87) and see *CP* IX, 486. With the death of her third husband John de Neville in 1358, the line of the Nevilles of Essex became extinct; see C. R. Young, *The Making of the Neville Family in England 1166–1400* (Woodbridge, Suffolk, 1990), p. 60. Alicia and John had tacitly acknowledged this when in 1357 they sold many of their Essex lands to William de Bohun, earl of Northampton.

5 I. S. Leadam and J. F. Baldwin (eds.), *Select Cases before the King's Council 1243–1482*, Selden Society 36 (Cambridge Mass., 1918), p. xxvi.

6 The petition is PRO sc 8/18/889. In their suits Margery and Alicia were joined by Sir John Lestraunge of Norfolk. For his career, including the episode of Margery's abduction, see J. S. Roskell et al. (eds.), *The House of Commons 1386–1421*, History of Parliament Trust, 4 vols. (Stroud, Glos., 1992), IV, 500–02, under Strange, Sir John. Additional warrants went out on July 8 and 28, and the document of July 28 directs Laurence de Bokesworth, bailiff of Stanton (Suffolk) to bring Margery in and to arrest John de Brewes. *CPR 1374–77*, pp. 299, 301.

7 Leadam and Baldwin, *Select Cases*, pp. xxv–xli.

8 It has been suggested that the charge of abduction was often a legal fiction, the wife having left the husband voluntarily. The resulting suits expressed the husband's desire either to get his wife back or to be compensated. Kelly, "Statutes," 351–419, and see also Kelly, "Meanings and Uses of *Raptus* in Chaucer's Time," *Studies in the Age of Chaucer* 20 (1998), 101–65. In Margery's case, Howard's imprisonment and the grants of protection suggest real jeopardy, though economic motives were perhaps a factor in the abduction. Of the nineteen King's Bench abduction cases from the fourteenth century summarized by Kelly, "Statutes," ten involve an annulment, suggesting that, in abduction cases, dissolution of the marriage and desire for financial compensation were linked.

9 *CCR 1377–81*, p. 204. In October Sir Robert Howard was directed to receive Margery from the Sheriff of Norfolk and a mandate was issued to the latter, *CPR 1377–81*, p. 307.

10 *CP* II, 69–70. Margery's story has certain similarities with the troubled history of a contemporary, Madame de Bedford's own daughter Philippe de Coucy, who was rejected by her husband Robert de Vere, earl of Oxford, in favor of the daughter of a Bohemian knight; they divorced in 1387 (*CP* X, 227–32). In this court scandal, sentiments were on the side of the wife, and the chroniclers say that Philippe had the sympathy of her husband's mother, Maud, Countess of Oxford (her own mother Madame de Bedford was now dead) (*Polychronicon* IX, 95). As Madame de Bedford had provided shelter and support for Margery, a younger woman in a difficult marriage, so her own daughter was helped by another powerful female courtier less than a decade later.

11 *CCR 1377–81*, pp. 222–23, 227–28. Howard's mainpernors, mostly knights, are listed in the latter pages, and include Sir Brian de Stapleton of Yorkshire and others.

12 The grants of protection are recorded on June 26, 1378, July 17, 1379, July 18, 1380 (*CPR 1377–81*, pp. 260, 374, 530), and August 7, 1381, (*CPR 1381–85*, p. 34.)

13 London, Guildhall Library, MS 9531/3, f. 325 v, Register Braybrooke.

14 *CP* IX, p. 471 cites Feet of Fines, Norfolk, 6 Ric. II, no. 93.

15 On November 17, 1382, John de Brewes sold the manor of Wyset to Lord Cobham and four other men (*CCR 1381–85*, pp. 222–23). Blomefield says (giving no source) that in 1383 John de Brewes settled various Nerford lands on William de Bergh and Lord Cobham as his trustees (*Norfolk*, V, pp. 305). After February 2, 1383, William de Bergh quitclaimed the manors of Shotisham and Therston to Lord Cobham and two other men (*CCR 1381–85*, p. 297).

16 Blomefield says (giving no source) that Margery conveyed by fine the manors of Panworth and Nerford, the moities of the manors of Holt and Cley with the advowson of Holt in 1382 (*Norfolk*, VI, pp. 231). On July 12, 1383, one Henry Perndon quitclaimed Holt and Cley to a group of four, including Cobham and de Bergh (*CCR 1381–85*, p. 384, and see *CPR 1396–99*, p. 544). For Penteney Priory, *CCR 1381–85* p. 389.

17 Alicia de Neville's will is also in Register Braybrooke, ff. 406v–407 (note 13 above). It is summarized by Blomefield, *Norfolk*, VI, 231 and printed in S. Bentley, *Excerpta Historica* (London, 1831), pp. 424–26. For the Cobham family see Nigel Saul, *Death, Art, and Memory in Medieval England: The Cobham Family and Their Monuments 1300–1500* (Oxford, 2001). He comments that the Nerfords' relation to the Cobhams remains an unsolved puzzle (private correspondence).

18 The *DNB* quotes Walsingham's description of Cobham as "an aged man, simple and upright" (IV, 612).

19 *CPR 1396–99*, p. 544.

20 Hilary Jenkinson, "Mary de Sancto Paulo, Foundress of Pembroke College Cambridge," *Archaeologia* 66 (1914–15), 401–46; her will is printed pp. 432–35. A portion of

her breviary survives as CUL MS DD.5.5, with a portrait of her in the vignette for St. Cecilia's day (f. 378) and with her arms throughout the volume (*Catalogue... University of Cambridge*, I, 244).

21 Records of Alicia de Neville's presentations to all but St. Peter's are found in R. C. Fowler and C. Jenkins (eds.), *Registrum Simonis de Sudbiria... 1362–1375*, 2 vols. Canterbury and York Society 34, 38 (Oxford, 1927–38), I, 232, 239, 243, 258(2), 260(2), 280, 281, 285. For lists of rectors at each parish, Richard Newcourt, *Repertorium Ecclesiasticum Parochiale Londinense... 2* vols. (London, 1708): St. Benet I, 299; St. Christopher I, 322–23; St. Margaret I, 407–08; St. Peter I, 523. Newcourt says that in 1380 Alicia de Neville confirmed to Thomas Coggeshall and others the manor of Leadenhall and the advowsons of two churches, St. Margaret and St. Peter, though these men did not present to St. Peter until 1395, after Alicia's death, while she presented to St Margaret from 1368 to 1392. Similarly she first presented to St. Benet in 1362 (Newcourt, ibid., I, 299, quoting Register Sudbury wrongly as Alicia de *Hereford*, Domina de Nevill). She is first listed as patron of St. Christopher in 1368. Newcourt says: "This Church has been in the Collation of the Bishops of London for above 300 Years; but before that, it appears to have been in the Noble Family of the Nevils, and by one of them probably given to the Bishops of London" (I, 322). For All Hallows, L. H. Butler, "Robert Braybrooke Bishop of London (1381–1404) and His Kinsmen," Ph.D. thesis, Oxford University (1951), p. 261.

22 George Hennessey, *Novum Repertorium Ecclesiasticum Parochiale Londinense* (repr. edn, London 1989), p. 281, and see Newcourt, *Repertorium*, preceding note.

23 Anthony Goodman, *The Loyal Conspiracy: The Lords Appellant under Richard II* (London, 1971), pp. 64, 75, 83.

24 Butler, "Robert Braybrooke," pp. 51, 92–105, 225, 426.

25 The wronged duchess of Ireland, Philippe de Coucy, whose book Sibyl de Felton bought for Barking after Philippe's death (B.N. Fr.1038, see Bell, *What Nuns Read*, pp. 115–16) was granted lands forfeited by her husband, to be overseen by a group of five including Braybrooke and Gloucester. Goodman, *Loyal Conspiracy*, p. 172.

26 Hustings Roll 113 (10). H. L. Hopkinson, "Ancient Bradestrete Identical with Thread-needle Street," *London Topographical Record* 13 (1923), 23–28; Hustings Roll 103 (239). The Worm's location is referred to in a 1451 document disposing of a tenement which, coincidentally, belonged to another vowed woman, Joan Gedney. Her property, "le Leadenporche" in the parish of St. Christopher, was just east of "a tenement sometime of dame Margery Nerford called the 'worme on the hope.'" *CCR 1447–54*, p. 263. It may be the Worm on the Hoop which is meant in a 1392 document listing ecclesiastical property in the City of London, although the tenement's location is not specified: Corporation of London Record Office MS 239A: "Quit rent from the tenements of... Lady de Nevyle to the church of St. Christopher 15s 11d." A. K. McHardy (ed.), *The Church in London 1375–1392*, London Record Society 13 (London, 1977), p. 39. Was the tenement then held by the church? When Alicia acquired it in 1384, she did so with William de Bergh, William Wangford, draper, and Richard Willesden.

27 *CPR 1391–96*, pp. 493, 570. Alicia's inquisition post-mortem, dated July 7, 1394, records the passage of her Essex lands to the heirs of Humphrey de Bohun, earl of Hereford. *Calendar of Inquisitions Post Mortem... [CIPM] Vol. XVII, 15–23 Richard II* (London 1988), pp. 207–08. The age given here for Margery, 32 and more, conflicts with the information in note 2 above; she was probably about 36. For other elements in Margery's inherited holdings, see *CIPM, Vol. XIV, 48–51 Edward III* (London 1952), p. 275 (Holt and Cleye).

28 *CPR 1405–08*, p. 292. The chaplain was to receive twenty shillings annually. Five years before she died, in 1412, Margery's income was listed as £6. J. C. L. Stahlschmidt, "London Subsidy temp. Henry IV," *Archaeological Journal* 44 (1887), 56–82, ref. p. 64.

29 Erbe (ed.), *Mirk's Festial*, p. 215.

30 William St. John Hope, *The History of the London Charterhouse from Its Foundation until the Suppression of the Monastery*. SPCK (London 1925), p. 42.

31 Edwin Freshfield (ed.), *Wills, Leases and Memoranda in the Book of Records of the Parish of St. Christopher le Stocks* (London 1895), p. iii. John Stow notes her burial in St. Christopher's, but dates it 1406. C. L. Kingsford (ed.), *A Survey of London*, 2 vols. (Oxford, 1908), I, 186.

32 Margery's will is Guildhall MS 9171/2, ff. 384r–v printed by Freshfield, not from this episcopal register but from the parish "Book of Records," Guildhall MS 4424. I have used Freshfield's printed text, checking it against MS 9171/2 and occasionally emending from the latter.

33 Christine's will is Guildhall MS 9171/2, f. 386.

34 Cloth of Westvale or Westphalia is found in the 1431–32 household accounts of John de Vere, Earl of Oxford, where it cost fourpence an ell (Woolgar, *Household Accounts*, II, 531). I am indebted for this information to Laurel Ann Wilson, Fordham University, Department of History.

35 Hope, *Charterhouse*, pp. 58, 66. Hope confuses Margery with her grandmother Alicia de Neville, p. 72, and consequently says that she died in 1394. The last, or twenty-fifth, cell was probably founded by a will of 1419, according to Hope, p. 157. Thus it is likely that Chamberlain acted before this date. Chamberlain may have drawn on Margery's and Christine's estates for a sum similar to the £100 left by the 1419 testator.

36 Hope's translation, *Charterhouse*, p. 66.

37 Hope, ibid., pp. 59–60. This section of the register was written when both Margery and William were alive, between 1397 and 1412. Guy of Burgh died sometime before 1398.

38 William de Bergh's will is Guildhall MS 9171/2, ff. 315v–316, dated May 10, 1414.

39 Daniel Lysons, *The Environs of London*, 4 vols. (London, 1792–96), II, 450, 454. *VCH Middlesex, Vol. X: Hackney Parish*, ed. T. F. T Baker (Oxford, 1995), p. 1.

40 A 1381 inventory from London jeweller Adam Ledyard lists many paternosters of various materials including four sets made of white amber priced at two shillings each. Ronald W. Lightbown, *Medieval European Jewellery* (London, 1992), p. 349, says paternosters had great sentimental value and "often figure as bequests, being handed down in a family or from great lady to confidential *demoiselle*," p. 353.

41 The episcopal register, Guildhall MS 9171/2, spells the name "Occlyf"; Freshfield, transcribing from the parish book of records, MS 4424, spells the name "occliffe." The date of Hoccleve's marriage is unknown. It occurred sometime between 1399, when he received an annuity which included a formula presuming a future award of a benefice, and 1411, when in his *Regiment* he wrote that, though originally intending to become a priest, he had married (J. A. Burrow, *Thomas Hoccleve* [Aldershot, Hants., 1994], pp. 11–12). The marriage has been speculatively linked with the increase in his annuity in 1409 (see M. C. Seymour, *Selections from Hoccleve* [Oxford, 1981], p. xiii) but if the Maud Hoccleve mentioned in the 1417 will were the poet's daughter, the marriage would have to be placed earlier, perhaps *c.* 1400–1402. A connection between Margery's household and the office of the Privy Seal, where Hoccleve worked, might have been made through John Prophet, privy seal clerk and later Keeper, who was related to Joan, Oldcastle's wife. Prophet's register (MS Harley 431) contains a letter from Prophet's nephew on behalf of his relative Joan, Lady Cobham, describing her destitute state (James Hamilton Wylie,

History of England under Henry the Fourth [London 1896], III, 295–96n). Prophet's 1416 will includes a bequest to her: "Lego dominae Johannae dominae meae de Cobham unum ciphum coopertum deauratum." Raine (ed.), *Testamenta Eboracensia*, III, 53–5, and see A. L. Brown, "The Privy Seal Clerks in the Fifteenth Century," in D. A. Bullough and R. L. Storey (eds.), *The Study of Medieval Records: Essays in Honour of Kathleen Major* (Oxford, 1971), pp. 276–81.

42 W. H. Frere, *Bibliotheca Musico-Liturgica*, 2 vols. (London 1894, 1932), II, 99 (no. 815). *A Catalogue of the Manuscripts Preserved in the Library of the University of Cambridge*, 5 vols. (Cambridge 1856–67), III, 199.

43 For Colchester, see Emden, *BRUO*, I, pp. 459–60 and Harvey, *Living and Dying* pp. 31, 80. The 1488 St. Christopher inventory is London, Guildhall Library MS 4424, f. 29, printed by Edwin Freshfield, "On the Parish Books of St. Margaret-Lothbury, St. Christopher-le-Stocks, and St. Bartholomew-by-the-Exchange, in the City of London," *Archaeologia* 45 (1877), 57–123, Appendix I.

44 H. Leith Spencer, *English Preaching in the Late Middle Ages* (Oxford, 1993), pp. 36–37.

45 Ibid., pp. 259, 230.

46 *VCH Cambridgeshire* II, 297 n56, citing *CPR 1391–96*, p. 74. Nigel Morgan, "Texts of Devotion and Religious Instruction Associated with Margaret of York," in Thomas Kren (ed.), *Margaret of York, Simon Marmion and 'The Visions of Tondal'* (Malibu, Calif., 1992), pp. 63–76, ref. p. 66.

47 For Joan Kyngeston: Bell, *What Nuns Read*, p. 210 (Dublin, MS Trinity College 209). For Cecily Welles: Donald Drew Egbert, "The So-Called 'Greenfield' *La Lumiere as Lais* and *Apocalypse*...," *Speculum* 11 (1930), 446–52 (London, BL MS Royal 15.D.11).

48 Nigel Morgan, "Texts and Images of Marian Devotion in Fourteenth-Century England," in Nicholas Rogers (ed.), *England in the Fourteenth Century: Proceedings of the 1991 Harlaxton Symposium* (Stamford, 1993), 34–57. L. F. Sandler, *Gothic Manuscripts 1285–1385*, A Survey of Manuscripts Illuminated in the British Isles 5 (London, 1986), nos. 80, 115, 53.

49 For Joan, see J. H. Wylie, *The Reign of Henry V*, 3 vols. (Cambridge, 1914–29), I, 278. Her 1434 brass survives at Cobham, Kent. Muriel Clayton, *A Collection of Rubbings of Brasses and Incised Slabs*... (London, 1915), p. 83. The bequest's wording, which distinguishes Oldcastle from Lord Cobham, rules out the possibility that the book was Oldcastle's.

50 J. G. Waller, "The Lords of Cobham, Their Monuments, and the Church," *Archaeologia Cantiana* 11 (1877), 49–112, ref. p. 85.

51 "Item lego et volo quod anachorita extra bysshopsgate melioribus post alios de omnibus et singulis libris meis non legatis in presenti testamento meo quemcunque seu quoscunque habere et eligere voluerit." Regarding Margery Pensax: Ann Warren discovered in the register of Archbishop Richard Scrope the March 20, 1399 permission granted this Hawton, Nottinghamshire, anchoress to choose a new cell and a prelate to seclude her: *Anchorites*, p. 78n. Four official documents survive from her subsequent time in London. On November 12, 1399, Henry IV granted her a pension of 40s yearly as the anchorite of St. Botolph Bishopsgate and on February 6, 1400, the order to pay was issued (*CCR 1399–1402*, p. 35). Subsequently, two months after his reign began, on May 31, 1413, Henry V increased her pension by half, to five marks yearly, and on November 22, 1414, the order to pay was issued (*CPR 1413–14* p. 29; *CCR 1413–19*, p. 151). Rotha Mary Clay says, "Since her name occurs in 1399 and 1413, she was probably that Bishopsgate anchoress to whom in 1417 a testator [i.e. Margery de Nerford] left a choice of books," and she cites de Nerford's will. "Further Studies in Mediaeval Recluses," *JBAA*, 3 rd ser. 16

(1953), 74–86, ref. 78–79. Warren agrees, speaking of Pensax's tenure at Bishopsgate as "at least eighteen years" [i.e. from 1399 to 1417] (*Anchorites*, p. 35).

Two subsequent references to the Bishopsgate anchorite are inconclusive. One is found in the will of Sir John Daubriggecourt, made July 20, 1415. "Item lego anachorite infra portam de Bysshopisgate supra murum versus Crepulgate v s." E. F. Jacob (ed.), *Register of Henry Chichele, Archbishop of Canterbury 1414–1443* (London, 1937–47), I, 51–55. I am grateful to Jennifer Collis, "The Anchorites of London in the Late Middle Ages," MA thesis, University of London (1992), p. 39 for this reference. Clay points out that the gender of *anachorita* is indefinite (*The Hermits and Anchorites of England*, [London, 1914], p. 73.) Finally, a woman was occupying the Bishopsgate cell still, or again, in 1426, when Thomas Beaufort, duke of Exeter, wrote: "Item lego mulieri recluse infra Bishopegate, London, xx s," John Nichols (ed.), *A Collection of the Wills . . . of the Kings and Queens of England* (London, 1780), p. 250. If the cell's occupant in 1426 was still Margery Pensax, her tenure there would have been 27 years.

52 Angus McIntosh, M. L. Samuels, and Michael Benskin (eds.), *A Linguistic Atlas of Late Medieval English* (Aberdeen, 1986), p. 298; Doyle, "Survey," I, 257 says it is addressed to a "ghostly brother," and, if made for a male reader, the manuscript is perhaps less likely to have belonged to Margery de Nerford before it was the anchorite's.

53 The 1424 will of John Whatley, discussed below, gives his name as David Fabian, but elsewhere it is Fyvyan.

54 R. M. Wilson, "The Contents of the Mediaeval Library," in F. Wormald and C. E. Wright (eds.), *The English Library before 1700* (London, 1958), pp. 85–112, ref. p. 89.

55 *Reparation du pecheur* is the last in a collection of ten moral tracts in French, produced in Ghent in the mid-1470s (Brussels, Bibliotheque Royale MS 9272–76), described as no. 21 in the appendix to Kren (ed.), *Margaret of York*. I am grateful to Nigel Morgan for this reference. A modern translation is found in Philip Schaff (ed.), *Select Library of the Nicene and Post-nicene Fathers IX* (New York, 1889), pp. 91–111, and see J. Dumortier (ed.), *Jean Chrysostome à Theodore* (Paris, 1966).

56 Other possibilities might be Chrysostom's letter to a young widow or his "De Virginitate," which emphasizes the miseries of married life in contrast with the worth of celibacy (see W. R. W. Stephens, *St John Chrysostom: His Life and Thought*, 3rd edn [London, 1883], pp. 92–100). Less likely but not impossible would be pseudo-Chrysostom on Matthew, a work much cited by Lollard commentators on the gospels. No English translation is known. Given the contemporary bequest by Peryne Clanvowe (1422) of "iiij quayres of Doctours on Mathewe" which Anne Hudson suggests might possibly be identified with the Wycliffite glossed gospels (*The Premature Reformation: Wycliffite Texts and Lollard History* [Oxford, 1988], p. 249), it seems possible that Margery's book might likewise have been a gospel commentary, though this suggestion, like the others above, is merely speculative.

57 Regarding female ownership of Chrysostom: an anonymous article says that the 1414 will of clerk William Corfe "mentions his books S. Gregory and S. Crisostom, which his mother, Margareta Butterley, had" ("Old Shropshire Wills: Part II," *Transactions of the Shropshire Archaeological and Natural History Society* 6 [1883], 319–25, ref. pp. 319–20; quoted in Cavanaugh, "Study," p. 209). Though this book was willed by Corfe to Oriel College (see Emden, *BRUO*, p. 487), the ownership attribution to Margaret Butterley seems to be based on a misreading of the will's Latin text. I am grateful to Dr. A. I. Doyle for his advice on Corfe's will, PCC 38 Marche; Prob 11/2B/301v.

58 Guildhall MS 9171/2 f. 384 has: "Item lego Johanni whatele ciui et mercere london librum meum de psalterio inglosatum existentem in duobus voluminibus." Whatley was four

times warden of the Mercers' Company, warden of London Bridge 1404–18, elected to Parliament in 1421, and collector of the wool custom 1427–29. Alfred B. Beaven, *The Aldermen of the City of London*, 2 vols. (London, 1908–13), I, p. 287. "Mercers' Company, Wardens' Accounts 1347, 1390–1463," for 1400–01, 1407–08, 1411–20, 1427–28. I am grateful to Anne F. Sutton, formerly Archivist to the Mercers' Company, for these references. For Whatley's biography, written by Carole Rawcliffe, see Roskell et al. (eds.), *House of Commons 1386–1421*, III, 825–26. For the will's other executor William Boson (or Bosom) of Bedfordshire, see ibid., II, 301–02.

59 Dorothy Everett, "The Middle English Prose Psalter of Richard Rolle of Hampole," *MLR* 17 (1922), 217–27, 337–50 and 18 (1923), 381–93; H. E. Allen, *Writings Ascribed to Richard Rolle...* (New York, 1927) who says, "Both volumes are large and expensive books... Both are written in two columns of fifty-two leaves each with the same type of decoration and handwriting" (p. 175); Hudson, *Reformation*, pp. 259–64, and "The Variable Text," in A. J. Minnis and C. Brewer (eds.), *Crux and Controversy in Middle English Textual Criticism* (Cambridge, 1992), pp. 49–60.

60 Henry J. Todd (ed.), *A Catalogue of the Archiepiscopal Manuscripts in the Library at Lambeth Palace* (London, 1812), p. 5; George F. Warner and Julius P. Gilson (eds.), *Catalogue of Western Manuscripts in the Old Royal and King's Collection* (London, 1921), II, 307. A second two-volume set of Rolle's works exists as well. H. R. Woudhuysen has called attention to a newly discovered MS of Rolle's psalm commentary sold at Christie's on Nov. 29, 2000, probably "the long lost second half" of BL Royal MS 18.D.I (*TLS* Nov. 24, 2000), and see the description of MS 14 in Christie's Sale Catalogue, date above, pp. 34–35, now BL Additional 74953. Anne Hudson says, "these two seem textually very close, but, despite a size comparable to the other pair, they are much less-well-produced books" (private communication).

61 Hudson, *Reformation*, pp. 262–64.

62 Phrase excerpted from BL Royal 18. C. xxvi in Everett, "Prose Psalter" (1923), p. 388.

63 Margery left twenty marks to the prioress of St. Mary Delapre, just outside the city walls of Northampton, "to spend for what will be of most use to them or to be given separately." Whether she was thinking of the prioress or the abbess is unclear. In 1417 the abbess was Katherine Wootten, elected March 8, 1407, died 1430 (R. M. Serjeantson, *A History of Delapre Abbey, Northampton* [Northampton, 1909], p. 29.) Besides the two books she bequeathed to the priory of Holy Trinity Aldgate, Margery left the prior ten pounds "for commending my soul to God with his devout prayers," and forgave the debt which he owed her. The prior at this time was William Harrington (elected 1407, died 1420. *VCH London* I, 474). The prior of the London Charterhouse John Maplested (*VCH Middlesex* I, 169) received one of her furred mantles. Besides the book she gave to Denny (below) the nuns received 40s in gold. Denny's abbess was either Agnes Bernard (occurs 1413) or Margery Milley (occurs 1419, 1430–31: *VCH Cambridgeshire* II, 302).

64 Everett, "Prose Psalter," p. 390.

65 Everett, "Prose Psalter," p. 391.

66 Michael P. Kuczynski, *Prophetic Song: The Psalms as Moral Discourse in Late Medieval England* (Philadelphia, 1995), pp. 173, 181. R. N. Swanson says, "Where books with heretical implications were transmitted, on closer examination that process was often dependent on their heresy not being fully appreciated: the books were translated not as vehicles for heresy but because they were felt to validate a particular form of orthodoxy (even if one which needed to be treated circumspectly." "Literacy, Heresy, History, and Orthodoxy: Perspectives and Permutations for the Later Middle Ages," in P. Biller

and A. Hudson (eds.), *Heresy and Literacy 1000–1530* (Cambridge, 1994), pp. 279–93, ref. p. 288.

67 Nicholas Watson, *Richard Rolle and the Invention of Authority* (Cambridge, 1991), p. 247.

68 Freshfield prints Whatley's will, Hustings Roll 160 [51], pp. 4–5.

69 Osbern acted as testamentary executor for many people: see Sharpe, *Letter Book I (1400–1422)*, pp. 6, 10, 44n, 57, 64, 84, 87, 91, 125, 177, 182, 201, 225, 231, 238, and *Letter Book K (Temp. Henry VI)*, pp. 58, 111, 120, 179. The earliest reference to him in these volumes is 1407, the latest 1434.

70 Details of how Margery arranged, in 1415 two years before her death, for her chantry to be supported, are summarized by Derek Keene and Vanessa Harding, *Historical Gazetteer of London Before the Great Fire: Cheapside* (London, Chadwyck-Healey, 1987 [microfiche]), 105/2, pp. 35–37. Two tenements provided support: the Worm and one in the parish of St. Mary Colchurch. The transfers of tenement ownership are Hustings Roll 144 (3) and 154 (46).

71 Keene and Harding, *Gazetteer*, 105/2, p. 38. C. J. Kitching (ed.), *London and Middlesex Chantry Certificate 1548*, London Record Society 16 (London, 1980), no. 76. Can Christian Vugham be identified with Christine Ipstans?

   The Worm's fortunes can be traced in the sixteenth century: a 1519 agreement between the parish and John Parnell, draper, allowed this tenant to make certain improvements to the property, and hence it is described in detail. (Guildhall MS, 4424, St. Christopher-le-Stocks "Book of Records," ff. 177–78v). Later in the century the Worm is called "a great house and two tenements," one on either side of it (f. 35).

72 The presentment took place sometime after June 4, 1410 (*CPR 1436–41*, pp. 279–80) and sometime before December 21, 1417, when Macclesfield granted Fyvyan and his successors, the rectors of St. Benet Fink, a yearly pension of six marks (*CPR 1422–29*, p. 156). David K. Maxfield, "St. Anthony's Hospital London: A Pardoner-Supported Alien Priory, 1219–1461," in J. L. Gillespie (ed.), *The Age of Richard II* (New York, 1997), pp. 225–47, ref. 236, implies that Fyvyan's appointment was made before 1414. Nevertheless Margery's will of October 31, 1417 says Fyvyan is "dwelling with me," and the date of the granted pension, since it is Margery's death date, suggests this was the moment at which Fyvyan transferred his allegiance. Hennessy says (p. 377) that Fyvyan's service at St. Benet Fink began in 1420; this must be incorrect. For Macclesfield's previous career as secretary to Richard II and Keeper of the Great Wardrobe and his many connections with other northwestern men, see Michael J. Bennett, *Community, Class, and Careerism: Cheshire and Lancashire Society in the Age of Sir Gawain and the Green Knight* (Cambridge, 1985), pp. 148, 150, 152, *passim*. The reading "Pilkington," Lancs. (from Margery de Nerford's will) for Fyvyan's former position seems most likely, given John Macclesfield's patronage of Fyvyan, but "Piltington" is also a possible reading and Ekwall says that Pilton, Northants. was formerly spelled "Pilkenton" in the twelfth and thirteenth centuries (Eilert Ekwall, *The Concise Oxford Dictionary of English Place-Names* [Oxford, 1960], p. 367.)

73 Regarding the school, Nicholas Orme says, "London was therefore one of the earliest of the large English towns to posses a free school, and for the next 100 years St. Anthony's enjoyed a considerable reputation." *English Schools in the Middle Ages* (London, 1973), p. 212, and see Maxfield, "St. Anthony's Hospital," pp. 237–39.

74 See Carpenter's biography in *BRUO* 1, 360–61. In addition Fyvyan was bequeathed 6s 8d and an English copy of Boethius' *Consolation of Philosophy* for acting as supervisor for the will of John Brynchele, cissor [tailor] of London. In his will, made July 4, 1420, Brynchele also left a *Canterbury Tales* to one of his executors, William Holgrave

(F. J. Furnivall, *The Fifty Earliest English Wills*, EETS os 78 (London, 1882), p. 136n; Caroline E. Spurgeon, *Five Hundred Years of Chaucer Criticism and Allusion 1357–1900*, 3 vols. [repr. edn New York, 1960], I, 25–6). I am grateful to Dr. A. I. Doyle for this reference.

75 The royal license to appropriate St. Benet Fink is dated July 13, 1439 (*CPR 1436–41*, p. 238). Episcopal permission is recorded in Register Gilbert (London, Guildhall Library MS, 9531/6, f. 183). The document itself is Windsor, Dean and Canons MS XV.37.9, dated June 14, 1441, see John Neale Dalton (ed.), *The Manuscripts of St. George's Chapel, Windsor Castle* (Windsor, 1957), p. 275. And see *VCH London* I, 582. A. F. Leach says that at the request of John Carpenter in 1440 Fyvyan and another clerk granted a rent of ten marks issuing out of the Cup on the Hoop and two other properties, to pay "John Bennet of London, clerk, yearly 8 marks and 4 yards of new cloth of gentleman's suit." He was to teach singing to the choristers of the hospital. Leach gives no reference. "St. Anthony's Hospital and School," in Walter Besant (ed.), *London City* (London, 1910), pp. 407–429, ref. p. 411.

76 Fyvyan's will is Guildhall MS 9171/5, f. 22v, excerpted in Hennessy, *Novum Repertorium*, p. 377. The will refers to the small bible which the bishop of Winchester "habet in custodia sua," not, as Hennessy translated, "left in my custody."

77 Thomas Brewer (ed.), *Memoir of the Life and Times of John Carpenter* (London, 1856), p. 97. "Historiae Provinciarum" is an account of the duties of an office (perhaps episcopal). Along with John Colop, the man behind the common profit manuscripts, Sudbury was one of four executors of John Killum's will; Killum's goods provided MS Lambeth 472. Colop was involved in the settlement of Sudbury's estate, when in 1439 Sudbury's son gave Colop an acquittance for an unspecified sum. It might be speculated that MS Douce 25, one of the common profit manuscripts whose inscription says it was made from the goods of "a certain person," was Colop's commission from Sudbury's estate, designated anonymously since Colop was not formally Sudbury's executor.

78 Walsingham recounts a 1387 incident in which a sermon preached at St. Christopher's by an Augustinian friar Peter (or William) Pateshull against the vices of his order caused a riot between the approving crowd (called Lollards by the chronicler) and several members of Pateshull's order who resented his criticisms (Thomas Walsingham, *Historia Anglicana*, ed. H. T. Riley, 2 vols. [London, 1864], II, 157–59). What role might de Bergh have played in this incident?

79 J. A. F. Thomson, "Knightly Piety and the Margins of Lollardy," in Aston and Richmond (eds.), *Lollardy and the Gentry*, pp. 95–111, ref. pp. 101–02.

80 Dorothy M. Owen (ed.), *John Lydford's Book* (London, 1974), pp. 108–12, cited in Margaret Aston, *Lollards and Reformers: Images and Literacy in Late Medieval Religion* (London, 1984), p. 64, n. 55, who corrects Owen's dating from *c.* 1395 to *c.* 1386.

81 The various uncertainties regarding identification of persons and of date are discussed by Anne Hudson (ed.), *Two Wycliffite Texts* . . . EETS os 301 (Oxford 1993), xlvi–lii.

82 Review of Pamela Gradon and Anne Hudson (eds.), *English Wycliffite Sermons IV, V* (Oxford, 1995), in *JEH* 49 (1998), 175–77. And see A. Hudson and H. L. Spencer, "Old Author, New Work: The Sermons of MS Longleat 4," *Medium Ævum* 53 (1984), 220–38. Indeed the dates make it possible that Margery read *Dives and Pauper*, and one of its surviving manuscripts is associated with Holy Trinity Aldgate, the neighboring monastery to which Margery had bequeathed books.

83 K. B. McFarlane, *Lancastrian Kings and Lollard Knights* (Oxford, 1972), p. 217.

84 Ibid., p. 225.

85 Peter Brown, *The Body in Society: Men, Women, and Sexual Renunciation in Early Christianity* (New York, 1988), p. 371.

86 J. Anthony Tuck, "Carthusian Monks and Lollard Knights: Religious Attitudes at the Court of Richard II," in P. Strohm and T. J. Heffernan (eds.), *Studies in the Age of Chaucer Proceedings, No. 1, 1984: Reconstructing Chaucer* (Knoxville Tenn., 1985), pp. 149–61.

3 A NORWICH WIDOW AND HER DEVOUT SOCIETY: MARGARET PURDANS

1 Margaret Purdans' will is Norwich Consistory Court (NCC) Register Caston, ff. 163v–165r. It was made July 10, 1481, and proved July 12, 1483. She had probably been revising the will for some time, since several bequests and reflections are crossed out, for instance that to Julian Lampett. Since the last mention of Lampett occurs in 1478 (Tanner, *Church*, p. 199) it seems likely that Lampett died between this date and 1481, the date of Purdans' will. Purdans could thus have been drafting the will as early as 1478. Selections translated from its Latin were published by Henry Harrod, "Extracts from Early Wills in the Norwich Registries," *Norfolk Archaeology* 4 (1855), 317–39; Purdans will pp. 335–37. More recently Tanner has commented on the will, suggesting her piety might be compared with that of Cecily Duchess of York (*Church*, p. 112), and see Gail McMurray Gibson, *The Theater of Devotion: East Anglian Drama and Society in the Late Middle Ages* (Chicago, 1989), p. 78.

2 Marcia Pointon, *Strategies for Showing: Women, Possession, and Representation in English Visual Culture 1665–1800* (Oxford, 1997), p. 40.

3 John Sell Cotman, *Engravings of Sepulchral Brasses in Norfolk and Suffolk*. 2 vols. (London, 1839), II, Appendix Plate 2. It is also reproduced in Peter Eade, *Some Account of the Parish of St. Giles, Norwich*, 2nd edn (London and Norwich, 1906), p. 161.

4 Richard Purdans' career is summarized in Basil Cozens-Hardy and Ernest A. Kent (eds.), *The Mayors of Norwich 1403 to 1835* (Norwich, 1938), p. 18. Blomefield prints his monumental brass inscription and provides other details: Francis Blomefield, *An Essay Towards a Topographical History of the County of Norfolk*, 11 vols. (London, 1805–10), III, pp. 123, 134, 136, 138, 163; IV, 240 (inscription). Discussion of Norwich politics and of Purdans' role can be found in Philippa Maddern, *Violence and Social Order in East Anglia 1422–1442* (Oxford, 1992), pp. 184–86, 200–01, 244.

5 Cozens-Hardy and Kent, *Mayors of Norwich*, pp. 28–29. Thomas and Margaret Elys appear in St. Peter Mancroft's stained glass, he in mayoral robes, she in a red dress with a fur skirt (though her head is lost). Blomefield records the inscription on his brass, now lost (*Norfolk* IV, 148), according to Christopher Woodforde, *The Norwich School of Glass-Painting in the Fifteenth Century* (Oxford, 1950), pp. 38–39.

6 For a detailed discussion of Hobart's character and connections, see Colin Richmond, *John Hopton, A Fifteenth-Century Suffolk Gentleman* (Cambridge, 1981), pp. 186–93. Also C. E. Moreton, *The Townshends and Their World: Gentry, Law, and Land in Norfolk, c. 1450–1551* (Oxford, 1992), pp. 93, 192. The letter in which John Paston II asks Margery to send him a medicinal plaster for Hobart, "the man that brought you and me togedyrs," is dated between 1489 and 1495. Norman Davis (ed.), *Paston Letters and Papers of the Fifteenth Century*, 2 vols. (Oxford, 1976), I, p. 628. Loddon church has a painting of Hobart and his wife, see Nikolaus Pevsner, *North-West and South Norfolk* (Harmondsworth, Mx, 1962), p. 249.

7 On the ward of St. Giles, see John Pound, *Tudor and Stuart Norwich* (Chichester, 1988), pp. 34–35. For Purdans' tax, Roger Virgoe, "A Norwich Taxation List of 1451," *Norfolk Archaeology* 40 (1989), 145–54. She is called *Domina* again in a c. 1457 list of about 600 persons assessed for money or armor or both. W. Hudson and J. C. Tingey (eds.), *The Records of the City of Norwich*, 2 vols. (Norwich, 1906–1910), 1, p. 407. For Elizabeth Clere, see Christopher Brooke, *A History of Gonville and Caius College* (Woodbridge, Suffolk, 1985), pp. 29, 31; Walter Rye, *Carrow Abbey* (Norwich, 1899), p. xxi; and Colin Richmond, "Elizabeth Clere: Friend of the Pastons," in Wogan-Browne et al. (eds.), *Medieval Women*, pp. 251–73.

8 Tanner, *Church*, p. 63. Ferneys' will is printed by Tanner, pp. 233–34.

9 Lillian J. Redstone, "Three Carrow Account Rolls," *Norfolk Archaeology* 29 (1946), 41–88; refs. pp. 43, 52, 53n.

10 Katherine Kerre's will is NCC Register Multon, ff. 89v–91r. It was made April 21, 1498 and proved June 16, 1498.

11 Saara Nevanlinna and Irma Taavitsainen (eds.), *St. Katherine of Alexandria: The Late Middle English Prose Legend in Southwell Minster MS 7* (Woodbridge, 1993), pp. xi–xii, 11, expanding the listing in *IPMEP* no. 28. And see J. Burke Severs (ed.), *Manual of Writings in Middle English* 11, pp. 599–602. One of these manuscript lives of St. Katherine, Cambridge, MS Gonville and Caius 390/610 was owned in the early sixteenth century by a nun of Ankerwyke (Bucks.), Alice Lego, while a *Gilte Legende* containing the life of St. Katherine (Bodleian MS Douce 372) belonged to a nun of Halliwell, Katherine Burton.

Katherine Kerre's book might even have been a separate quire containing one of Bokenham's *Legendys*, since it has recently been suggested that BL MS Arundel 327, the unique manuscript of Bokenham's work, was transcribed from a series of independent booklets. A.S.G. Edwards, "The Transmission and Audience of Osbern Bokenham's *Legendys of Hooly Wummen*," in A. J. Minnis (ed.), *Late-Medieval Religious Texts and Their Transmission* (Woodbridge, 1994), pp. 157–68, ref. p. 159.

12 Moreton, *Townshends*, p. 9.

13 Dame Joan Blakeney's will is NCC Register Popy, ff. 315v–317 and 362–63 (draft). It was made March 16, 1502 (i.e. probably 1503) and proved June 20, 1504. See also Blomefield, *Norfolk* IV, pp. 338, 432; VII, pp. 131–32. At Bishop Goldwell's 1492 visitation of Norwich priory one of the faults noted was that a certain precious object of the Blessed Virgin given to the high altar by "Dominam de Blakeney" had been alienated by the priory's sacristan. A. Jessopp (ed.), *Visitations of the Diocese of Norwich 1492–1532*, Camden Society n.s. 43 (London, 1888), p. 4. Her brother Sir Roger Townshend's 1492 will (PCC 2 Vox) has an intensely pious preface beseeching God "for the merits of his bitter and glorious passion to have mercy on me and to take me unto his mercy which is above all works . . . the which cometh only of the grace, charity and infinite mercy of our saviour Christ Jesus of the which number of contrite sinners I meekly and humbly beseech him that I may be one and come of the number predestinate to be saved." Despite these apparently reforming sentiments, he prays for the souls in purgatory.

14 C. E. Moreton, "The 'Library' of a Late-Fifteenth-Century Lawyer," *The Library* 13 (1991), 338–46. The 1494/95 inventory is NRO MS, 1503, 1 D 2. Roger's son listed twenty-one books belonging to his father in BL Additional MS 41139, f. 23v, in the early sixteenth century. There is some overlap between the two lists. Moreton has written more about Townshend in "The 'Diary' of a Late Fifteenth-Century Lawyer," in S. Michalove and A. C. Reeves (eds.), *Estrangement, Enterprise and Education in Fifteenth-Century England* (Sutton, 1998), pp. 27–45.

15 For Norman's (St. Paul's) hospital sisters see *VCH Norfolk* II, 447–48, and Carole Rawcliffe, *Medicine for the Soul: The Life, Death and Resurrection of an English Medieval Hospital, St. Giles, Norwich, c. 1249–1550* (Sutton, 1999), p. 173. Just five years after Purdans made her will, in 1486, a sister of Norman's, Dame Katherine Peckham, was teaching a boy to read. In his 1558 will Londoner Thomas Salter recalled and dated her instruction. Carole Rawcliffe, *The Hospitals of Medieval Norwich* (Norwich, 1995), p. 69.

16 Joan Elys was probably the daughter of former Norwich mayor Thomas Elys who with his wife is remembered in the Purdans' will, since in the 1477 will of Robert Grond the nun Joan Elys received 6s 8d and Thomas Elys, alderman of Norwich, was the will's supervisor. Rye, *Carrow Abbey*, p. xix, and for other references to her, pp. xx and 49. The prioress of Carrow in 1481, the date of Margaret Purdans' will, was probably Joan Spalding (*VCH Norfolk* II, 854).

17 Oliva, *Convent and Community*, p. 78, says Alice Erle was prioress of Blackborough from 1434 (*VCH Norfolk* II, 433) to 1462. The *VCH* lists the next prioress Margaret Geyton as holding office in 1480 (II, 351). The Purdans will suggests that Alice Erle may have continued in office in the 1470s.

18 Etheldreda Wulmer was elected in 1469 (*VCH Norfolk* II, 408–09). For the history of Crabhouse nunnery and the heroic building campaign of Margery Daubenay, Audrey Wulmer's predecessor as prioress (1420–44), see Mary Bateson, "The Register of Crabhouse Nunnery," *Norfolk Archaeology* 4 (1892), 1–71. It was composed after 1476, near the time Purdans was drafting her will.

19 Thetford's prioress was probably Joan Eyton, elected 1477 (*VCH Norfolk* II, 356).

20 A rubbing from Alice Yaxley's brass inscription, collected by the Suffolk historian David Elisha Davy, is found in BL Additional MS 32483, f. 37.

21 BL Additional MS 19156, ff. 321v–322, a nineteenth-century pedigree of Yaxley from the collections of David Elisha Davy of Rumburgh Hill, Suffolk, made for a parochial history of Suffolk.

22 Sister Mary Patrick Candon, R.S.M., "The Doctrine of the Hert," Ph.D. thesis, Fordham University, 1963. The manuscripts are Bodleian Laud 330; Cambridge, Trinity College B.14.15 (301), owned by the abbess of the London minoresses, Christine St. Nicolas (d. 1455), who left it to the house after her death (these two contain only *Doctrine*); Durham Cosin v.iii.24 and Cambridge, Fitzwilliam McClean 132 (these two contain *Doctrine* plus the *Tree & xii Frutes of the Holy Goost*).

23 J. J. Vaissier (ed.), *A Devout Treatyse Called the Tree & xii Frutes of the Holy Goost* (Groningen, 1960), p. xvii. McIntosh, Samuels, and Benskin (eds.), *Linguistic Atlas*, I, 87.

24 The Durham manuscript carries on f. ii in "a set 15th-century bookhand" the following lines: "O Ihesu ful of myght markyd in þi mageste / Save our Kyng bothe day and nyght / In euery place wher so he be. / Quod Welles" (Vaissier, *Tree*, p. xx).

25 Candon, *Doctrine*, pp. xli, lvii.

26 Alice Catelyn's 1524 will is NCC Register Palgrave, ff. 216r–v. For the frequency of friendship between mistress and maid see Barron, "Introduction," in Barron and Sutton (eds.), *Medieval London Widows*, p. xxxiii.

27 Sister rather than mother since Alice Barley was still living in 1498 when Katherine Kerre's will left her a smock cloth of holland.

28 For the Barleys, A. B. Emden, *A Biographical Register of the University of Cambridge* (Cambridge, 1963) (hereafter *BRUC*), pp. 38–39; Tanner, *Church*, pp. 44, 46. They witnessed Elizabeth Clere's will: Richmond, "Elizabeth Clere," p. 271.

29 Tanner, *Church*, p. 124, for Gonville and Caius' founding. Barley's glass: *BRUC*, p. 39 and P. Lasko and N. J. Morgan, *Medieval Art in East Anglia 1300–1520* (London and Norwich, 1974), no. 96.

30 Brooke, *Gonville and Caius*, p. 40.

31 Alan B. Cobban, "Pembroke College: Its Educational Significance in Late Medieval Cambridge," *TCBS* 10 (1991), pp. 1–16, ref. pp. 12–13.

32 For Cokerham, *BRUC*, p. 147; for Damlett, p. 176. Damlett's will is London, Guildhall MS 9171/6, f. 189r–v.

33 Caroline M. Barron, "The Expansion of Education in Fifteenth-Century London," in J. Blair and B. Golding (eds.), *The Cloister and the World* (Oxford, 1996), pp. 219–45, ref. p. 231.

34 Damlett's bequest to Syon of Master Philip de Greves, chancellor of Paris, on the Sunday gospels, is mentioned in Mary Bateson (ed.), *Catalogue of the Library of Syon Monastery, Isleworth* (Cambridge, 1898), p. xxiv. Besides the books listed in Emden, *BRUC*, Damlett's name appears in a collection which includes an imperfect text of the *Manuel de péchés*, Stonyhurst College MS 27 (Ker, *MMBL* IV, 397–99).

35 Roger Virgoe, "Hugh Atte Fenne and Books at Cambridge," *TCBS* 10 (1991), 92–98.

36 For Damlett's opposition to Pecock see V. H. Green, *Bishop Reginald Pecock: A Study in Ecclesiastical History and Thought* (Cambridge, 1945), pp. 37, 63, 69n.

37 Damlett's intellectual and pastoral interests have been analyzed (using, among other sources, the marginal jottings in his many books) by R. M. Ball, "The Opponents of Bishop Pecock," *JEH* 48 (1997), 230–62. Damlett has been called a man "of a charming modesty," since his will "forbids an expensive funeral but allows a 'modesta et honesta refeccio amicorum et aliorum.'" F. R. H. DuBoulay, "The Quarrel between the Carmelite Friars and the Secular Clergy of London 1464–1468," *JEH* 6 (1955), 156–74.

38 Fewer than fifty such bowls survive – among them one given to Pembroke, Damlett's college, by a contemporary, Richard Sokborn, elected fellow in 1470. See E. Alfred Jones, *The Old Plate of the Cambridge Colleges* (Cambridge, 1910), plate XVIII.

39 *BRUC*, p. 458; Tanner, *Church*, pp. 31, 41, 47–8, 124. His shroud brass is reproduced in Cotman, *Engravings*, II, plate 107. Poringland owned the *Sermones de sanctis* of Bonaventure and Petrarch's *De remediis utriusque fortune*.

40 Tanner, *Church*, p. 232.

41 Ibid., p. 231.

42 Blomefield, *Norfolk*, III, p. 604; IX. p. 340.

43 *BRUC*, pp. 552–53. M. B. Tait, "The Bridgettine Monastery of Syon . . . ," Ph.D thesis, Oxford University (1975), p. 296.

44 Another contemporary Norwich woman's will, Isabel Lyston's made in 1491, left to her daughter Margery London "an englyssh boke called *partonope* and myn englysshe boke of seynt Margaretes lyfe." Her daughter's husband William, named one of the executors, was at that time a Norwich alderman, later mayor of the city (NCC Register Wolman, f. 171v). Again we have a glimpse of what Norwich women of the governing class read.

45 *BRUC*, p. 563 (Stubbe); pp. 241–42 (Framingham); pp. 194–95 (Drentall); p. 249 (Fyske).

46 She left 3s 4d to John Castre who at Bishop Goldwell's 1492 visitation was identified as a friar and accused of sexual immorality with Isabella Chapman junior (Tanner, *Church*, p. 187).

47 Virgoe, "Taxation List," pp. 149–51. The other woman is Dame (*Domina*) Margaret Wetherby, the widow of Thomas Wetherby, Richard Purdans' predecessor as mayor

and his political enemy. She lived at Carrow where she had a house in the monastery precincts; she appears in the 1455 accounts, see Redstone, "Carrow Account Rolls," p. 43.

48 Richard Firth Green, *A Crisis of Truth: Literature and Law in Ricardian England* (Philadelphia, 1999), p. 274.

49 Susan Foister, "Paintings and Other Works of Art in Sixteenth-Century English Inventories," *Burlington Magazine* 123 (May 1981), 273–82. Nicholas Mander says that stained cloths (water-soluble paint on linen) originated in royal apartments, moved downward to the halls "and later the upstairs rooms, of the Tudor manor house," and by the mid-sixteenth century were found "in the halls and parlours of the farm and town houses of the yeoman and merchant." "Painted Cloths: History, Craftsmen and Techniques," *Textile History* 28 (1997), 119–48, ref. p. 119. For an idea of their cost, a 1452 inventory prices two stained cloths with images of St. John the Evangelist and St. John of Beverley at 6s each. Oliver Baker, *In Shakespeare's Warwickshire and the Unknown Years* (London, 1937), quoting *TE* III, 135.

50 For an object recalling Purdans' gift to Eston, a gold fifteenth-century reliquary cross from Suffolk decorated with an incised crucifixion, see Hugh Tait (ed.), *Jewelry 7000 Years: An International History and Illustrated Survey from the Collections of the British Museum* (New York, 1987), no. 524.

51 Charles Oman, *English Church Plate* (Oxford, 1957), pp. 76–8. Only about twenty English paxes survive; the majority, unlike Margery's two, are carved with the crucifixion and Mary and John. They are surveyed by J. F. Williams, "A Wooden Pax at Sandon," *TEAS* n.s. 21 (1937), 37–44.

52 Green, *Crisis*, p. 273.

53 Gibson, *Theater*, chapter 4.

54 Samuel Tymms (ed.), *Wills and Inventories from the . . . Commisssary of Bury St. Edmunds*, Camden Society 49 (London, 1850), p. 36. Baret's will (p. 19) mentions an image of Our Lady painted by Robert Pygot, whose panel of St. Etheldreda illustrates this book's introduction. Nicholas J. Rogers, "Fitzwilliam Museum MS3-1979: A Bury St. Edmunds Book of Hours and the Origins of the Bury Style," in Daniel Williams (ed.), *England in the Fifteenth Century: Proceedings of the 1986 Harlaxton Symposium* (Suffolk, 1987).

55 The children of Richard Yaxley senior and his second wife Alice Purdans were Elizabeth and Richard junior, as Margaret Purdans' will makes clear. The children of Richard Yaxley's first marriage with Rose Goldwell were John, Robert, Alice, and Philippa. See BL MS Additional 19156, ff. 321v–322 and also the 1481 will of Jankyn Smyth, printed in Tymms, *Bury Wills*, pp. 55–61. Perhaps it is Richard and Alice's daughter Elizabeth Yaxley who, at the time of her 1530 will was living at Carrow (Rye, *Carrow Abbey*, p. 52) and who some time before 1510 had filed a successful defamation suit against Dominus John Levenham. E. D. Stone and B. Cozens-Hardy (eds.), *Norwich Consistory Court Depositions 1499–1512 and 1518–1530*, Norfolk Record Society 10 (1938), no. 119.

56 Charles Oman mentions a surviving fifteenth-century gimmel ring which, like Baret's, recalls virtuous love. It was engraved with the Annunciation angel and inscribed inside "en bon." *British Rings 800–1914* (London, 1974), no. 68G (Dalton 746), and for double-stone rings, see nos. 17A and B.

57 Tanner, *Church*, pp. 64–5, 202–03. Roberta Gilchrist and Marilyn Oliva, *Religious Women in Medieval East Anglia*, Studies in East Anglian History 1 (Norwich, 1993), Table 3: Informal Female Religious Communities in the Diocese of Norwich, pp. 95–6.

4 ORTHODOXY: THE FETTYPLACE SISTERS AT SYON

An earlier version of this chapter was published as "The Books and Lives of Three Tudor Women," in Jean R. Brink (ed.), *Privileging Gender in Early Modern England*, Sixteenth-Century Essays and Studies 23 (Kirksville, Mo., 1993), pp. 5–17.

1 J. Renton Dunlop, whose manuscript collections concerning the family are contained in three volumes, BL Additional MSS 42763, -64, -65, calls the Fettyplaces "a most remarkable family for their ancient descent, aristocratic alliances, acquisition of estates, and public benefactions . . . " and notes that "their prosperity . . . lasted for nearly 400 years," Additional MS 42763, f. 3 v.

2 Will of Richard Fettyplace, PRO PCC 1 Fettyplace, Prob 11 /17/1, made August 11, 1510, proved May 15, 1511. At his father's death in 1507, John Kyngeston was "aged 16 and more." *CIPM* 2nd ser. III (20–24 Henry VII) (London, 1955), p. 537. According to Stanford E. Lehmberg, Susan's marriage was arranged through the offices of her uncle Anthony Fettyplace, since John Kyngeston was his ward. *Sir Thomas Elyot*, p. 191.

3 Syon cellaress's foreign accounts PRO SC 6/Hen 8/2214, 2215 (1514–15) through SC 6/Hen 8/2244 and 2245 (1536–37) show yearly board amounts for Susan Kyngeston ranging from a high of £33 18s 3d (she occasionally paid for the boarding of others besides herself) to a low of 55s, the charge for 1536–37, the last year in which she appears in the accounts. The inventory is PRO LR 2/112; it is quoted in F. R. Johnston, "Syon Abbey" in *VCH Middlesex* I, 188. Later writers (e.g. Alan Neame, Diane Watt) have for the most part followed Johnston in misidentifying Susan Kyngeston as the wife of Sir William Kingston, Constable of the Tower and Captain of the Guard.

4 Will of Alice Beselles, PRO PCC 8 Porch, Prob 11/22/59.

5 PRO SC 6/Hen 8/2224 (1520–21); SC 6/Hen 8/2227 and 2228 (1523–24); SC 6/Hen 8/2229 and 2230 (1524–25); SC 6/Hen 8/2231 and 2232 (1525–26).

6 Will of William Beselles, PRO PCC 6 Holder, Prob 11/18/45 r–v, made May 4, 1515. Alice was the daughter of Sir Richard Starecourt of Stanton Harcourt (Berks.), Knight of the Order of the Bath in 1465 (Dunlop, BL Addl. 42763, f. 103).

7 This pioneering Latin dictionary, which later developed into polyglot form, is discussed by DeWitt Starnes and Ernest William Talbert, who call it the period's "standard work of reference for students of Latin." They note that despite Vives' expressed dissatisfaction with its "comprehensiveness, scholarliness, and accuracy" he nonetheless recommended its use in his 1523 educational prescriptions for Princess Mary. *Classical Myth and Legend in Renaissance Dictionaries* (Chapel Hill, 1955), pp. 11–13. Mary Bateson (ed.), *Catalogue of the Library of Syon Monastery, Isleworth* (Cambridge, 1898), A 38.

8 For Elizabeth as sole heir of William and Alice Beselles, see *VCH Berkshire*, IV, 456–57. Since Richard Fettyplace was dead by May 15, 1511 (see note 2 above), the date of Elizabeth Beselles Fettyplace's second marriage to Richard Elyot falls sometime between the middle of 1511 and the middle of 1514, when in April of the latter year Richard Elyot was named as a trustee in John Kyngeston's will, indicating he had married into the Fettyplace–Kyngeston alliance. For details of Richard Elyot's career, Henry Herbert Stephen Croft (ed.), *The Boke Named the Gouernour*. 2 vols. (London, 1880), I, xxvii–xxxiv. For Dunlop's belief that she was a vowess, BL Additional 42763, f. 361.

9 *STC* 6157, *A Swete and Deuoute Sermon of Mortalitie of Man* and *The Rules of a Christian Lyfe by Picus erle of Mirandula*, Thomas Berthelet (1534), A3 v. St. Cyprian's "On the Mortality" is translated in *The Ante-Nicene Fathers of the Third Century: Hippolytus, Cyprian, Caius, Novatian*, vol. 5 (repr. edn, Grand Rapids, Mich., 1951), pp. 469–75. Croft's suggestion that the Dorothy referred to in Thomas Elyot's preface

is Dorothy Danvers Fettyplace, widow of John Fettyplace (d. 1524) cannot be correct, since she remarried and died in 1560 as the widow of Sir Anthony Hungerford (*Boke*, p. cv).

10 Joyce Leigh, More's dedicatee, has been variously identified. For a summary of the controversy see A. S. G. Edwards, K. G. Rodgers, C. H. Miller (eds.), *The Complete Works of St. Thomas More Vol. 1: English Poems, Life of Pico, the Last Things* (New Haven, 1997), p. xl. Edwards, the work's latest editor, accepts the minoress as More's recipient because of the connection referred to in More's letters between himself and Joyce's brother Edward Lee (or Leigh), later Archbishop of York (*DNB* xi, 788–90). More's *Life* was published by John Rastell (*STC* 19897.7); a second edition, by Wynkyn de Worde, appeared about 1525 (*STC* 19898). For analysis of More's changes to his text, see Stanford E. Lehmberg, "Sir Thomas More's Life of Pico della Mirandola," *Studies in the Renaissance* 3 (1956), 61–74. Pico's twelve rules for the Christian life appear in both More's 1510 translation (in verse) and in Elyot's 1534 sermon (in prose). Fisher's "Spiritual Consolation" was not printed until *c.* 1578 (*STC* 10899). It is edited, together with another work dedicated to Elizabeth White, "The Wayes to Perfect Religion," in John E. B. Mayor (ed.), *The English Works of John Fisher, Part 1*, EETS es 27 (London, 1876).

11 For the first reading, Lehmberg, *Sir Thomas Elyot*, p. 129. For the second, John M. Major, *Sir Thomas Elyot and Renaissance Humanism* (Lincoln, Nebraska, 1964), p. 106. For the third, Pearl Hogrefe, *The Life and Times of Sir Thomas Elyot, Englishman* (Ames, I., 1967), p. 212.

12 Lehmberg, *Sir Thomas Elyot*, pp. 128–29; Hogrefe, *Life and Times*. Thomas Elyot and Susan Kyngeston were probably approximate contemporaries. Although neither's birthdate is known, Elyot's is usually assigned to about 1490. If Susan were already married in 1510 when her father made his will (see note 2 above), a birthdate around 1490 or slightly later would appear likely.

13 The most comprehensive treatment of the Nun's life is Alan Neame, *The Holy Maid of Kent: The Life of Elizabeth Barton 1506–1534* (London, 1971). David Knowles provides a judicious assessment in *The Religious Orders in England: Vol III, The Tudor Age* (Cambridge, 1961), pp. 182–91. See also A. Denton Cheney, "The Holy Maid of Kent," *TRHS* 18 (1904), 107–29.

14 *L&PH8*, vi, nos. 1464, 1465. The marchioness was Gertrude, daughter of William Blount, fourth Lord Mountjoy (*DNB* iv, 1262). Muriel St. Clare Byrne points out, in another context, that the countess of Salisbury, the marchioness of Exeter, Lady Willoughby, and Lady Lisle were "all devoted adherents of Katherine of Aragon" (*The Lisle Letters*, 6 vols. [Chicago, 1981], i, 351n); all but the third were among those Hugh Rich told of the Nun's revelations.

15 Neame, *Holy Maid*, pp. 170–71. The Nun's superior was probably also a supporter. Neame points out that the 1547 will of Canterbury St. Sepulchre prioress Philippa John calls Henry VIII "Supreme Head in Hell" (p. 348).

16 *L&PH8*, vi, no. 1468.

17 Sidney Lee, *DNB* i, 1266, says that Rich was not executed, but Neame's account differs. The examination of [blank] of Syon survives, Paul Friedmann, *Anne Bolyn: A Chapter of English History 1527–1536*, 2 vols. (London, 1884), i, p. 245 n. 2. John Morris, Syon's receiver, was questioned, but not until April 1535 (*L&PH8* viii, no. 592).

18 Will of Sir John Kyngeston, PRO PCC 23 Fettyplace, Prob 11/17/34. Will of Sir Thomas Fettyplace, PRO PCC 32 Bodfelde, Prob 11/21/248–50. Will of Dorothy Fettyplace Codryngton, PRO PCC 13 Thower, Prob 11/24/99ᵛ. Will of Sir William Fettyplace,

PRO PCC 6 Jankyn, Prob 11/23/ 42v–45. Pearl Hogrefe has summarized this same material independently, *Life and Times*, pp. 29–30.

19 Will of Susan Fettyplace Kyngeston, PRO PCC 28 Alenger, Prob 11/28/ 218v–219, made June 25, 1540, proved May 11, 1541.

20 That Susan Kyngeston's school may have been open to both boys and girls is suggested by the similar will of Syon steward John Morris (PRO PCC 14 Alenger, Prob 11/28/ 107–107v), proved in 1540. Morris established a chantry school in Farnham, Surrey, where upon successful recitation before the sacrament of three paters, three aves, and the creed for the founder's soul, boys were to receive 4d, girls 8d.

21 A. F. Leach, "Childrey School," in *VCH Berkshire* II, 275. The indenture establishing a perpetual chantry at Childrey with almshouse and school is described by John Nichols, *Bibliotheca Topographica Britannica* (London, 1790), IV, pt 2, pp. 68*–83*; quotations are taken from Nichols' translation of the Latin document. Strickland Gibson discovered a copy of the indenture, made between Queen's College, Oxford; John Collysforde, rector of Lincoln College, Oxford; and William Fettyplace, preserved as binders' waste: "Fragments from Bindings at the Queen's College Oxford," *The Library* 4th ser. 12 (1931–2), 429–33.

22 The will of another uncle, Sir Thomas Fettyplace (see note 18 above), acknowledges the difficulties of an Oxford student's life: it left £20 to provide "to some pour scoler a Cote / to some a gown / or other Clothing or money or suche thinge as shalbe thought moost necessary."

23 The *VCH Berkshire*, IV, 225 describes her (probably palimpsest) brass, including the ring. Just under two feet in height, it is one of fewer than half a dozen brasses on which the subject is explicitly identified as a vowess, although many women costumed as widows on their memorial brasses may have taken vows. For the pedigree of Purefoy of Shalston, Lipscomb, *History*, III, 71. Dunlop's observation comes from BL Additional MS 42763, f. 360v. The joint brass of Sir John and Lady Susan Kyngeston is described in Elias Ashmole, *The Antiquities of Berkshire*, 3 vols. (London, 1719), II, 211–12; it is reproduced by T. H. Morley, *Monumental Brasses of Berkshire* (n.p., 1924), p. 77.

24 Croft, *Boke*, I, 313.

25 Register Fitzjames, London, Guildhall MS 9531/9, ff. cxxviij–cxxx does not indicate her presence at the abbatial election of 1518.

26 Brussels Bibl. Royale IV, 481. Watson (ed.), *Supplement*, pp. 64, 118. Christopher de Hamel, *Syon Abbey: The Library of the Bridgettine Nuns and Their Peregrinations after the Reformation*, Roxburghe Club (Otley, 1991), pp. 74–5, 88, 91, 105, 123, 130, 135. Bell, *What Nuns Read*, pp. 176–7.

27 Oxford, Bodleian 4° W.2.Th.Seld., *STC* 25421. Ker (ed.), *MLGB*, p. 186. De Hamel, *Syon*, pp. 126–27, 148. Bell, *What Nuns Read*, p. 196.

28 Southwark Diocesan Archives no. 72, *STC* 16217. Not in Ker–Watson, *MLGB*. De Hamel, *Syon*, p. 148. Not in Bell, *What Nuns Read*. For Amesbury pension list, *L&PH8* XIV(ii), no. 646. Will of James Yate, PRO PCC 11 Pynnyng, Prob 11/30/86ᵛ–87, made May 23, 1543, proved July 16, 1544.

29 J. R. Fletcher, notebook no. 5, "History of Syon Abbey 1539–63," Exeter Record Office. George James Aungier, *The History and Antiquities of Syon Monastery* (London, 1840), p. 99, note 2. For Daniel Rock, C. W. Dutschke and R. H. Rouse (eds.), *Medieval and Renaissance Manuscripts in the Claremont Libraries* (Berkeley, 1980), p. 321. His ownership of Eleanor Fettyplace's missal is mentioned in "Antiquities and Works of Art Exhibited," *Archaeological Journal* 21 (1864), 179.

30 Oxford, Bodleian Auct. D.4.7, *SC* II, pt I, p. 134. Ker, *MLGB*, p. 186. A. Jefferies Collins, *The Bridgettine Breviary of Syon Abbey*, Henry Bradshaw Society no. 96 (Worcester, 1969), pp. xlv–xlvii. De Hamel, *Syon*, pp. 66, 75, 108, 117, 127. Bell, *What Nuns Read*, p. 194. It is described, and its initial reproduced in Otto Pächt and J. J. G. Alexander, *Illuminated Manuscripts in the Bodleian Library Oxford*, 3 vols. (Oxford, 1973), III, no. 938 and plate LXXXIX. Both *SC* and Kathleen L. Scott assign the breviary to *c.* 1420: *Later Gothic Manuscripts 1390–1490, A Survey of Manuscripts Illuminated in the British Isles*, 2 vols. (London, 1996), II, 154. The Sir William Bowes who died on September 14, 1432 might be the grandson of Maud Bowes of Streatham and Dalton named in her 1420 will; see *Wills and Inventories Illustrative . . . of the Northern Counties*, Surtees Society 2 (London 1835), pp. 63–65, and also Robert Surtees, *History and Antiquities of the County Palatine of Durham . . .* 4 vols. (London, 1840), IV, 107, pedigree of Bowes of Streatham.

For Collins' quotation, see *Bridgettine Breviary*, p. v. Elizabeth Yate's book is Oxford, University College MS 25, which includes a printed Sarum psalter of 1522 (*STC* 16260). Ker, *MLGB*, p. 187; De Hamel, *Syon*, pp. 97–8, 107, 119, 127. Bell, *What Nuns Read*, pp. 197–8. Collins, pp. xlviii–xlix. For the 1428 Syon list, Aungier, *Syon*, pp. 51–2, from London, Guildhall Library MS 9531/5, f. 69.

31 Syon *Martyrology*, BL Additional MS 22285, f. 46v. Fletcher notebook no. 5.

32 For Manwaring, see C. B. Heberden (ed.), *Brasenose College Register 1509–1909*, 2 vols. (Oxford, 1909), I, 84, and Joseph Foster (ed.), *Alumni Oxonienses . . . 1500–1714*, 4 vols. (Oxford, 1891), III, 960.

33 Brass and inscription are reproduced in Morley, *Monumental Brasses*, p. 23. The chancery suit is PRO CI/405/29.

34 The rule notes that the entrant must arrange for "bokes, beddynge, profession rynge, dyner, offerynge, and suche other." James Hogg (ed.), *The Rewyll of Seynt Sauioure. Vol. 4: The Syon Additions for the Sisters . . . BL MS Arundel 146* (Salzburg, 1980), p. 83 (f. 44a).

35 PCC 13 Thower, Prob 11 /24/99ᵛ. (Codryngton's unusual specification of "a graduat man to preach" on the Sunday before her husband's obit may owe something to the Fettyplace interest in education.) "A monk or nun can not acquire or have any proprietary rights. When a man becomes 'professed in religion,' . . . if he has made a will, it takes effect at once as though he were naturally dead," Frederick Pollock and Frederick William Maitland, *The History of English Law before the Time of Edward I.* 2 vols. (Cambridge, 1968), I, 434–35.

36 Vaissier (ed.), *Tree* p. xxxviii. The will signature is transcribed in the PCC copy, "Dorathe Cotherington"; the *Tree* signature is "Dorothe Corderynton," according to Vaissier, p. xxxvii. For Ampleforth Abbey C. V. 130, see Watson, *Supplement*, pp. 64, 110; Bell, *What Nuns Read*, p. 176.

37 Vaissier analyzes the annotations in the Ampleforth Abbey copy and in Margaret Windsor's copy at Trinity College, Cambridge. I hope to write at more length about the Folger copy of *Tree*.

38 The 1539 pension list is *L&PH8* XIV(ii), no. 581 (or 206). Aungier prints the *c.* 1554 list (p. 98) from BL Additional MS 8102. For Fletcher's statement that Dorothy Codryngton lived at Buckland, his notebook no. 5.

39 "Private Devotion in England on the Eve of the Reformation," Ph.D. thesis, University of Durham (1974), p. 18.

40 David Knowles, *The Religious Orders in England*, 3 vols. (Cambridge, 1948–61), III, 216–17. Susan Brigden, *London and the Reformation* (Oxford, 1989), p. 226.

41 A thirteenth-century Latin bible with historiated initials and medieval fore-edge painting is likely to have been owned by another woman of the Fettyplace family. Its sixteenth-century signature "Dorothee Fettiplace" may belong to Susan, Eleanor, and Dorothy's sister-in-law, Dorothy Danvers Fettyplace, wife of their brother John Fettyplace the elder. Her will was proved 5 February 1560 (PCC Mellershe 12). For the bible, Oxford, Bodleian Lat. bib. d. 8, see Pächt and Alexander, *Illuminated Manuscripts*, III, no. 488.

5 HETERODOXY: ANCHORESS KATHERINE MANNE AND ABBESS ELIZABETH THROCKMORTON

A version of this chapter was delivered as a talk at the 1991 Early Book Society conference in Dublin.

1 To Claire Cross's classic article " 'Great Reasoners in Scripture': the Activities of Women Lollards 1380–1530," in Derek Baker (ed.), *Medieval Women*, Studies in Church History Subsidia (Oxford, 1978), pp. 359–80 can be added Margaret Aston, "Lollard Women Priests?" *JEH* 31 (1980), 441–61, and Shannon McSheffrey, *Gender and Heresy: Women and Men in Lollard Communities 1420–1530* (Philadelphia, 1995).

2 George Townsend (ed.), John Foxe, *Acts and Monuments*, 8 vols. (London, 1843; repr. edn, New York, n.d.) IV, 642. Clay, *Hermits and Anchorites*, p. 79. Tanner, *Church*, pp. 248–52 (will of Robert Jannys, PRO PCC 1 Thower). Whether Katherine Manne might have been connected with the Lollard teacher Thomas Man, executed in 1518, who worked in London, Essex, Norfolk, and Suffolk, is unknown. For Thomas Man, see Hudson, *Reformation*, p. 449.

3 For a detailed treatment of Bilney's life and thought see John F. Davis, *Heresy and Reformation in the South-East of England, 1520–1559* (London and New Jersey, 1983), especially pp. 47–54.

4 Foxe, *Acts*, IV, 642.

5 Bilney's words during his last hours and their interpretation were much discussed, Thomas More asserting (in the *Confutation of Tyndale's Answer*) that Bilney had re-canted. Foxe, in rebuttal, printed Matthew Parker's eyewitness testimony and Edward Rede's eyewitness notes. The most detailed account of the political context of Bilney's death is provided by John Guy, *The Public Career of Sir Thomas More* (Brighton, 1980), pp. 166–71. Using More's November 1531 Star Chamber inquiry into Bilney's death (*L&PH8*, V, 522, 560, 569 and SP 1/68) Guy frames the execution as a struggle between ecclesiastical jurisdiction (Pelles and Nix, chancellor and bishop of Norwich, and More) and temporal (Bilney had appealed to the king as head of the church, and Rede's notes were preparation for his announced intention to raise the issue of jurisdiction in the 1532 Parliament). Guy's reading is supported by John F. Davis' earlier suggestion, based on a dispatch of the imperial ambassador Chapuys, that in the 1534 imprisonment of Bishop Nix "a subsidiary charge concerned his having burnt Bilney without waiting for the king's writ," "The Trials of Thomas Bylney and the English Reformation," *The Historical Journal* 24 (1981), 775–90, ref. p. 787. See also Stanford E. Lehmberg, *The Reformation Parliament 1529–1536* (Cambridge, 1970), p. 118, n. 1.

6 Foxe *Acts*, IV, appendix III, who identifies the document as PRO Treasury of the Receipt of the Exchequer, second ser. nos. 1884–90; Rede's notes are no. 1887. Guy, *Public Career*, p. 170, gives the modern reference as SP 1/66, ff. 296–317 (*L&PH8*, V, 372).

7 Paul L. Hughes and James F. Larkin (eds)., *Tudor Royal Proclamations* (hereafter *TRP*), 3 vols. (New Haven and London, 1964–69), I, 129. A royal and ecclesiastical

commission had met to review various problematic books from May 11 to May 24, 1530.
A. G. Dickens says, "Many readers of moderate or even conservative views studied
[Tyndale's New Testament] with eagerness over the next decade. Perusing contempo-
rary records one encounters it in the most unlikely places." *The English Reformation*
(New York, 1964), p. 72.

8 *L&PH8* iv(iii), no. 6385.

9 Foxe *Acts*, iv, 652.

10 For Bayfield see Foxe *Acts*, iv, 680–83. For Robert Necton: John Strype, *Ecclesiastical
Memorials*, 3 vols. (Oxford, 1882), i/i, no. 22, summarized in *L&PH8* iv(ii), no. 4030.
The Necton brothers' connection is supported by Guy's discovery of a 1528 bond of
£100 for Robert Necton to which Thomas Necton stood surety, cited in *Public Career*,
p. 108 (PRO Star Chamber 2/31), and by Robert Necton's reference in his confession to
being "at Norwiche at his [unnamed] brother's house."

11 The letter was discovered in the PRO by James Gairdner who published it as "A
Letter Concerning Bishop Fisher and Sir Thomas More," *EHR* 7 (1892), 712–15. It
was subsequently included in *L&PH8*, Addenda i, pt i, 357–58, and has been printed
in a modernized version by Elizabeth Nugent (ed.), *The Thought and Culture of the
English Renaissance: An Anthology of Tudor Prose 1481–1555*, 2 vols. (Cambridge, 1954), ii,
pp. 547–49. Nugent says the letter is held by the Parkminster Charterhouse, Horsham
(p. 549). Quotations are taken from Gairdner.

12 *TRP* i, 158.

13 Foxe *Acts*, iv, Appendix iii, for Bilney's words.

14 For More's words, *The Confutation of Tyndale's Answer*, Book viii, 892, in Louis
A. Schuster, Richard C. Marius, James P. Lusardi, and Richard J. Schoeck (eds.), *The
Complete Works of St. Thomas More*, viii, pt ii, (New Haven and London, 1973).

15 A. B. Emden, *A Biographical Register of the University of Cambridge to 1500* (Cambridge,
1963), pp. 148–49 (hereafter *BRUC*).

16 John Venn (ed.), *The Annals of Gonville and Caius College by John Caius, M.D.*,
Cambridge Antiquarian Society Octavo Series 40 (Cambridge, 1904), p. 27.

17 Brooke, *Gonville and Caius*, pp. 48, 103.

18 Emden, *BRUC*, p. 620.

19 Foxe *Acts*, iv, 655.

20 Emden, *BRUC*, pp. 229–30 for Fisher; pp. 84–85 for Bouge (listed under Bownge).

21 Carol B. Rowntree in her directory of English Carthusians calls him John Bourg, "also
Bownge and Burg. Monk of Axholme. In 1526 sent to Hull as guest. Still there in 1529."
"Studies in Carthusian History in Later Medieval England," Ph.D. thesis, University
of York (1981), p. 493. I am grateful to Dr. Rowntree for her suggestions regarding
Carthusian spirituality.

22 Tanner, *Church*, p. 182, but this name has no prefix; surely Bouge would have been
"magister."

23 For Jannys' will see Tanner, *Church*, pp. 248–52.

24 John F. Pound, "The Social and Trade Structure of Norwich 1525–1575," *Past and Present*
34 (1966), 49–69, reference p. 51.

25 Clay, *Hermits and Anchorites*, p. 79; printed in F. I. Dunn, "Hermits, Anchorites and
Recluses: A Study with Reference to Medieval Norwich," in F. D. Sayer (ed.), *Julian
and Her Norwich* (Norwich, 1973). The last year in which her 20s annuity was paid was
1555.

26 Dunn, "Hermits," quotes and interprets the 1550 document: Manne will have "ffree
libertye to occupie within this Citie so long as she shall kepe her shoppe [i.e. mind

her own business] and be soole and unmarryed," p. 25. The phrase "shut your shop," i.e. hold your tongue, is recorded by *OED* only from 1868, by *MED* not at all, hence it seems likely that the document is instead describing Manne's economic position as *femme sole* and that she was, in fact, at this time a shopkeeper.

For a detailed survey of the *femme sole*'s position, see Caroline M. Barron, "The 'Golden Age' of Women in Medieval London," *Reading Medieval Studies* 15 (1989), 35–58.

27 Ann K. Warren, *Anchorites and Their Patrons in Medieval England* (Berkeley, 1985), ch. 7.

28 Patrick Collinson, review of Perez Zagorin, *Ways of Lying* (Cambridge, Mass., 1990), *TLS*, March 1, 1991. Greg Walker concludes that at his trial Bilney played the lawyer, in "Saint or Schemer? The 1527 Heresy Trial of Thomas Bilney Reconsidered," *JEH* 40 (1989), 219–38, reprinted in *Persuasive Fictions: Faction, Faith and Political Culture in the Reign of Henry VIII* (Aldershot, Hants., 1996).

29 Davis, *Heresy and Reformation*, pp. 30–33.

30 Tanner, *Church*, p. 29, although in 1522, 39 out of 52 beneficed London priests were graduates, a much higher percentage (Tanner, quoting *VCH London* I, 245.)

31 Strype, *Ecclesiastical Memorials*, I/2, no. 89. As the earliest printed edition is dated November 15, 1533 (it may or may not be Tyndale's translation), Monmouth probably sent the abbess a manuscript version – unless a lost edition was printed earlier. J. A. Gee, "John Byddell and the First Publication of Erasmus' Enchiridion in English," *ELH* 4 (1937), 43–59.

32 John W. O'Malley (ed.), *Collected Works of Erasmus: Enchiridion...*, vol. 66 (Toronto, 1988), pp. 3–4. Jonathan Goldberg, *Desiring Women Writing* (Stanford, 1997), p. 109.

33 The text of *Image of Love* is printed as Appendix A and discussed by E. Ruth Harvey in T. M. C. Lawler et al. (eds.), *The Complete Works of St. Thomas More*, vol. 6, pt 2 (New Haven and London, 1981).

34 A. W. Reed, *Tudor Drama* (London, 1926), pp. 166–68.

35 Essex Record Office D/DP F234. Bell, *What Nuns Read*, p. 119.

36 Byrne (ed.), *Lisle Letters*, III, 452.

37 P. S. Allen, H. M. Allen, and H. W. Garrod (eds.), *Opus Epistolarum Des. Erasmi Roterdami*, 12 vols. (Oxford, 1906–58), VII, 283–85, no. 1925 (excerpts).

38 Knowles, *Religious Orders*, III, 152. The relevant 1513 letters from Erasmus to William Gonnell are translated by Francis Morgan Nichols, *The Epistles of Erasmus*, 3 vols. (New York, 1962), II, nos. 264, 267, 270, 272, and in 1514 nos. 278, 279, 286, 288. Four of the letters are translated in D. F. S. Thomson and H. C. Porter, *Erasmus and Cambridge* (Toronto, 1963), pp. 159–65.

39 The story has been retold by Susan Brigden, *London and the Reformation* (Oxford, 1989), p. 110. For more detail see John T. Day, "William Tracy's Posthumous Legal Problems," in John A. R. Dick and Anne Richardson (eds.), *William Tyndale and the Law*, Sixteenth-Century Essays and Studies 25 (Kirksville, Mo., 1994), 103–13.

40 Tyndale has been fortunate in his biographers: R. Demaus, *William Tindale* (London, 1871); J. T. Mozley, *William Tyndale* (London, 1937). The most recent is David Daniell, *William Tyndale: A Biography* (New Haven and London, 1994). I am grateful to Janet Wilson, Trinity College, Dublin, for helpful material on early Protestantism in Gloucestershire. And see Caroline Litzenberger, *The English Reformation and the Laity: Gloucestershire 1540–1580* (Cambridge, 1997), esp. p. 29ff.

41 T. Nash, *Collections for the History of Worcestershire*, 2 vols., 2nd edn (London, 1799), I, facing 452 ("Pedigree of Throckmorton"). G. Andrews Moriarty calls this a copy of the

Throckmorton pedigree by Browne Willis in London, BL Additional 5841. "The Early Throckmortons," *Miscellanea Geneologica et Heraldica*, 5th ser. VI, pts 6 and 7 (1927), 228–53. Also see John Fetherston (ed.), *The Visitation of the County of Warwick in the Year 1619, taken by William Camden*...Harleian Society Publications 12 (London, 1877), p. 87 ("Pedigree of Throckmorton").

42 Brigden, *London and the Reformation*, p. 110.

43 The first edition is *STC* 3274.5. The second edition's two issues are *STC* 3275 (general audience) and *STC* 3276 (Denny).

44 *VCH Cambridgeshire* II, 302.

45 Bridget Cusack, "A Critical Edition of Willam Bonde's *Consolatori*... ", M.A. thesis, University of London (1963), p. 48. The statutes are Pembroke College Deeds Coll. A.12, quoted in Hilary Jenkinson, "Mary de Sancto Paulo, Foundress of Pembroke College Cambridge," *Archaeologia* 66 (1915), 401–30, note 4. For Fewterer, see M. B. Tait, "The Bridgettine Monastery of Syon," Ph.D. thesis, Oxford University (1975), p. 277. Or is it possible that the spiritual friend at Syon might have been Richard Reynolds, with whom in 1531 or 1532 Elizabeth Throckmorton's nephew Sir George discussed his political and religious difficulties over the king's divorce? Guy, *Public Career*, p. 211.

46 "Books Connected with the Vere Family and Barking Abbey," *TEAS* 25 (1958), 222–43.

47 See under Denny, Ker, *MLGB* and its continuation by Watson, *Supplement*. Also *Catalogue of Western Manuscripts in the Bodleian*... (Oxford, 1895–1953), no. 4109. Bell, *What Nuns Read*, pp. 134–35. A Denny business manuscript containing "the proceedings on the appropriation of the churches" of Eltisley (Camb.) and Bydenham (Beds.) *c.* 1512 survives at Ely; see A. Gibbons (ed.), *Ely Episcopal Records: A Calendar and Concise View of the Episcopal Records* ... (Lincoln, 1891), p. 153. A partial eighteenth-century transcript of the court rolls of Denny Abbey and Waterbeach 1327–1630 made by William Cole is in BL Additional 5837, ff. 129v–163v (orig. fol.).

48 "Vernacular Books of Religion," in Jeremy Griffiths and Derek Pearsall (eds.), *Book Production and Publishing in Britain 1375–1475* (Cambridge, 1989), p. 333. Ms Hatton 18 also bears the name of John Fakun, whom the *VCH Cambridgeshire* (II, 281) identifies as vice-warden of the Cambridge Franciscan house and a contemporary of Elizabeth Throckmorton's; he was one of twenty-four signers of the friary's undated surrender.

49 John W. Clay (ed.), *North Country Wills*, Surtees Society 116 (Durham, 1899), pp. 48–49.

50 London, BL Additional MS 5833, mod. fol. 183v. Cited in Bourdillon, *Order of Minoresses*, p. 83. Also in *VCH Cambridgeshire* II, 302.

51 Sir Robert's will: PRO PCC 2 Maynwaryng (Prob 11/20/9v). Fetherston, *Visitation of... Warwick*, 87, 173.

52 Elizabeth Englefield's will: PRO PCC 4 Pynnyng, Prob 11/30/25–28. William Dugdale, *Antiquities of Warwickshire*, 2 vols. (London, 1730), II, 755. *VCH Warwickshire* III, 85. *VCH Cambridgeshire* II, 302. A wooden gate from Denny carved with Abbess Elizabeth Throckmorton's name remains: E. A. B. Barnard, "A 16th-Century Dole-Gate from Denny Abbey," *Proceedings of the Cambridge Antiquarian Society* 29 (1928), 72–5.

53 "Instructions for a Devout and Literate Layman," in Jonathan G. Alexander and Margaret T. Gibson (eds.), *Medieval Learning and Literature* (Oxford, 1976), pp. 398–422.

54 Francis James Thacker, "The Monumental Brasses of Worcestershire, Part II," *Transactions of the Worcestershire Archaeological Society* n.s. 4 (1926–27), 129–56, prints John Throckmorton's will (PRO PCC 32 Luffenham) and reproduces his brass. His wife Eleanor and their son Thomas endowed the Throckmorton chantry at Fladbury after

his death, in 1448, though the *VCH Worcestershire* comments "the actual foundation does not appear to have taken place until 1460" (III, 363).

55 The announcement is in Box 61, folder 1, according to Edward Wilson, "A Middle English Manuscript at Coughton Court, Warwickshire, and British Library MS Harley 4012," *Notes and Queries* 222 (July–August 1977), 295–303.

56 Ibid., 298. The Coughton Court manuscript is now London, Lambeth Palace MS 3597.

57 His daughter Elizabeth Throckmorton Englefield specifies the same daily votive masses in her 1543 will, PRO PCC 4 Pynnyng, Prob 11/30/25–28. For additional information on Sir Robert Throckmorton's life see the entry for his son Sir George in S. T. Bindoff, *The House of Commons 1509–1558*, 3 vols. (London, 1982), III, 450–51.

58 Ibid., III, 451; *VCH Berkshire* II, 103. J. Foster, *Alumni Oxonienses* (repr. edn, 1968), III, 1484. His will, PRO PCC 5 Dyngeley, Prob 11/27/40.

59 Dugdale, *Warwickshire*, II, 895. Her will, PRO PCC 1 Thower, Prob 11/24/7–7v.

60 The manuscript's English material has been edited by Nita Scudder Baugh, *A Worcestershire Miscellany Compiled by John Northwood c. 1400* (Philadelphia, 1956); see esp. p. 15, note 1. *Catalogue of Additions to the Manuscripts in the British Museum* (London, 1906–10), p. 150.

61 *VCH Warwickshire* V, 17, 43; VI, 269. Goditha's Christian name probably derives from her grandmother, Goditha Bosom, wife of Sir Robert Olney (inscription in Fladbury church, *VCH Worcestershire* III, 361). Her daughter Margaret Olney married Sir Thomas Throckmorton and received the Cistercian letter of confraternity mentioned above.

62 Dugdale, *Warwickshire*, I, 477. Three successive generations of these female brasses have not fared well. Goditha Bosom Olney's brass inscription remains at Fladbury and is reproduced by Thacker, "Monumental Brasses," but Thomas Dingley's drawing of the monument, made between 1660 and 1685, indicates the inscription may originally have accompanied a brass figure, absent by Dingley's time. See *History from Marble, compiled in the reign of Charles II by Thomas Dingley*, introduction by John Gough Nichols, 2 vols. Camden Society 94, 97 (Westminster, 1867, 1868), vol. 97, p. ccxcviii. A similar fate seems to have befallen her daughter Margaret Olney Throckmorton's brass, from which only a partial inscription remains (Thacker, "Monumental Brasses" p. 152). Margaret's daughter Goditha Throckmorton Peyto's brass has likewise been removed, along with those of her children, although the brass of her husband Edward Peyto remains. The whole was intact when Dugdale saw it and is engraved in his first edition of *Warwickshire*, I, 656; here five children are shown, one girl and four boys. The children's brasses disappeared in the eighteenth century (Thacker, "Monumental Brasses," p. 153; Dingley, "History," ibid.) Goditha's brass disappeared between 1868, when Nichols comments that "this slab remains as Dingley drew it" i.e. with Goditha's brass present, and 1926, when Thacker noted its absence.

63 *Catalogue of Additions to the Manuscripts in the British Museum* (London, 1906–10), p. 150. Baugh, *Worcestershire Miscellany*, 15, note 1. Dugdale, *Warwickshire* I 472, 477. For William Peyto see John R. H. Moorman, *The Grey Friars in Cambridge 1225–1538* (Cambridge, 1952), pp. 200–01, and Joseph Gillow, *A...Bibliographical Dictionary of the English Catholics...*, 5 vols. (London, 1885–1903), V, 300–03, as well as *DNB*. The Easter 1532 sermon is recorded in PRO CSP Span. IV/2, 934.

64 A contemporary conversation in 1531 or 1532 between Elizabeth Throckmorton's two nephews, George Throckmorton, son of Sir Robert, and William Peyto, illustrates the political and theological intensity of the 1520s and 1530s, an atmosphere in which the religious houses were deeply involved. Peyto, in prison since his Easter sermon, advised his cousin Throckmorton that the latter's spiritual and political duty as a

member of parliament was to oppose the Boleyn marriage. Throckmorton's October 1537 retrospective account includes similar encouragements which he received from Thomas More and from Richard Reynolds of Syon (PRO SP 1/125, ff. 247–56, printed in Guy, *Public Career*, Appendix 2). Hence in Monmouth's statement that both the abbess of Denny and a friar of Greenwich asked him for the *Enchiridion*, it is tempting to identify the latter as Peyto since he might have learned of the translation from his aunt the abbess. In addition his role in the period's religious controversies was a most active one, although the same might be said of such other Greenwich Observants as John West, John Ryckes, or Henry Elstow.

6 WOMEN OWNERS OF RELIGIOUS INCUNABULA: THE PHYSICAL EVIDENCE

An earlier version of this chapter was presented at the 1993 conference "Women and the Book in the Middle Ages" held at St. Hilda's College, Oxford. Some of the material in this chapter has been treated more briefly in Erler, "Devotional Literature," in Lotte Hellinga and J. B. Trapp (eds.), *The Cambridge History of the Book in Britain. Vol. III: 1400–1557* (Cambridge, 1999), pp. 495–525.

1 White, "Early Print and Purgatory," Appendix I: *STC* Books Published 1475–1499.

2 I excluded devotional texts which survived in only one or two examples. I selected both generally popular titles (*Speculum Vite Christi*; *Scale of Perfection*) and less popular ones (Bernard's *Meditations*; *Life of St. Katherine*). The percentage seen is higher for the primers: 30 out of 36 extant copies, or about 83 percent. A list of all copies known to me (not only copies listed in *STC*) is provided below for each of the titles discussed. The women whose names appear in these volumes did not always acquire their books immediately upon publication, of course, but I have tried to exclude owners later than fifty years after the book's publication, or after the Dissolution.

3 This classification is tentative, since several of the women owners have been identified only provisionally or not at all.

Nuns (14): Palmer, Sewell, Clement, Bridgettine community of Syon (2), Necollson, Purefeye, Morepath/Palmer, Nevell/Dely, Wyllowby/Symond, Fabyan (?), Burton, Efflyn, Woodward.

Aristocrats (5): Margaret Beaufort/Elizabeth of York, Parr, Grey (?), Elizabeth of York, Pole.

Gentry (6): Porter, Withypoll, Massey, Verney, Regent, Throckmorton/Englefield.

Unknown: (6): Elizabeth, anonymous bedeswoman, Woodhowse, Alford, Fench/Roydon, Stafforton. The number of nuns at the Dissolution has been estimated to be about 1,500 (J. C. Russell, "The Clerical Population of Medieval England," *Traditio* 2 [1944], Table 9, p. 212; p. 181). R. Neville Hadcock judges the number of nuns 1534–1540 to range between 1,599 and 1,920 Knowles and Hadcock, *Medieval Religious Houses*, p. 364.)

4 Knowles, *Religious Orders*, II, pp. 240–44. Barking's acounts, for instance, include the office of "lady of the pension," the nun responsible for distributing these sums (e.g. PRO SC 6/Hen 8/928). Each nun received at least £1 13s annually, the principal obedientiaries more, according to Sturman, "Barking Abbey," p. 481.

5 Kerre's will is NRO NCC Register Multon, ff. 89v–91r. For *Scale* and *Vitas Patrum* in Margaret Beaufort's accounts: Susan Powell, "Lady Margaret Beaufort and her Books," *The Library*, 6th ser. 20 (1998), 197–240, refs. n. 65, n. 118, n. 119.

6 Although de Worde produced three editions of the primer in 1494, two survive only in single fragments (*STC* 15876 and 15878); the copies of the remaining edition, *STC* 15875, are discussed here.

7 Lambeth Palace 1494.6. *Collected Papers of Henry Bradshaw* (Cambridge 1889), pp. 274–75. Bradshaw concluded that Dendermonde commissioned this engraving from a Flemish artist whose initials, G. M., he found both on the St. Katherine engraving and on another religious illustration which he reproduced. For the binding, Howard M. Nixon and Mirjam M. Foot, *The History of Decorated Bookbinding in England* (Oxford, 1992), p. 15.

8 Bodley Arch.G.e.43. The note slips made by N. R. Ker and others in preparation for his *MLGB* are deposited in Duke Humfrey's library at the Bodleian. Of a thirteenth-century Latin bible belonging to Syon (Bodley Auct. D.3.1 [2665]) the annotator says "vellum markers throughout the book projecting from fore edge (cf. Harley 42, Bodley 630, Rawl. C 941, etc.)." He also records the tabs' presence in other Syon volumes: Bodley 212; Brasenose 16; Oxford St. John's A.9.5, 6, 7 (printed books), Cambridge Emmanuel College 32.6.49 (printed book); Aberdeen UL 134. Fore-edge markers in the form of miniature leather buttons are found in a mid-fifteenth-century Brigittine breviary from Marienwater Abbey in North Brabant. Svato Schulz (ed.), *Medieval and Renaissance Manuscript Books in the Library of Congress, A Descriptive Catalogue* (Washington D.C., 1989), p. 202.

9 BL C.21.c.20. T. A. Birrell, "The Printed Books of Dame Margaret Nicollson: A Pre-Reformation Collection," in J. Bakker et al. (eds.), *Costerus: Essays on English and American Literature* (Amsterdam, 1987), pp. 27–33. Birrell identified the volume's owner with the Benedictine nun of Elstow (Beds.) More recently Carol Meale has discovered a contemporary of the same name at the Gilbertine house of Wotton (Yorks.) ("The Miracles of Our Lady," in Derek Pearsall (ed.), *Studies in the Vernon Manuscript* [Woodbridge, Suffolk 1990], p. 132n.) Eileen Power summarized the 1529 and 1530 controversies over Elstow's abbatial election, in which Margaret Necollson testified, from Bishop Langland's register: *Nunneries*, pp. 46–51.

10 J. C. T. Oates, *A Catalogue of the Fifteenth-Century Printed Books in the University Library Cambridge* (Cambridge, 1954), no. 4150 (Inc.4.J.1.2 [3570]) transcribes "oncle wan you do on thys loke / I pray you remember wo wrete thys in your bo[ke] / your louuynge nys Kateryn parr." Susan E. James, *Kateryn Parr, The Making of a Queen* (Aldershot, Hants., 1999), pp. 26, 30–31, Figs. 3, 4, 5, 7, 9.

 Besides the copy associated with Katherine Parr, Cambridge University Library owns a second copy of the 1494 primer (Inc.4.J.1.2.[3571]) which is wanting its calendar. The soiled state of its first leaf, a i, suggests it was lost early on. Perhaps Margaret Necollson's detached calendar, the first item in her collection, might have belonged to the CUL copy, but the two have not been compared.

11 Christopher de Hamel, *A History of Illuminated Manuscripts* (Oxford, 1986), ch. 6 "Books for Everybody," pp. 159–85. Roger S. Wieck, *Time Sanctified: The Book of Hours in Medieval Art and Life* (New York and Baltimore, 1988).

12 Anonymous: *STC* 15880, BL copy (IA 41332), [Pigouchet?] (1495). Margaret Grey: *STC* 15881.3, Bodley Arch. B.f.42 (Paris, E Jehannot, 1495?). Elizabeth of York: *STC* 15889, Pigouchet for Vostre [1498], Folger copy. Margaret Porter: *STC* 15886, Arch.G.e.38, Pynson 1497. Elizabeth Woodhowse: *STC* 15887, PML ch.L. 1482. Pigouchet for Simon Vostre, 1498. Fench/Roydon: *STC* 15887, Lambeth Palace 1498.6.

13 The 1427 will of Lady Elizabeth Fitzhugh, for instance, leaves two psalters, one covered in red and one in blue, two primers, one covered in red and one in blue, and a

green-covered book of prayers. *Wills and Inventories Illustrative... of the Northern Counties*, Part I, Surtees Society 2 (London, 1835), pp. 74–75.

14 Anne Reed: *STC* 15880, Bodley Douce 24, Paris, Pigouchet? (1495). For Freville, A. W. Franks, "The Geneological History of the Freville Family," *Publications of the Cambridge Antiquarian Society* 2, no. 14 (1848), 21–29. Rede's will is summarized in G. C. Moore Smith, *The Family of Withypoll*, Walthamstow Antiquarian Society Publications 34, 1936. More information on Paul Withypoll is provided in Bindoff, *The House of Commons*, III, 649–51.

15 Anne Withypoll's manuscript primer is described by M. R. James, "Description of the Ancient Manuscripts in the Ipswich Public Library," *Proceedings of the Suffolk Institute of Archaeology and Natural History* 22 (1935), 95–99, where it is no. 7, and, more recently, by Ker, *MMBL* II, 990–92. It may be her name which appears in London, Society of Antiquaries MS 252, an English verse *Boccus and Sydrac* on fol. I: "My lady Anne Redes boke."

16 *STC* lists copies of 14042, the first edition of *Scale*, at L, C, G², LINC, M+; F, HN, PML, ROS, Y[Mellon] = 10+ copies, the + sign indicating others unlisted. I am indebted to Katharine F. Pantzer for information that the following copies also exist: L⁴⁴, C⁴, C⁵, M², Copenhagen RL, Perryville, Mo., Y = 7 copies. In addition there is one leaf of 14042 at L². I have seen the copies or received information on their inscriptions for all except L⁴⁴ and Perryville, Mo.

17 The inscription reads: "Dedit hunc librum in Ihu Christi dilectione Antonio bolney pia mater Katherina Palmere Anno dni M.D.xlvj." Her signature, in a different hand, follows. Oates,*Catalogue*, no. 4118, CUL Inc.3.J.1.2.[3534]. For Syon's life after the Dissolution, John Rory Fletcher, *The Story of the English Bridgettines of Syon Abbey* (South Brent, Devon, 1933), pp. 37–39, and De Hamel, *Syon*. For Bolney, who was at Gonville Hall as a pensioner from 1520 to 1523, John Venn and J. A. Venn, *Alumni Cantabrigienses*, Part I, vol. I (Cambridge, 1922), p. 175.

18 Rosenbach copy, see "Walter Hilton's *Scale of Perfection*: The London Manuscript Group Reconsidered," *Medium Ævum* 52 (1983), 189–216, ref. p. 201. Among the manuscripts which Grenehalgh used was BL Harley 6576, Trinity College Cambridge B.15.18 (354) and perhaps others, according to Sargent.

19 The drawing is reproduced as plate 10 in Michael Sargent, "James Grenehalgh: The Biographical Register,"*Sonderdruck aus Analecta Cartusiana Kartausermystik und-Mystiker*, 4 (1984), 20–54. It also appears as the frontispiece to Margaret Deanesly's *The Incendium Amoris of Richard Rolle of Hampole* (Manchester, 1915).

20 Eric Colledge, "*The Recluse*: A Lollard Interpolated Version of the *Ancren Riwle*," *RES* 15 (1950), 1–15, 129–45, ref. pp. 140–41.

21 PML. ch.L.f 1804. Sargent, "Walter Hilton's *Scale*," p. 207. For John Clement and Margaret Giggs, *DNB* IV, 489. Dorothy's sister Margaret was elected prioress of St. Ursula's in 1569, see Joseph Gillow, *Biographical Dictionary of the English Catholics*, 5 vols. (London, 1885), I, 500–01. According to John Morris, S. J., *The Troubles of Our Catholic Forefathers...* 2 vols. (London, 1872–75), Dorothy was a Franciscan nun who was obliged by poverty to leave her monastery and came to live at St.Ursula's (I, 40).

22 The royal copy (Yale–Mellon) is described by P. J. Croft, *Lady Margaret Beaufort... Elizabeth of York and Wynkyn de Worde* (London, 1958). See also *Fifty-Five Books Printed before 1525... An Exhibition from the Collection of Paul Mellon* (Grolier Club, n.p., 1968).

23 Cambridge, St. John's College A.I.7. The start of a following word is visible, perhaps a majuscule C. This single-word signature is also found at the end of a devotional

miscellany associated with the Throckmorton family *olim* Coughton Court manuscript, now Lambeth Palace MS 3597. It has been suggested that the "Elyzbeth [*sic*]" on its f. 95 might be either the wife of Sir Robert Throckmorton (1451–1519) or his sister, abbess of Denny Elizabeth Throckmorton. In the absence of any identifying title, the lay Elizabeth may be more likely. Edward Wilson, "A Middle English Manuscript at Coughton Court, Warwickshire, and British Library MS Harley 4012," *Notes & Queries* 222 (July–August 1977), 295–303, ref. p. 298. It is difficult to say whether the signature "Elizabeths" in the St. John's and the Lambeth manuscripts are in the same hand. The forms of majuscule "E" and minuscule "h" and "b" are similar, and both signatures are positioned at the leaf's center bottom margin, below the text.

24 Of the 18+ partial or complete copies listed by *STC*, 3 are fragments. To the copies listed in *STC* may be added: *STC* 3259 = L²(frag); 3260 = L² and a second copy at L; 3262 = Cant. for a total of 4 fragments and 18 largely complete copies. Of these 18, I have seen 15 (not O⁷ or Stevens Cox or Cant.). I am much indebted to Katharine F. Pantzer for help in locating these non-*STC* copies.

25 BL IB 55119. Seymour de Ricci, *A Census of Caxtons*, Bibliographical Society Illustrated Monograph 15 (Oxford, 1909), p. 14. Christopher de Hamel has suggested the seminary may have been Downside Abbey in Devon (*Syon*, p. 148).

26 For the pedigree of Purefoy of Shalston, see George Lipscomb, *The History and Antiquities of the County of Buckingham*, 4 vols. (London, 1847), III, 71. Susan Kyngeston's brass is reproduced in III, 75. Regarding the dates of Susan Purefeye's Syon membership, Syon accounts show boarding charges for her in 1532–33 and 1533–34, probably her period of novitiate (SC 6/ Hen 8/ 2239, 2240, 2241, 2242). Her pension is recorded in George J. Aungier, *The History and Antiquities of Syon Monastery* (London, 1840), p. 89, from *L&PH8*, XIV ii. 581 (Nov. 25, 1539). For its 1554 payment, see G. A. J. Hodgett (ed.)., *The State of the Ex-Religious and Former Chantry Priests in the Diocese of Lincoln 1547–1574 from Returns in the Exchequer*, Lincoln Record Society 58 (Hereford, 1959), p. 99. Her death date is given in BL Additional MS 22285, f. 68v.

The Syon catalogue records manuscripts of the *Speculum Vite Christi* at M3, M6, M7, M76 (an incorrect entry) and M 89 (Bateson [ed.], *Catalogue*.

27 Love's *Mirror* is BL IB 55527. For Elizabeth Massey's household membership, Michael K. Jones and Malcolm G. Underwood, *The King's Mother: Lady Margaret Beaufort, Countess of Richmond and Derby* (Cambridge, 1992), p. 278. Margaret Beaufort's will is printed by C. H. Cooper, *Memoir of Margaret, Countess of Richmond and Derby* (Cambridge, 1874).

28 Joyce Bazire and Eric Colledge (eds.), *The Chastising of God's Children and the Treatise of Perfection of the Sons of God* (Oxford, 1957).

29 *STC* 5065. *STC* lists 9+ copies: I have been able to trace 10 more. Copies of *Chastising*: L, C(2), G², LEEDS, M, LINC, COP. RL (lost), L⁴, C⁶, C¹⁷, O(frag.), Göttingen, Harleian Cat (lost), F, HN, IND, PML(2). I am grateful to Katherine F. Pantzer for her help in locating these copies. Of the sixteen surviving I have seen or have information on all but LEEDS.

30 These three examples of religious ownership are noted in Bazire and Colledge (eds.), *Chastising*. A. I. Doyle observed the presence of the Morepath–Palmer inscription in Cambridge, Sidney Sussex College BB.2.14 (p. 38). The Newell–Dely copy is Göttingen University Library, 4° Theol. Mor. 138/53 Inc.; the inscription was discovered by de Ricci, *Census*, pp. 111–12. The Campsey inscription, recorded in *Catalogus Bibliothecae Harleianae* from a book now lost, was also noted by Doyle. "On the last *Leaf*, there is a *Memorandum*, written by a Nun of Campessey, named *Elyzabeth Wyllowby*, That she gives this Book to Dame *Cateryne Symonde*, under the Condition,

That, in no wise, she sell it, or give it from the House of Campessey: But she shall give it to one of her Sisters." Vol. III, London 1744, no. 1560. Summarized by Ker, *MLGB*, p. 238, and see Bell, *What Nuns Read*, p. 125.

Regarding age: Morepath's and Palmer's death dates come from the Syon *Martyrology*, BL Additional 22285, ff. 61v, 68. Though Mary Nevell died in 1557 or 1558 and Awdry Dely in 1579 (BL Additional MS 22285, ff. 192, 60, 35), in both 1539 and 1557 pension lists, which reflect seniority, their names are separated by only two and three others (Aungier, *History*, pp. 90, 97). Perhaps Wyllowby was slightly older than Symond: both were present at elections in 1514 and 1526; Bell adds the information (p. 126) that by the 1532 visitation Wyllowby's name had disappeared. M. R. James noted the presence of another Wyllowby–Symonde *ex dono* inscription in a fifteenth-century *Scale* manuscript: *A Descriptive Catalogue of the Manuscripts in the Library of Corpus Christi College Cambridge*. 2 vols. (Cambridge, 1912), II, 24–25. It is no. 268; James transcribes "Md that I Elizabeth Wylby / (erasure) N . . . of . . . ossee Gyffe thys boke / (bottom of leaf cut off)," and see Bell, *What Nuns Read*, p. 123.

31 Constance L. Rosenthal, *The Vitae Patrum in Old and Middle English Literature* (Philadelphia, 1936), pp. 14–15, 33.

32 In an unpublished lecture on the Dutch printer Gheraert Leeu, Lotte Hellinga has noted that of the six inscribed copies of Leeu's 1480 edition of this work in Dutch (*Vanden leven der heiliger vnderen under woestinen*), five belonged to women's religious houses, one to a beguine.

33 For Elizabeth de Burgh, James Westfall Thompson, *The Medieval Library* (Chicago, 1939), p. 645. For the minoress' and Barking books, Bell, *What Nuns Read*, pp. 116, 151. Sibyl de Felton's purchase suggests a personal connection between herself and the duchess, perhaps even the latter's residence at Barking, although she was buried at the London Charterhouse according to Hope (ed.), *Charterhouse*, p. 100.

34 This large number of surviving copies is accounted for by Edward Hodnett's detective work, which discovered a re-issue of the 1495 edition (*STC* 14507) printed around 1529, with some sheets reprinted and with a woodcut of St. Bernard which did not appear in the original edition (*English Woodcuts 1480–1535, Additions & Corrections* [London 1973], no. 854, Fig. 72 and p. 10). Thus some of the twenty-six copies known to me, though dated 1495, are not incunabula, and were not produced nor acquired until the early sixteenth century. No effort has been made to distinguish the edition from which the surviving copies come (all are dated 1495). Copies of *Vitas Patrum*: L(2), L², O(2), CUL (3), C², C⁴, DUR, LINC, M, ST, G², Blackburn Pub. Lib., F, HN, ILL, NY, Y, PML, LC, IND, Gordan, Mellon. Of this number I have seen fifteen. I am grateful to Katharine F. Pantzer for supplying locations for several copies not in *STC*.

35 Erler, "Devotional Literature," pp. 522–23.

36 Lambeth Palace 1495.4. Nicolas (ed.), *Privy Purse*, pp. 8, 30, 36, 39, 43, 55, 57, 84, 91, 99, 228. Eleanor's relationship to the countess is shown in N. H. Nicolas, "Pedigrees Showing the Relationship between Many of the Nobility and Gentry and the Blood Royal . . .," *Collectanea Topographica et Genealogica* I (1834), no. XII, p. 310 (from BL Harley MS 1074). For her legacy: Cooper, *Memoir of Margaret*, p. 133. Meg Ford has suggested a later name: Eleanor Verney Greville, the great-granddaughter of London mayor Ralph Verney, who married John Greville of Milcote, Warwickshire, about 1527 – hence the signature would precede her marriage (private correspondence).

37 *L&PH8* XV, 547 for 1539; Dugdale *Monasticon* I, 438 note b for 1553; Sturman, "Barking Abbey," p. 438, lists the community's membership in 1499, 1527, 1556, 1559. The absence

of a prefixing "Dame" might indicate ownership before she joined the community or ownership by a lay Martha Fabyan (see note following).

38 Robert Fabyan died in 1513; his will mentions only daughters Mary and Joan, but it was not unusual for a child in religion to be omitted from a parental will, and Fabyan's tomb sculpture was ordered to show six daughters. Since his home was at Theydon Garnon in southwest Essex, close to Barking Abbey, circumstantial evidence supports the possibility that Martha Fabyan was his daughter. PRO Prob 11/17/ 12, printed in Henry Ellis (ed.), *The New Chronicles of England and France* (London, 1811).

In addition the 1541 will of John Fabyan, gentleman, of St. Clement Danes (Guildhall MS 9171/11) leaves four nobles yearly to his sister Martha out of his Essex lands, together with a black gown, a mourning black cloak, a featherbed and sheets, all bequests which would not be unsuitable for a nun. A. G. Thomas and I. D. Thornley indicate that this John is not the chronicler's son, but might be his grandson, the son of Robert Fabyan (*The Great Chronicle of London*, London, 1938, p. xlv). Finally, the chronicler's son Anthony had a daughter named Martha (P. Boyd, *Genealogist's Magazine* 7 [1935–37], 10–11. I owe this reference to Meg Ford). There would thus seem to be two Martha Fabyans who were granddaughters of the chronicler. Whether either is to be identified with the nun of Barking or the owner of *Vitas Patrum* is not clear.

39 Glasgow, Hunterian Collection BV.2.13. R. E. Lewis and A. McIntosh, *A Descriptive Guide to the Manuscripts of the Prick of Conscience*, Medium Ævum Monographs, n.s. 12 (Oxford, 1982), p. 35. The Foyle MS was lot 77 at Christie's Foyle sale, July 11, 2000, see catalogue, pp. 232–33, where a Worcestershire provenance is suggested (following Lewis), and a date of 1465, based on a lost manuscript note. The Christie's cataloguer believed a different, later, hand wrote the second part of the ownership inscription, concluding "that Margaret owned the book after her cousin."

40 Oates, *Catalogue* 4121 [3538]. C. F. R. Palmer, "History of the Priory of Dartford, in Kent," *Archaeological Journal* 36 (1879), 241–71, refs. pp. 269–71. Lee, *Nunneries*, pp. 119–31. Godfrey Anstruther, *A Hundred Homeless Years, English Dominicans 1558–1658* (London, 1958), pp. 6–15. The volume has another inscription; Oates, *Catalogue*, transcribes "diesen boech hoort to hindre Jaij (Faij?) up de boter mart." ("This book belongs to [name] at the butter market.") I am grateful to Livia Visser-Fuchs for discussing the language with me.

41 The *Royal Book* is BL c.10.b.22 (*STC* 21429). *STC* lists copies at L, C (2), M; F, HN, CB, HD, PML; there is also a copy at LC. I have seen L, M, F, PML, LC.

42 PRO PCC 1 Thower, Prob 11/24/4.

43 Goditha's sister Mary had married Thomas Burdett sometime before 1510; the Mary Burdett mentioned in Goditha's will is probably her daughter, Goditha's niece. Bindoff, *House of Commons*, I, 546–47.

44 Ibid., I, 100.

45 Sir Robert Throckmorton's will is PRO PCC 2 Maynwaryng, Prob 11/20/9v.

46 Bindoff, *House of Commons*, I, 100. *DNB* VI, 790. Geoffrey de C. Parmiter, "Plowden, Englefield and Sandford: I. 1558–65," *Recusant History* 13 (1976), 159–77.

47 Elizabeth Englefield's will is PRO PCC 4 Pynnyng, Prob 11/30/ 25–28. Her brass (with her husband and children) is described by Elias Ashmole, *The Antiquities of Berkshire*, 3 vols. (London, 1719), I, 10–11.

48 Nov. 21, 1537 is the date of probate of his father's will, which looks forward to the marriage (PRO PCC 11 Dyngeley, Prob 11/27/89).

49 *VCH Berkshire* III, 407. For an assessment of Englefield's political stance see Joel Hurstfield, *The Queen's Wards: Wardship and Marriage under Elizabeth I* (London, 1958), pp. 244–45.

50 Alan Coates, *English Medieval Books: The Reading Abbey Collections from Foundation to Dispersal* (Oxford, 1999), pp. 131–42, and for a summary of material on the Englefields, p. 128, n. 23.

51 See BL Additional MSS 42763, 42764, 42765, manuscript collections made by J. Renton Dunlop on the history of the Fettyplace family.

52 Jane I. Gilroy, "The Reception of Bridget of Sweden's 'Revelations' in Late Medieval and Early Renaissance England," Ph.D. thesis, Fordham University (1999), pp. 238–42. The manuscripts are BL Arundel 197; CUL ii.6.40 (nun of Shaftesbury); Pepys 2125 (address to "sister," later changed to "friend"); Bodley 423 (written by Stephen Dodesham, addressed to "gode brother or sustur"); Princeton, Garrett 145 (Syon).

53 Bodleian Tanner 191, a copy of de Worde's 1507 edition (*STC* 21430) was given to Margery Bakon. Marilyn Oliva says that she occurs in a Bruisyard pension list from 11–13 Elizabeth, PRO E 178/3251 (*Convent and Community*, p. 114) and see Watson, *Supplement*, p. 77.

54 PRO PCC 4 Pynnyng, Prob 11/30/25–28.

55 Additional women's names which have not yet been investigated are found in other incunabula; some of these may come from later in the sixteenth century, beyond the period examined here. For instance, according to de Ricci, the Royal College of Physicians' copy of Caxton's *Recueil* bears the name of Elizabeth Carew, and de Ricci lists another copy, sold in 1833 to Beriah Botfield, "which belonged in 1518 to Agnes Cole" (*Census*, p. 5). Frans Korsten notes that the St. John's College Cambridge copy of Caxton's [1489] *Dictes . . . of the philosophers* (*STC* 6829) is inscribed "Margrett Conyers." (*A Catalogue of the Library of Thomas Baker* [Cambridge, 1990], no. 43).

56 This consistency may be seen as part of a larger continuity in spiritual reading. Edward Meek points out that "the same titles were being acquired [by parish clergy] in 1520 as in 1420." He continues: "The fact that few books are specifically described as printed shows that the degree of intellectual continuity between the ages of script and print was much greater than might have been expected." "Printing and the English Parish Clergy in the Later Middle Ages," *TCBS* 11 (1997), 112–26, ref. p. 126.

57 Paul Morgan, "Frances Wolfreston and 'Hor Bouks'", *The Library* 11 (1989), 197–219. Tessa Watt, *Cheap Print and Popular Piety 1550–1640*, Cambridge Studies in Early Modern British History (Cambridge, 1991), pp. 315–17. Morgan points out that Frances Wolfreston owned a copy of the 1519 edition of *Orchard of Syon* (*STC* 4815), now in the Copenhagen Royal Library.

Select bibliography

Aarts, F. G. A. M. (ed.), þe *Pater Noster of Richard Ermyte. A Late Middle English Exposition of the Lord's Prayer . . .*, The Hague, 1967.

Allen, Hope Emily, *Writings Ascribed to Richard Rolle, Hermit of Hampole, and Materials for His Biography*, New York, 1927.

Allen, P. S. and Allen, H. M. and H. W. Garrod (eds.), *Opus Epistolarum Des. Erasmi Roterdami*, 12 vols., Oxford, 1906–58.

Anstruther, Godfrey, *A Hundred Homeless Years, English Dominicans 1558–1658*, London, 1958.

Ashdown-Hill, John, "Norfolk Requiem: The Passing of the House of Mowbray," *The Ricardian* 12 (2001), 198–217.

Ashley, Kathleen and Pamela Sheingorn (eds.), *Interpreting Cultural Symbols: Saint Anne in Late Medieval Society*, Athens, Ga., 1990.

Ashmole, Elias, *The Antiquities of Berkshire*, 3 vols., London, 1719–23.

Aston, Margaret, "Lollard Women Priests?" *JEH* 31 (1980), 441–61.

  Lollards and Reformers: Images and Literacy in Late Medieval Religion, London, 1984.

Aston, Margaret and Colin Richmond (eds.), *Lollardy and the Gentry in the Later Middle Ages*, Stroud, Glos. and New York, 1997.

Aungier, George James, *The History and Antiquities of Syon Monastery*, London, 1840.

Bainbridge, Virginia R., *Gilds in the Medieval Countryside: Social and Religious Change in Cambridgeshire c. 1350–1558*, Woodbridge, Suffolk, 1996.

Baker, Oliver, *In Shakespeare's Warwickshire and the Unknown Years*, London, 1937.

Ball, R. M., "The Opponents of Bishop Pecock," *JEH* 48 (1997), 230–62.

Barker, Nicholas, "Provenance," *The Book Collector* 45 (1996), 157–70.

Barnard, E. A. B., "A Sixteenth-Century Dole-Gate from Denny Abbey," *Proceedings of the Cambridge Antiquarian Society* 29 (1928), 72–75.

Barratt, Alexandra, "Books for Nuns: Cambridge University Library MS Additional 3042," *Notes and Queries* 242 [n.s. 47], 3 (September 1997), 310–19.

  Women's Writing in Middle English, London and New York, 1992.

Barron, Caroline, "The Expansion of Education in Fifteenth-Century London," in J. Blair and B. Golding (eds.), *The Cloister and the World: Essays in Medieval History in Honour of Barbara Harvey* (Oxford, 1996), pp. 219–45.

Select bibliography

"The 'Golden Age' of Women in Medieval London," *Reading Medieval Studies* 15 (1989), 35–58.

"Introduction: The Widow's World," in Barron and Sutton, *Widows*, pp. xiii–xxxiv.

Barron, Caroline M. and Anne F. Sutton (eds.), *Medieval London Widows 1300–1500*, London and Rio Grande, 1994.

Bartlett, Anne Clark, *Male Authors, Female Readers: Representation and Subjectivity in Middle English Devotional Literature*, Ithaca, 1995.

Baskerville, Geoffrey, "Married Clergy and Pensioned Religious in Norwich Diocese 1555, Pt. 2," *EHR* 48 (1933), 199–228.

Bateson, Mary, "The Register of Crabhouse Nunnery," *Norfolk Archaeology* 4 (1892), 1–71.

Bateson, Mary (ed.), *Catalogue of the Library of Syon Monastery, Isleworth*, Cambridge, 1898.

Baugh, Nita Scudder (ed.), *A Worcestershire Miscellany Compiled by John Northwood c. 1400*, Philadelphia, 1956.

Bazire, Joyce and Eric Colledge (eds.), *The Chastising of God's Children and the Treatise of Perfection of the Sons of God*, Oxford, 1957.

Beadle, Richard, "Medieval Texts and Their Transmission, 1350–1500: Some Geographical Criteria," in M. Laing and K. Williamson (eds.), *Speaking in Our Tongues: Proceedings of a Colloquium on Medieval Dialectology and Related Disciplines* (Cambridge, 1994), pp. 69–91.

Beadle, Richard, and A. J. Piper (eds.), *New Science out of Old Books: Studies in Manuscripts and Early Printed Books in Honour of A. I. Doyle*, Aldershot, Hants., 1995.

Beaven, Alfred B., *The Aldermen of the City of London*, 2 vols., London, 1908–13.

Bell, David N., *What Nuns Read: Books and Libraries in Medieval English Nunneries*, Kalamazoo, Mich., 1995.

Bennett, Michael J., *Community, Class, and Careerism: Cheshire and Lancashire Society in the Age of Sir Gawain and the Green Knight*, Cambridge, 1985.

Bentley, Samuel, *Excerpta Historica*, London, 1831.

Bestul, Thomas, "The Collection of Anselm's Prayers in British Library MS Cotton Vespasian D.xxvi," *Medium Ævum* 47 (1978), 1–5.

Bindoff, S. T., *The House of Commons 1509–1558*, 3 vols., London, 1982.

Birrell, T. A., "The Printed Books of Dame Margaret Nicollson: A Pre-Reformation Collection," in J. Bakker, T. A. Birrell, J. A. Verleun, and J. v. d. Vriesenaerde (eds.), *Costerus: Essays on English and American Literature and a Sheaf of Poems Presented to David Wilkinson* (Amsterdam, 1987), pp. 27–33.

Blaauw, W., "Episcopal Visitations of the Benedictine Nunnery of Easebourne," *Sussex Archaeological Collections* 9 (1857), 1–32.

Blomefield, Francis (ed.), *An Essay Toward a Topographical History of the County of Norfolk*, 10 vols., London, 1800–10.

Boffey, Julia, "Some London Women Readers and a Text of The Three Kings of Cologne," *The Ricardian* 10 (1996), 387–96.

Bokenham, Osbern, *Legendys of Hooly Wummen*, ed. Mary S. Serjeantson, EETS os 206, London, 1938.

Botfield, Beriah (ed.), *Manners and Household Expenses of England in the Thirteenth and Fifteenth Centuries*, Roxburghe Club no. 57, London, 1841.

Bourdillon, A. F. C., *The Order of Minoresses in England*, British Society of Franciscan Studies 12, Manchester, 1926.

Bradshaw, Henry, *Collected Papers*. Cambridge University Press, 1889.

Breay, Claire (ed.), *The Cartulary of Chatteris Abbey*, Woodbridge, Suffolk, 1999.

Brewer, Thomas (ed.), *Memoir of the Life and Times of John Carpenter*, London, 1856.

Bridges, John. *The History and Antiquities of Northamptonshire . . .* , 2 vols., Oxford, 1791.

Brigden, Susan, *London and the Reformation*, Oxford, 1989.

Brooke, Christopher, *A History of Gonville and Caius College*, Woodbridge, Suffolk, 1985.

Brown, A. L. "The Privy Seal Clerks in the Fifteenth Century," in D. A. Bullough and R. L. Storey (eds.), *The Study of Medieval Records: Essays in Honour of Kathleen Major* (Oxford, 1971), pp. 276–81.

Brown, Peter, *The Body in Society: Men, Women, and Sexual Renunciation in Early Christianity*, New York, 1988.

Brundage, James A. and Elizabeth M. Makowski, "Enclosure of Nuns: The Decretal *Periculoso* and Its Commentators," *JMH* 20 (1994), 143–55.

Burgess, Clive, "'A Fond Thing Vainly Invented': An Essay on Purgatory and Pious Motive in Late Medieval England," in S. Wright (ed.), *Parish, Church, and People: Local Studies in Lay Religion 1350–1750* (London, 1988), pp. 56–84.

Burrow, J. A., *Thomas Hoccleve*, Aldershot, Hants., 1994.

Burton, Janet E., *Monastic and Religious Orders in Britain 1000–1300*, Cambridge, 1994.

"Yorkshire Nunneries in the Middle Ages: Recruitment and Resources," in J. C. Appleby and P. Dalton (eds.), *Government, Religion and Society in Northern England 1000–1700* (Stroud, Glos, 1997), pp. 104–16.

Butler, Audrey, "Clemence Tresham, of Rushton and Syon," *Northamptonshire Past and Present* 5 (1974), 91–93.

Butler, L. H., "Robert Braybrooke Bishop of London (1381–1404) and His Kinsmen," Ph.D. thesis, Oxford University, 1951.

Byrne, Muriel St. Clare (ed.), *The Lisle Letters*, 6 vols., University of Chicago Press, 1981. Abridged edition, University of Chicago Press, 1983.

Candon, Sister Mary Patrick, R.S.M. "The Doctrine of the Hert," Ph.D. thesis, Fordham University, 1963.

Carter, Patrick, "Barking Abbey and the Library of William Pownsett: A Bibliographical Conundrum," *TCBS* 10 (1998), 263–71.

A Catalogue of the Manuscripts Preserved in the Library of the University of Cambridge, 5 vols., Cambridge, 1856–67.

Cavanaugh, Susan H., "A Study of Books Privately Owned in England: 1300–1450," Ph.D. thesis, University of Pennsylvania, 1980.

Cheney, Denton, "The Holy Maid of Kent," *TRHS* 18 (1904), 107–29.

Christ, Karl, *The Handbook of Medieval Library History*. Reprint edition. Metuchen, N.J. and London, 1984.

Christie's Sale Catalogue, "The Library of William Foyle, Part I: Medieval and Renaissance Manuscripts" (Tuesday, July 11, 2000), 218–20.

Christine de Pizan, *The Book of the City of Ladies*, trans. Earl Jeffrey Richards, New York, 1982.

Clay, John W. (ed.), *North Country Wills*, Surtees Society 116, Durham, 1899.

Clay, Rotha Mary, "Further Studies in Mediaeval Recluses," *JBAA*, 3rd ser. 16 (1953), 74–86.

The Hermits and Anchorites of England, London, 1914.

Claydon, Muriel, *A Collection of Rubbings of Brasses and Incised Slabs...* London, 1915.

Coates, Alan, *English Medieval Books: The Reading Abbey Collections from Foundation to Dispersal*, Oxford, 1999.

Cobban, Alan B., "Pembroke College: Its Educational Significance in Late Medieval Cambridge," *TCBS* 10 (1991), 1–16.

Coldicott, Diana K., *Hampshire Nunneries*, Chichester, Sussex, 1989.

Colledge, Eric, "*The Recluse*: A Lollard Interpolated Version of the *Ancren Riwle*," *RES* 15 (1950), 1–15, 129–45.

Collins, A. Jefferies (ed.), *The Bridgettine Breviary of Syon Abbey*, Henry Bradshaw Society 96, Worcester, 1969.

Collinson, Patrick, review of Perez Zagorin, *Ways of Lying* (Cambridge, Mass. 1990) in *TLS* March 1, 1991.

Collis, Jennifer, "The Anchorites of London in the Late Middle Ages," MA thesis, University of London, 1992.

Connolly, Margaret (ed.), *Contemplations of the Drede and Love of God*, EETS 303, Oxford, 1993.

Cooke, Kathleen, "The English Nuns and the Dissolution," in J. Blair and B. Golding (eds.), *The Cloister and the World: Essays in Medieval History in Honour of Barbara Harvey* (Oxford, 1996), pp. 287–301.

Cooper, C. H., *Memoir of Margaret, Countess of Richmond and Derby*, Cambridge, 1874.

Cotman, John Sell, *Engravings of Sepulchral Brasses in Norfolk and Suffolk*, 2 vols., London, 1839.

Cozens-Hardy, Basil and Ernest A. Kent (eds.), *The Mayors of Norwich 1403 to 1835*, Norwich, 1938.

Crawford, Anne, "Victims of Attainder: The Howard and de Vere Women in the Late Fifteenth Century," *Reading Medieval Studies* 15 (1989), 59–74.

Croft, Henry Herbert Stephen (ed.), *The Boke Named the Gouernour*, 2 vols., London, 1880.

Croft, P. J., *Lady Margaret Beaufort... Elizabeth of York and Wynkyn de Worde*, London, 1958.

Cross, Claire, *The End of Medieval Monasticism in the East Riding of Yorkshire*, East Yorkshire Local History Society no. 47, Beverley, 1993.

" 'Great Reasoners in Scripture': The Activities of Women Lollards 1380–1530," in D. Baker (ed.), *Medieval Women*, Studies in Church History Subsidia (Oxford, 1978), pp. 359–80.

"A Medieval Yorkshire Library." *Northern History* 25 (1989), 281–90.

Cross, Claire and Noreen Vickers (eds.), *Monks, Friars and Nuns in Sixteenth-Century Yorkshire*, Yorkshire Archaeological Society 150, Huddersfield, 1995.

Cusack, Bridget, "A Critical Edition of William Bonde's *Consolatori . . .* ", MA thesis, University of London, 1963.

Cyprian, Saint, "On the Mortality," trans. in *Ante-Nicene Fathers of the Third Century: Hippolytus, Cyprian, Caius, Novatian*, vol 5, Grand Rapids, Mich. 1951.

Dalton, John Neal (ed.), *The Manuscripts of St. George's Chapel, Windsor Castle*, Windsor, 1957.

Daniell, David, *William Tyndale: A Biography*, New Haven and London, 1994.

Darlington, Ida (ed.), *London Consistory Court Wills 1492–1547*, London Record Society 3 (1967).

Davis, G. R. C. (ed.), *Medieval Cartularies of Great Britain*, London, 1958.

Davis, John F., *Heresy and Reformation in the South-East of England, 1520–1559*, London and New Jersey, 1983.

"The Trials of Thomas Bylney and the English Reformation," *The Historical Journal* 24 (1981), 775–90.

Davis, Norman (ed.), *Paston Letters and Papers of the Fifteenth Century*, 2 vols., Oxford, 1971, 1976.

Day, John T., "William Tracy's Posthumous Legal Problems," in J. A. R. Dick and A. Richardson (eds.), *William Tyndale and the Law*, Sixteenth-Century Essays and Studies 25 (Kirksville, Mo., 1994), pp. 103–13.

Dean, Ruth J. and M. Domenica Legge (eds.), *The Rule of St. Benedict: A Norman Prose Version*, Oxford, 1964.

Deanesly, Margaret, *The Incendium Amoris of Richard Rolle of Hampole*, Manchester, 1915.

De Hamel, Christopher, *A History of Illuminated Manuscripts*, Oxford, 1986.

Syon Abbey, The Library of the Bridgettine Nuns and Their Peregrinations after the Reformation, Roxburghe Club, Otley, 1991.

Demaus, R., *William Tindale*, London, 1871.

Denise, Sister M., "The *Orchard of Syon*: An Introduction," *Traditio* 14 (1958), 269–93.

De Ricci, Seymour, *A Census of Caxtons*, Bibliographical Society Illustrated Monograph 15, Oxford, 1909.

Dickens, A. G., *The English Reformation*, New York, 1964.

Dingley, Thomas, *History from Marble, Compiled in the Reign of Charles II by Thomas Dingley*, 2 vols., Camden Society 94, 97, Westminster, 1867, 1868.

Dobson, R. B., *Durham Priory 1400–1450*, Cambridge, 1973.

Dodwell, Barbara, "The Monastic Community," in I. Atherton, E. Fernie, C. Harper-Bill, and H. Smith (eds.), *Norwich Cathedral, Church, City and Diocese 1096–1996* (London and Rio Grande, 1996), pp. 231–54.

Dowling, Maria, *Humanism in the Age of Henry VIII*, London, 1986.

Doyle, A. I. "Book Production by the Monastic Orders in England (*c.* 1375–1530): Assessing the Evidence," in L. L. Brownrigg (ed.), *Medieval Book Production: Assessing the Evidence* (Los Altos Hills, 1990), pp. 1–19.

"Books Connected with the Vere Family and Barking Abbey," *TEAS* n.s. 25 (1958), 222–43.

"The English Provincial Book Trade before Printing," in P. Isaac (ed.), *Six Centuries of the Provincial Book Trade in Britain* (Winchester, 1990), pp. 13–29.

"Stephen Dodesham of Witham and Sheen," in P. Robinson and R. Zim (eds.), *Of the Making of Books: Medieval Manuscripts, Their Scribes and Readers, Essays Presented to M. B. Parkes* (London, 1997), pp. 94–115.

"The Study of Nicholas Love's *Mirror*, Retrospect and Prospect," in S. Oguro, R. Beadle, and M. Sargent (eds.), *Nicholas Love at Waseda: Proceedings of the International Conference, 20–22 July, 1995* (Cambridge and Rochester, NY, 1997), pp. 163–74.

"A Survey of the Origins and Circulation of Theological Writings in English in the 14th, 15th and Early 16th Centuries with Special Consideration of the Part of the Clergy Therein," Ph.D. thesis, University of Cambridge, 1954.

DuBoulay, F. R. H., "The Quarrel between the Carmelite Friars and the Secular Clergy of London 1464–1468," *JEH* 6 (1955), 156–74.

Dugdale, William, *Antiquities of Warwickshire*, 2 vols., London, 1730.

Monasticon Anglicanum, ed. J. Caley, H. Ellis, and B. Bandinel. 6 vols. in 8 (1817–30).

Dumortier, Jean (ed.), *Jean Chrysostome à Theodore*, Paris, 1966.

Dunn, F. I. "Hermits, Anchorites and Recluses: A Study with Reference to Medieval Norwich," in F. D. Sayer (ed.), *Julian and Her Norwich* (Norwich, 1973).

Dutschke, C. W. and R. H. Rouse, *Medieval and Renaissance Manuscripts in the Claremont Libraries*, Berkeley, 1980.

Dutton, Anne M., "Passing the Book: Testamentary Transmission of Religious Literature to and by Women in England 1350–1500," in L. Smith and J. H. M. Taylor, (eds,) *Women, the Book and the Godly: Selected Proceedings of the St. Hilda's Conference 1993, Vol. I* (Cambridge, 1995), pp. 41–54.

Eade, Peter, *Some Account of the Parish of St. Giles, Norwich*, 2nd edn, London and Norwich, 1906.

Edwards, A. S. G., "The Transmission and Audience of Osbern Bokenham's *Legendys of Hooly Wummen*," in A. J. Minnis (ed.), *Late-Medieval Religious Texts and Their Transmission* (Woodbridge, Suffolk, 1994), pp. 157–68.

Egbert, Donald Drew, "The So-Called 'Greenfield' *La lumiere as lais* and *Apocalypse . . .*," *Speculum* 11 (1930), 446–52.

Ekwall, Eilert (ed.), *The Concise Oxford Dictionary of English Place-Names*, Oxford, 1960.

Ellis, Henry (ed.), *The New Chronicles of England and France*, London, 1811.

Elm, Kaspar, "Die Stellung der Frau in Ordenswesen, Semireligiosentum und Häresie zur Zeit der Heiligen Elisabeth," in *Sankt Elisabeth, Fürstin, Dienerin, Heilige*, Sigmaringen, 1981.

Select bibliography

"Vita Regularis sine Regula: Bedeutung, Rechtsstellung und Selbstverständnis des Mittelalterlichen und frühneuzeitlichen Semireligiosentums," in F. Smahel (ed.), *Häresie und Vorzeitige Reformation im Spätmittelalter* (Munich, 1998).

Erbe, Theodore (ed.), *Mirk's Festial: A Collection of Homilies by . . . John Mirk*, EETS ES 96, London, 1905.

Erler, Mary C., "The Abbess of Malling's Gift Manuscript (1520)," in F. Riddy (ed.), *Prestige, Authority, and Power in Late Medieval Manuscripts and Texts*, (York, 2000), pp. 147–57.

"Bishop Richard Fox's Manuscript Gifts to his Winchester Nuns: A Second Surviving Example," *JEH* 52 (2001), 1–4.

"Devotional Literature," in L. Hellinga and J. B. Trapp (eds.), *The Cambridge History of the Book in Britain. Vol. III: 1400–1557* (Cambridge, 1999), pp. 495–525.

"Exchange of Books between Nuns and Laywomen: Three Surviving Examples," in Beadle and Piper (eds.), *New Science*, pp. 360–73.

"Pasted-In Embellishments in English Manuscripts and Printed Books *c.* 1480–1533," *The Library* sixth ser. 14 (1992), 185–206.

"Three Fifteenth-Century Vowesses," in Barron and Sutton, *Widows*, pp. 165–84.

Evans, John, "Extracts from the Private Account Book of Sir William More, of Loseley, in Surrey, in the Time of Queen Mary and of Queen Elizabeth," *Archaeologia* 36 (1855), 284–310.

Everett, Dorothy, "The Middle English Prose Psalter of Richard Rolle of Hampole," *MLR* 17 (1922), 217–27; 18 (1923), 281–93.

Fetherston, John (ed.), *The Visitation of the County of Warwick in the Year 1619, taken by William Camden . . .*, Harleian Society Publications 12, London, 1877.

Fifty-Five Books Printed before 1525 . . . An Exhibition from the Collection of Paul Mellon, Grolier Club, no place, 1968.

Fisher, John. *The English Works of John Fisher, Part I*, ed. John E. B. Mayor, EETS ES 27, London, 1876.

Fletcher, J. R., "History of Syon Abbey 1539–1563," notebook, deposited at Exeter University Library.

The Story of the English Bridgettines of Syon Abbey, South Brent, Devon, 1933.

Fletcher, John, "Slices from a Deep Cake: Dating Panel Paintings of St. Etheldreda from Ely," *Country Life* (March 28, 1974), 728–30.

"Four Scenes from the Life of St. Etheldreda," *Antiquaries Journal* 54 (1974), 287–89.

Foister, Susan, "Paintings and Other Works of Art in Sixteenth-Century English Inventories," *Burlington Magazine* 123 (May 1981), 273–82.

Foster, Joseph (ed.), *Alumni Oxonienses . . . 1500–1714*, 4 vols., Oxford, 1891.

Fowler, R. C. and C. Jenkins (eds.), *Registrum Simonis de Sudbiria Diocesis Londoniensis, A.D. 1362–1375*, 2 vols., Canterbury and York, Society 34, 38, London, 1927–38.

Foxe, John, *Acts and Monuments*, ed. George Townsend, 8 vols., London, 1843.

Franks, A. W., "The Genealogical History of the Freville Family," *Publications of the Cambridge Antiquarian Society* 2, no. 14 (1848), 21–29.

Frere, W. H., *Bibliotheca Musico-Liturgica*, 2 vols., London, 1894, 1932.

Freshfield, Edwin, "On the Parish Books of St. Margaret-Lothbury, St. Christopher-le-Stocks, and St. Bartholomew-by-the-Exchange, in the City of London," *Archaeologia* 45 (1877), 57–123.

Freshfield, Edwin (ed.), *Wills, Leases and Memoranda in the Book of Records of the Parish of St. Christopher le Stocks*, London, 1895.

Friedmann, Paul, *Anne Boleyn: A Chapter of English History 1527–1536*, 2 vols., London, 1884.

Furnivall, F. J. (ed.), *The Fifty Earliest English Wills*, EETS os 78, London, 1882.

Gairdner, James, "A Letter Concerning Bishop Fisher and Sir Thomas More," *EHR* 7 (1892), 712–15.

Gee, J. A., "John Byddell and the First Publication of Erasmus' Enchiridion in English." *ELH* 4 (1937), 43–59.

Gibbons, A. (ed.), *Ely Episcopal Records: A Calendar and Concise View of the Episcopal Records*, Lincoln, 1891.

Gibson, Gail McMurray, *The Theater of Devotion: East Anglian Drama and Society in the Late Middle Ages*, Chicago, 1989.

Gibson, Strickland, "Fragments from Bindings at the Queens College Oxford," *The Library* 4th ser. 12 (1931–32), 429–33.

Gilchrist, Roberta, *Gender and Material Culture: the Archaeology of Religious Women*, London, 1994.

Gilchrist, Roberta and Marilyn Oliva, *Religious Women in Medieval East Anglia*. Studies in East Anglian History 1, Norwich, 1993.

Gillespie, Vincent, "*Lukynge in haly bukes*: *Lectio* in Some Late Medieval Spiritual Miscellanies," *Analecta Cartusiana* 106 (1984), 1–27.

"Vernacular Books of Religion," in J. Griffiths and D. Pearsall, (eds.), *Book Production and Publishing in Britain 1375–1475* (Cambridge, 1989), pp. 317–44.

Gillow, Joseph, *A . . . Bibliographical Dictionary of the English Catholics . . .* , 5 vols., London, 1885–1903.

Gilroy, Jane I, "The Reception of Bridget of Sweden's 'Revelations' in Late Medieval and Early Renaissance England," Ph.D. thesis, Fordham University, 1999.

Goldberg, Jonathan, *Desiring Women Writing*, Stanford, 1997.

Goldberg, P. J. P., "Lay Book Ownership in Late Medieval York: The Evidence of Wills," *The Library* 6th ser. 16 (1994), 181–89.

Goodman, Anthony, *The Loyal Conspiracy: The Lords Appellant under Richard II*, London, 1971.

Görlach, Manfred, *Studies in Middle English Saints' Legends*, Heidelberg, 1998.

Green, Richard Firth, *A Crisis of Truth: Literature and Law in Ricardian England*, Philadelphia, 1999.

Green, V. H., *Bishop Reginald Pecock: A Study in Ecclesiastical History and Thought*, Cambridge, 1945.

Guy, John, *The Public Career of Sir Thomas More*, Brighton, 1980.

Hackett, M. B., "William Flete and the De Remediis Contra Temptaciones," in J. A. Watt, J. B. Morrall, and F. X. Martin (eds.), *Medieval Studies Presented to Aubrey Gwynn, S. J.*, (Dublin, 1961), pp. 330–48.

Select bibliography

Hanna III, Ralph (ed.), *The Index of Middle English Prose. Handlist XII: Smaller Bodleian Collections* ... (Woodbridge, Suffolk, 1997).

Harley, Marta Powell (ed.), *The Myrour of Recluses: A Middle English Translation of Speculum Inclusarum*, Rutherford, N.J., 1995.

Harris, Barbara J. "A New Look at the Reformation: Aristocratic Women and Nunneries 1450–1540," *JBS* 3 (1993), 89–113.

Harrod, Henry, "Extracts from Early Wills in the Norwich Registries," *Norfolk Archaeology* 4 (1855), 317–19.

Hartshorne, C. H., "Illustrations of Domestic Manners during the Reign of Edward I," *JBAA* 18 (1862), 60–75, 145–52, 213–20, 318–32.

Harvey, Barbara, *Living and Dying in England 1100–1540, The Monastic Experience*, Oxford, 1993.

Harvey, E. Ruth (ed.), "Image of Love," in T. M. C. Lawler, G. Marc'hadour, and R. C. Marius (eds.), *Complete Works of More*, vol. 6, New Haven, 1981.

Heberden, C. B. (ed.), *Brasenose College Register 1509–1909*, 2 vols., Oxford, 1909.

Hennessey, George, *Novum Repertorium Ecclesiasticum Parochiale Londinense*, reprint edn London, 1989.

Herrtage, Sidney J. H. (ed.), *Early English Versions of the Gesta Romanorum*, EETS ES 33, London, 1879.

Hicks, Michael, "The Last Days of Elizabeth, Countess of Oxford," *EHR* 103 (1988), 76–95.

Hill, Betty, "Some Problems in Washington, Library of Congress MS Faye-Bond 4," in J. Lachlan Mackenzie and R. Todd (eds.), *In Other Words: Transcultural Studies in Philology, Translation, and Lexicology Presented to Hans Heinrich Meier* ..., (Dordrecht, 1989), pp. 35–44.

Hodgett, G. A. J., *The State of the Ex-Religious and Former Chantry Priests in the Diocese of Lincoln 1547–1574 from Returns in the Exchequer*, Lincoln Record Society 58, Hereford, 1959.

Hodnett, Edward, *English Woodcuts 1480–1535. Additions & Corrections*, London, 1973.

Hogg, James (ed.), *The Rewyll of Seynt Sauioure and Other Middle English Brigittine Legislative Texts*, 4 vols., Salzburg, 1978–80.

Hogrefe, Pearl, *The Life and Times of Sir Thomas Elyot, Englishman*, Ames, Ia, 1967.

Hope, William St. John (ed.), *The History of the London Charterhouse from Its Foundation until the Suppression of the Monastery*, London, 1925.

Hopkinson, H. L., "Ancient Bradestrete Identical with Threadneedle Street," *London Topographical Record* 13 (1923), 23–28.

Horn, Joyce M. (ed.), *The Register of Robert Hallum, Bishop of Salisbury 1407–17*, Canterbury and York Society 72, Torquay, 1982.

Horstmann, Carl, "Marienlegenden," *Anglia* 3 (1880), 320–25.

Hudson, Anne, *The Premature Reformation: Wycliffite Texts and Lollard History*, Oxford, 1988.

Hudson, Anne (ed.), *Two Wycliffite Texts* ..., EETS os 301, Oxford, 1993.

Hudson, Anne and H. L. Spencer, "Old Author, New Work: The Sermons of MS Longleat 4," *Medium Ævum* 53 (1984), 220–38.

Hudson, W. and J. C. Tingey (eds.), *The Records of the City of Norwich*, 2 vols., Norwich, 1906–10.

Hughes, Jonathan, *Pastors and Visionaries: Religious and Secular Life in Late Medieval Yorkshire*, Woodbridge, Suffolk, 1988.

Hughes, Paul L. and James F. Larkin (eds.), *Tudor Royal Proclamations*, 3 vols., New Haven and London, 1964–69.

Jacob, E. F. (ed.), *Register of Henry Chichele, Archbishop of Canterbury 1414–1443*, 4 vols., London, 1938–47.

James, M. R., "Description of the Ancient Manuscripts in the Ipswich Public Library," *Proceedings of the Suffolk Institute of Archaeology and Natural History* 22 (1935), 95–99.

James M. R. (ed.), *A Descriptive Catalogue of the Manuscripts in the Library of Corpus Christi College Cambridge*, 2 vols., Cambridge, 1912.

James, M. R. and E. G. Millar (eds.), *The Bohun Manuscripts*, Roxburghe Club, Oxford, 1936.

James, Susan E., *Kateryn Parr, The Making of a Queen*, Aldershot, Hants., 1999.

Jenkinson, Hilary, "Mary de Sancto Paulo, Foundress of Pembroke College Cambridge," *Archaeologia* 66 (1914–15), 401–46.

The Jerusalem Bible: Reader's Edition, New York, 1966.

Jessopp, A. (ed.), *Visitations of the Diocese of Norwich 1492–1532*, Camden Society n.s. 43, London, 1888.

Johnston, F. R., "Syon Abbey," in *VCH Middlesex* I.

Jolliffe, P. S., "Middle English Translations of the *De Exterioris et Interioris Hominis Compositione*," *Mediaeval Studies* 36 (1974), 259–77.

Jones, E. Alfred, *The Old Plate of the Cambridge Colleges*, Cambridge, 1910.

Jones, Michael K. and Malcolm G. Underwood, *The King's Mother: Lady Margaret Beaufort, Countess of Richmond and Derby*, Cambridge, 1992.

Keene, Derek and Vanessa Harding (eds.), *Historical Gazeteer of London before the Great Fire: Cheapside*, London, 1987.

Kelly, Henry Ansgar, "Meanings and Uses of *Raptus* in Chaucer's Time," *Studies in the Age of Chaucer* 20 (1998), 101–65.

'A Neo-Revisionist Look at Chaucer's Nuns," *Chaucer Review* 31 (1996), 115–32.

"Statutes of Rapes and Alleged Ravishers of Wives: A Context for the Charges Against Thomas Malory, Knight," *Viator* 28 (1997), 351–419.

Ker, N. R., "Oxford College Libraries before 1500," in A. G. Watson (ed.), *Books, Collectors and Libraries: Studies in the Medieval Heritage* (London and Rouncevert, 1985), pp. 301–20.

Ker, N. R. (ed.), *Medieval Libraries of Great Britain: A List of Surviving Books*, 2nd edn, London, 1964.

Medieval Manuscripts in British Libraries, 4 vols., London, 1969–92.

Kerr, Berenice M., *Religious Life for Women c. 1100 – c. 1350, Fontevraud in England*, Oxford, 1999.

Kirby, Joan (ed.), *The Plumpton Letters and Papers*, Camden 5th ser. vol. 8, Cambridge, 1996.

Kitching, C. J. (ed.), *London and Middlesex Chantry Certificate 1548*, London Record Society 16, London, 1980.

Knowles, David, *The Religious Orders in England*, 3 vols., Cambridge, 1948–61.

Knowles, David and R. Neville Hadcock, *Medieval Religious Houses: England and Wales*, London, 1953.

Korsten, Frans (ed.), *A Catalogue of the Library of Thomas Baker*, Cambridge, 1990.

Krochalis, Jeanne, "The Benedictine Rule for Nuns: Library of Congress, MS 4," *Manuscripta* 30 (1986), 21–34.

Kuczynski, Michael P., *Prophetic Song: The Psalms as Moral Discourse in Late Medieval England*, Philadelphia, 1995.

Labarge, Margaret Wade, "Eleanor de Montfort's Household Rolls," *History Today* 11 (1961), 490–500.

Laing, M. and K. Williamson (eds.), *Speaking in Our Tongues: Proceedings of a Colloquium on Medieval Dialectology and Related Disciplines*, Cambridge, 1994.

Langton, William (ed.), *Visitation of Lancashire...1533*, Chetham Society 98, Manchester, 1876.

Lasko, P. and N. J. Morgan, *Medieval Art in East Anglia 1300–1520*, Norwich and London, 1974.

Lawless, Catherine, "'A Widow of God'? St. Anne and Representations of Widowhood in Fifteenth-Century Florence," in C. Meek (ed.), *Women in Renaissance and Early Modern Europe*, Dublin, 2000.

Leach, A. F., "Childrey School," in *VCH Berkshire*, II. 275–76.

"St. Anthony's Hospital and School," in W. Besant (ed.), *London City* (London, 1910), pp. 407–29.

Leadam, I. S. and J. F. Baldwin (eds.), *Select Cases before the King's Council 1243–1482*, Selden Society 36, Cambridge, Mass., 1918.

Lee, Paul, *Nunneries, Learning and Spirituality in Late Medieval English Society: The Dominican Priory of Dartford*, York, 2001.

Lehmberg, Stanford E., *The Reformation Parliament 1529–1536*, Cambridge, 1970.

Sir Thomas Elyot, Tudor Humanist, Austin, Tx., 1960.

"Sir Thomas More's Life of Pico della Mirandola," *Studies in the Renaissance* 3 (1956), 61–74.

Lewis, R. E. and A. McIntosh (eds.), *A Descriptive Guide to the Manuscripts of the Prick of Conscience*, Medium Ævum Monographs n.s. 12, Oxford, 1982.

Leyerle, Blake, "John Chrysostom on the Gaze," *Journal of Early Christian Studies* 1 (1993), 159–74.

Lightbown, Ronald W., *Medieval European Jewellery*, London, 1992.

Lipscomb, George, *The History and Antiquities of the County of Buckingham*, 4 vols., London, 1847.

Litzenberger, Caroline, *The English Reformation and the Laity: Gloucestershire 1540–1580*, Cambridge, 1997.

Loftus, E. A. and H. F. Chettle, *A History of Barking Abbey*, Barking, 1954.

Logan, F. Donald, *Runaway Religious in Medieval England c. 1240–1540*, Cambridge, 1996.

London, Vera C. M. (ed.), *The Cartulary of Canonsleigh Abbey...*, Devon and Cornwall Record Society n.s. 8, 1965.

Lowndes, G. Alan, "History of the Priory at Hatfield Regis Alias Hatfield Broad Oak," *TEAS* n.s. 2 (1884), 117–52.

Lysons, Daniel, *The Environs of London*, 4 vols., London, 1792–96.

McFarlane, K. B., *Lancastrian Kings and Lollard Knights*, Oxford, 1972.

McGerr, Rosemarie Potz (ed.), *The Pilgrimage of the Soul*, New York, 1990.

McHardy, A. K., (ed.), *The Church in London 1375–1392*, London Record Society 13, London, 1977.

McIntosh, Angus, M. L. Samuels, and Michael Benskin (eds.), *A Linguistic Atlas of Late Medieval English*, 4 vols., Aberdeen, 1986.

McKitterick, David, "The Survival of Books," *The Book Collector* 43 (1994), 9–26.

McSheffrey, Shannon, *Gender and Heresy: Women and Men in Lollard Communities 1420–1530*, Philadelphia, 1995.

Madden, Frederick (ed.), *Privy Purse Expenses of Princess Mary*, London, 1831.

Maddern, Philippa, *Violence and Social Order in East Anglia 1422–1442*, Oxford, 1992.

Major, John M., *Sir Thomas Elyot and Renaissance Humanism*, Lincoln, Nebr., 1964.

Makowski, Elizabeth, *Canon Law and Cloistered Women: Periculoso and Its Commentators 1298–1545*, Washington D.C., 1997.

Mander, Nicholas, "Painted Cloths: History, Craftsmen and Techniques," *Textile History* 28 (1997), 110–48.

Manion, Margaret M., Vera F. Vines, and Christopher de Hamel (eds.), *Medieval and Renaissance Manuscripts in New Zealand Collections*, Melbourne, 1989.

Maxfield, David K., "St. Anthony's Hospital London: A Pardoner-Supported Alien Priory, 1219–1461," in J. L. Gillespie (ed.), *The Age of Richard II* (New York, 1997), pp. 225–47.

Meale, Carol, "'..alle the Bokes that I haue of Latyn, Englisch, and Frensch': Laywomen and their Books in Late Medieval England," in Meale (ed.), *Women and Literature*, pp. 128–58.

"The Miracles of Our Lady: Context and Interpretation," in Derek Pearsall, (ed.), *Studies in the Vernon Manuscript* (Woodbridge, Suffolk, 1990), pp. 115–36.

Meale, Carol, (ed.), *Women and Literature in Britain 1150–1500*, Cambridge, 1993.

Meek, Edward, "Printing and the English Parish Clergy in the Later Middle Ages," *TCBS* 11 (1997), 112–26.

Mierow, C. C. trans., *The Letters of St. Jerome*, in *Ancient Christian Writers* 33, Westminster, Md., 1963.

Moore Smith, G. C., *The Family of Withypoll*, Walthamstow Antiquarian Society Publications 34, Walthamstow, 1936.

Moorman, R. H., *The Grey Friars in Cambridge 1225–1538*, Cambridge, 1952.

Moran, Jo Ann Hoeppner, *The Growth of English Schooling 1340–1548: Learning, Literacy, and Laicization in Pre-Reformation York Diocese*, Princeton, N.J., 1985.

More, Thomas, *English Poems, Life of Pico, the Last Things*, ed. A. S. G. Edwards, K. G. Rodgers, and C. H. Miller, vol. 1 in *Complete Works of St. Thomas More*, New Haven, 1997.

Select bibliography

A Dialogue Concerning Heresies, ed. T. M. C. Lawler, G. Marc'hadour, and R. C. Marius, vol. 6 in *Complete Works of St. Thomas More*, New Haven, 1981.

The Confutation of Tyndale's Answer, ed. L. A. Schuster, R. C. Marius, J. P. Lusardi, and R. J. Schoeck, vol. 8, in *Complete Works of St. Thomas More*, New Haven, 1973.

Moreton, C. E., "The 'Diary' of a Late Fifteenth-Century Lawyer," in S. Michalove and A. C. Reeves (eds.), *Estrangement, Enterprise and Education in Fifteenth-Century England* (Sutton, 1998), pp. 27–45.

"The 'Library' of a Late-Fifteenth-Century Lawyer," *The Library* 13 (1991), 338–46.

The Townshends and Their World: Gentry, Law, and Land in Norfolk, c. 1450–1551, Oxford, 1992.

Morgan, Nigel, *Early Gothic Manuscripts (1) 1190–1250* and *(2) 1250–85*, London, 1982, 1988.

"Texts and Images of Marian Devotion in Fourteenth-Century England," in N. Rogers (ed.), *England in the Fourteenth Century: Proceedings of the 1991 Harlaxton Symposium* (Stamford, 1993), pp. 34–57.

"Texts of Devotion and Religious Instruction Associated with Margaret of York," in T. Kren (ed.), *Margaret of York, Simon Marmion and 'The Visions of Tondal'* (Malibu, Calif., 1992), pp. 63–76.

Morgan, Paul, "Frances Wolfreston and 'Hor Bouks,'" *The Library* 11 (1989), 197–219.

Moriarty, G. Andrews, "The Early Throckmortons," *Miscellanea Genealogica et Heraldica*, 5th ser. VI, pts. vi and vii (1927), 228–53.

Morley, T. H., *Monumental Brasses of Berkshire*, n.p., 1924.

Morris, John, S. J., *The Troubles of Our Catholic Forefathers...*, 2 vols., London, 1872–75.

Mozley, J. T., *William Tyndale*, London, 1937.

Munro, C. (ed.), *Letters of Queen Margaret of Anjou*, Camden Society no. 86, London, 1863.

Nash, T. (ed.), *Collections for the History of Worcestershire*, 2 vols., 2nd edn, London, 1799.

Naughton, Joan, "Books for a Dominican Nuns Choir: Illustrated Liturgical Manuscripts at Saint-Louis de Poissy, c. 1330–1350," in M. M. Manion and B. J. Muir (eds.), *The Art of the Book, Its Place in Medieval Worship* (Exeter, 1998), pp. 67–110.

Neame, Alan, *The Holy Maid of Kent: The Life of Elizabeth Barton 1506–1534*, London, 1971.

Nevanlinna, Saara and Irma Taavitsainen (eds.), *St. Katherine of Alexandria: The Late Middle English Prose Legend in Southwell Minster MS 7*, Woodbridge, Suffolk, 1993.

Newcourt, Richard, *Repertorium Ecclesiasticum Parochiae Londinense...*, 2 vols., London, 1708.

New Interpreter's Bible, Vol. III, Nashville, Tenn., 1999.

Nichols, Francis Morgan (ed.), *The Epistles of Erasmus*, 3 vols., New York, 1962.

Nichols, John, *Bibliotheca Topographica Britannica*, 8 vols., London, 1780–90.

Nichols, John, (ed.), *A Collection of All the Wills... of the Kings and Queens of England*, London, 1780.

Nicolas, N. H. "Pedigrees Showing the Relationship between Many of the Nobility and Gentry and the Blood Royal . . . ," *Collectanea Topographica et Genealogica* 1 (1834), no. XII.

Nicolas, N. H. (ed.), *Privy Purse Expenses of Elizabeth of York*, London, 1830.

Nixon, Howard M. and Mirjam M. Foot, *The History of Decorated Bookbinding in England*, Oxford, 1992.

Nugent, Elizabeth (ed.), *The Thought and Culture of the English Renaissance: An Anthology of Tudor Prose 1481–1555*, 2 vols., Cambridge, 1954.

Oates, J. C. T., *A Catalogue of the Fifteenth-Century Printed Books in the University Library Cambridge*, Cambridge, 1954.

"Old Shropshire Wills: Part II," *Transactions of the Shropshire Archaeological and Natural History Society* 6 (1883), 319–25.

Oliva, Marilyn, *The Convent and the Community in Late Medieval England: Female Monasteries in the Diocese of Norwich, 1350–1540*, Woodbridge, Suffolk, 1998.

Oliva, Marilyn and Roberta Gilchrist, *Religious Women in Medieval East Anglia: History and Archaeology c. 1100–1540*, Studies in East Anglian History 1, Norwich, 1993.

O'Malley, John W. (ed.), *Collected Works of Erasmus: Enchiridion . . .*, vol. 66, Toronto, 1988.

Oman, Charles, *English Church Plate*, Oxford, 1957.

British Rings 800–1914, London, 1974.

O'Mara, V. M. (ed.), *A Study and Edition of Selected Middle English Sermons*, Leeds Texts and Monographs n.s. 13, Leeds, 1994.

Orme, Nicholas, *English Schools in the Middle Ages*, London, 1973.

Owen, Dorothy M., *John Lydford's Book*, London, 1974.

Pächt, Otto and J. J. G. Alexander (eds.), *Illuminated Manuscripts in the Bodleian Library Oxford*, 3 vols., Oxford, 1973.

Palmer, C. F. R., "History of the Priory of Dartford, in Kent," *Archaeological Journal* 36 (1879), 241–71.

"Notes on the Priory of Dartford, in Kent," *Archaeological Journal* 39 (1882), 177–79.

Pantin. W. A., "Instructions for a Devout and Literate Layman," in J. J. G. Alexander and M. T. Gibson (eds.), *Medieval Learning and Literature* (Oxford, 1976), pp. 398–422.

Parmiter, Geoffrey de C., "Plowden, Englefield and Sandford: I. 1558–85," *Recusant History* 13 (1976), 159–77.

Parrey, Yvonne, " 'Devoted Disciples of Christ': Early Sixteenth-Century Religious Life in the Nunnery at Amesbury," *BIHR* 67 (1994), 240–48.

Paxton, Catherine, "The Nunneries of London and Its Environs in the Later Middle Ages," Ph.D. thesis, University of Oxford, 1993.

Peck, Russell A. (ed.), *Heroic Women from the Old Testament in Middle English Verse*, Kalamazoo, 1991.

Pevsner, Nikolaus, *North-West and South Norfolk*, Harmondsworth, Mx, 1962.

Pezzini, Domenico, " 'The Meditacion of Oure Lordis Passyon' and Other Bridgettine Texts in MS Lambeth 432," *Analecta Cartusiana. Studies in St. Birgitta and the Bridgettine Order* 1 (1993), 276–95.

Pickering, O. S. and V. M. O'Mara (eds.), *Index of Middle English Prose. Handlist XII, Manuscripts in Lambeth Palace Library...*, Woodbridge, Suffolk, 1999.

The Plumpton Letters and Papers, ed. J. Kirby, Camden 5th ser. 8, Cambridge, 1996.

Pointon, Marcia, *Strategies for Showing: Women, Possession, and Representation in English Visual Culture 1665–1800*, Oxford, 1997.

Pollard, William F., "Bodleian MS Holkham Misc. 41: A Fifteenth-Century Bridgettine Manuscript and Prayer Cycle," *Birgittiana* 3 (1997), 43–53.

"The Festis and the Passion of Oure Lord Ihesu Crist," in M. Glasscoe (ed.), *The Medieval Mystical Tradition in England. Exeter Symposium IV. Papers Read at Darlington Hall, July 1987* (Woodbridge, Suffolk, 1987), pp. 47–61.

Pollock, Frederick and F. W. Maitland, *The History of English Law before the Time of Edward I*, 2 vols., Cambridge, 1968.

Polychronicon Ranulphi Higden, (ed.) Joseph Rawson Lumby. Rerum Britannicarum Medii Ævi Scriptores vol. 9, London, 1886.

Pound, John F., "The Social and Trade Structure of Norwich 1525–1575," *Past & Present* 34 (1966), 49–69.

Tudor and Stuart Norwich, Chichester, 1988.

Powell, Susan, "Lady Margaret Beaufort and Her Books," *The Library* 6th ser. 20 (1998), 197–240.

Power, Eileen, *Medieval English Nunneries c. 1275 to 1535* (Cambridge, 1922).

Powicke, F. M. and C. R. Cheyney (eds.), *Councils & Synods with Other Documents Relating to the English Church AD 1205–1313*, 2 vols., Oxford, 1964.

Raine, James (ed.), *Testamenta Eboracensia*, 6 vols., Surtees Society 4, 30, 45, 53, 79, 106, Durham, 1836–1902.

Raines, F. R. (ed.), *Examynytyons Towcheynge Cokeye More...*, Chetham Society Miscellanies 2 (1855).

Ramsay, Nigel, "The Cathedral Archives and Library," in P. Collinson, N. Ramsay, and M. Sparks (eds.), *A History of Canterbury Cathedral*, Oxford (1995), pp. 341–407.

Rawcliffe, Carole, *The Hospitals of Medieval Norwich*, Norwich, 1995.

Medicine for the Soul: The Life, Death and Resurrection of an English Medieval Hospital, St. Giles, Norwich, c. 1249–1550, Stroud, Glos., 1999.

Redgard, John, *Medieval Framlingham: Select Documents 1270–1524*, Suffolk Record Society 27, Ipswich, 1985.

Redstone, Lillian, "Three Carrow Account Rolls," *Norfolk Archaeology* 29 (1946), 41–88.

Reed, A. W., *Tudor Drama*, London, 1926.

Rhodes, J. T., "Private Devotion in England on the Eve of the Reformation," Ph.D. thesis, University of Durham, 1974.

Richmond, Colin, "Elizabeth Clere: Friend of the Pastons," in J. Wogan-Browne, R. Voaden, A. Diamond, A. Hutchison, C. M. Meale, and L. Johnson (eds.), *Medieval Women: Texts and Contexts in Late Medieval Britain: Essays for Felicity Riddy* (Turnhout, Belgium, 2000), pp. 251–73.

John Hopton, A Fifteenth-Century Suffolk Gentleman, Cambridge, 1981.

The Paston Family in the Fifteenth Century: The First Phase, Cambridge, 1990.

"Thomas Lord Morley (d. 1446) and the Morleys of Hingham," *Norfolk Archaeology* 39 (1942), 1–12.

Rickert, Margaret, *Painting in Britain: The Middle Ages*, Baltimore, Md., 1954.

Riddy, Felicity, *Sir Thomas Malory*, Leiden, 1987.

" 'Women Talking about the Things of God': A Late Medieval Sub-Culture," in Meale (ed.), *Women and Literature*, pp. 104–27.

Robertson, Elizabeth, *Early English Devotional Prose and the Female Audience*, Knoxville, Tenn., 1990.

Rogers, Nicholas J., "Fitzwilliam Museum MS 3–1979: A Bury St. Edmunds Book of Hours and the Origins of the Bury Style," in D. Williams (ed.), *England in the Fifteenth Century: Proceedings of the 1986 Harlaxton Symposium* (Woodbridge, Suffolk, 1987), pp. 229–44.

Rosenthal, Constance L., *The Vitae Patrum in Old and Middle English Literature*, Philadelphia, 1936.

Roskell, J. S., L. Clark and C. Rawcliffe (eds.), *The House of Commons 1386–1421*, History of Parliament Trust, 4 vols., London, 1992.

Ross, C. D., "The Household Accounts of Elizabeth Berkeley, Countess of Warwick, 1420–21," *TBGAS* 70 (1951), 81–105.

Rouse, Richard H. and Mary A. Rouse (eds.), *Registrum Angliae de Libris Doctorum et Auctorum Veterum*, Corpus of British Medieval Library Catalogues, London, 1991.

Rowntree, Carol B., "Studies in Carthusian History in Later Medieval England," Ph.D. thesis, University of York, 1981.

The Rule of Benedict: A Guide to Christian Living, trans. Monks of Glenstal Abbey, Dublin, 1994.

Russell, D. W., "The Manuscript Source of the Fragment, Rylands French MS 6," *BJRL* 71 (1989), 41–47.

Russell, Josiah Cox, "The Clerical Population of Medieval England," *Traditio* 2 (1944), 177–212.

Rye, Walter, *Carrow Abbey*, Norwich, 1889.

Salu, M. B., trans., *The Ancrene Riwle*, London, 1955.

Sandler, Lucy Freeman, *Gothic Manuscripts 1285–1385*, A Survey of Manuscripts Illuminated in the British Isles, 2 vols., London and Oxford, 1986.

Sargent, Michael, "James Grenehalgh: The Biographical Register," *Sonderdruck aus Analecta Cartusiana Kartausermystik und-Mystiker*, 4 (1984), 20–54.

"Walter Hilton's *Scale of Perfection*: The London Manuscript Group Reconsidered," *Medium Ævum* 52 (1983), 189–216.

Saul, Nigel, *Death, Art, and Memory in Medieval England: The Cobham Family and Their Monuments 1300–1500*, Oxford, 2001.

Scase, Wendy, "Reginald Pecock, John Carpenter and John Colop's 'Common-Profit' Books: Aspects of Book Ownership and Circulation in Fifteenth-Century London," *Medium Ævum* 61 (1992), 261–74.

Scattergood, John, "Two Unrecorded Poems from Trinity College Dublin MS 490," *RES* 38 (1987), 46–49.

Schaff, Philip (ed.), *Select Library of the Nicene and Post-Nicene Fathers IX*, New York, 1889.

Schulenburg, Jane Tibbetts, "Strict Active Enclosure and Its Effects on the Female Monastic Experience (*ca.* 500–1100)," in John A. Nichols and Lillian Thomas Shank (eds.), *Distant Echoes: Medieval Religious Women*, 2 vols. (Kalamazoo, Mich., 1984), pp. 51–86.

Schulz, Svato (ed.), *Medieval and Renaissance Manuscript Books in the Library of Congress, A Descriptive Catalogue*, Washington D.C., 1989.

Scott, Kathleen L., *Later Gothic Manuscripts 1390–1490, A Survey of Manuscripts Illuminated in the British Isles*, 2 vols., London, 1996.

Serjeantson, R. M., *A History of Delapre Abbey, Northampton*, Northampton, 1909.

Severs, J. Burke, *Manual of Writings in Middle English*, vol. 2, Hamden, Conn., 1970.

Seymour, M. C. (ed.), *Selections from Hoccleve*, Oxford, 1981.

Sharpe, Reginald R. (ed.), *Calendar of the Letter Books, Preserved among the Archives of the Corporation of the City of London at Guildhall, A.D. 1298–1498, Books A-L*, London, 1899–1912.

Sharpe, R., J. P. Carley, R. M. Thomson, A. G. Watson (eds.), *English Benedictine Libraries: The Shorter Catalogues*, Corpus of British Medieval Library Catalogues, vol. 4, London, 1996.

Silber, Ilana F., *Virtuosity, Charisma, and Social Order: A Comparative Sociological Study of Monasticism in Theravada Buddhism and Medieval Catholicism*, Cambridge, 1995.

Spencer, H. Leith, *English Preaching in the Late Middle Ages*, Oxford, 1993.

Spurgeon, Caroline E., *Five Hundred Years of Chaucer Criticism and Allusion 1357–1900*, 3 vols., repr. edn, New York, 1960.

Stahlschmidt, J. C. L., "London Subsidy temp. Henry IV," *Archaeological Journal* 44 (1887), 56–82.

Starnes, DeWitt and E. W. Talbert, *Classical Myth and Legend in Renaissance Dictionaries*, Chapel Hill, 1955.

Stephens, W. R. W., *St. John Chrysostom: His Life and Thought*, 3rd edn, London, 1883.

Stone, E. D. and Basil Cozens-Hardy, *Norwich Consistory Court Depositions 1499–1512 and 1518–1530*, Norfolk Record Society 10, n.p., 1938.

Stow, John, *A Survey of London*, ed. C. L. Kingsford, 2 vols., Oxford, 1908.

Strype, John, *Ecclesiastical Memorials*, 3 vols., Oxford, 1882.

Sturman, Winifred, "Barking Abbey, A Study in Its External and Internal Administration from the Conquest to the Dissolution," Ph.D. thesis, University of London, 1961.

Surtees, Robert, *History and Antiquities of the County Palatine of Durham . . .*, 4 vols., London, 1840.

Tait, Hugh (ed.), *Jewelry 7000 Years: An International History and Illustrated Survey from the Collections of the British Museum*, New York, 1987.

Tait, M. B., "The Bridgettine Monastery of Syon . . ." Ph.D. thesis, University of Oxford, 1975.

Takamiya, Toshiyuki, "'On the Evils of Covetousness': An Unrecorded Middle English Poem," in Beadle and Piper (eds.), *New Science*, pp. 189–206.

Tanner, Norman, *The Church in Late Medieval Norwich 1370–1532*, Pontifical Institute of Mediaeval Studies, Studies and Texts 66, Toronto, 1984.

Thacker, Francis James, "The Monumental Brasses of Worcestershire, Part II," *TWAS* n.s. 4 (1926–27), 129–56.

Thomas, A. G. and I. D. Thornley (eds.), *The Great Chronicle of London*, London, 1938.

Thompson, A. Hamilton (ed.), *Visitations of Religious Houses in the Diocese of Lincoln*, 3 vols., Canterbury and York Society 17, 24, 33, London 1915, 1919, 1927.

Thompson, E. Margaret, *The Carthusian Order in England*, London, 1930.

Thompson, E. Maunde, G. F. Warner, F. G. Kenyon, and J. P. Gilson (eds.), *New Palaeographical Society Facsimiles of Ancient Manuscripts*, 2 vols., London, 1903–12.

Thompson, James Westfall, *The Medieval Library*, Chicago, 1939.

Thomson, D. F. S. and H. C. Porter, *Erasmus and Cambridge*, Toronto, 1963.

Thomson, J. A. F., "Knightly Piety and the Margins of Lollardy," in Aston and Richmond, *Lollardy and the Gentry*, pp. 95–111.

Tillotson, John H., *Marrick Priory: A Nunnery in Late Medieval Yorkshire*, Borthwick Paper No. 75, York, 1989.

"Visitation and Reform of the Yorkshire Nunneries in the Fourteenth Century," *Northern History* 30 (1994), 1–21.

Timmins, T. C. B. (ed.), *The Register of John Chandler, Dean of Salisbury 1404–17*, Wiltshire Record Society 39, Devizes, 1984.

Todd, Henry J. (ed.), *A Catalogue of the Archiepiscopal Manuscripts in the Library at Lambeth Palace*, London, 1812.

Tolhurst, J. B. L., (ed.), *The Ordinal and Customary of the Benedictine Nuns of Barking Abbey: University College, Oxford, MS 169*, 2 vols., Henry Bradshaw Society 65, 66, London, 1927–28.

Tuck, J. Anthony, "Carthusian Monks and Lollard Knights: Religious Attitudes at the Court of Richard II," in P. Strohm and T. J. Heffernan (eds.), *Studies in the Age of Chaucer Proceedings, No. 1, 1984: Reconstructing Chaucer* (Knoxville, Tenn., 1985), pp. 149–61.

Tymms, Samuel (ed.), *Wills and Inventories from the . . . Commissary of Bury St. Edmunds*, Camden Society 49, London, 1850.

Vaissier, J. J., (ed.), *A Devout Treatyse Called the Tree & xii Frutes of the Holy Goost*, Groningen, 1960.

Van Engen, John, "Friar Johannes Nyder on Laypeople Living as Religious in the World," in F. J. Felten and N. Jaspert (eds.), *Vita Religiosa im Mittelalter: Festschrift für Kaspar Elm zum 70. Geburtstag* (Berlin, 1999).

Venn, John (ed.), *The Annals of Gonville and Caius College by John Caius, M. D.*, Cambridge Antiquarian Society Octavo Series 40, Cambridge, 1904.

Venn, John and J. A. Venn (eds.), *Alumni Cantabrigienses*, Part I, vol. 1, Cambridge, 1922.

Virgoe, Roger, "Hugh atte Fenne and Books at Cambridge," *TCBS* 10 (1991), 92–98.

"A Norwich Taxation List of 1451," *Norfolk Archaeology* 40 (1989), 145–54.

Walcott, Mackenzie E. C., "Inventories and Valuations of Religious Houses at the Time of the Dissolution, from the Public Record Office," *Archaeologia* 43 (1871), 201–49.

Walker, Greg. "Saint or Schemer? The 1527 Heresy Trial of Thomas Bilney Reconsidered," *JEH* 40 (1989), 219–38, reprinted in *Persuasive Fictions: Faction, Faith and Political Culture in the Reign of Henry VIII,* Aldershot, Hants., 1996.

Walker, Sue Sheridan (ed.), *Wife and Widow in Medieval England,* Ann Arbor, Mich., 1993.

Waller, J. G., "The Lords of Cobham, Their Monuments, and the Church," *Archaeologica Cantiana* 11 (1877), 49–112.

Walsingham, Thomas, *Historia Anglicana,* ed. H. T. Riley, 2 vols., London, 1864.

Ward, Jennifer C., English Noblewomen and the Local Community in the Later Middle Ages," in D. Watt (ed.), *Medieval Women in Their Communities* (Cardiff, 1997), pp. 186–203.

English Noblewomen in the Later Middle Ages, New York, 1992.

Warner, George F. and Julius P. Gilson, *Catalogue of Western Manuscripts in the Old Royal and King's Collection,* London, 1921.

Warren, Ann K., *Anchorites and Their Patrons in Medieval England* (Berkeley, 1985).

Watson, Andrew G., *A Descriptive Catalogue of the Medieval Manuscripts of All Souls College Oxford,* Oxford, 1997.

Watson, Nicholas, *Richard Rolle and the Invention of Authority,* Cambridge, 1991.

Watt, Tessa, *Cheap Print and Popular Piety 1550–1640,* Cambridge Studies in Early Modern British History, Cambridge, 1991.

Weightman, Christine, *Margaret of York, Duchess of Burgundy 1446–1503,* New York, 1989.

Whitaker, T. D., *History of... Whalley,* 2 vols., London, 1876.

White, Robyn, "Early Print and Purgatory: the Shaping of an Henrician Ideology," Ph.D. thesis, Australian National University, 1994.

Whitwell, Robert Jowitt, "An Ordinance for Syon Library, 1482," *EHR* 25 (1910), 121–23.

Wieck, Roger S., *Time Sanctified: The Book of Hours in Medieval Art and Life,* New York and Baltimore, 1988.

Williams, J. F., "A Wooden Pax at Sandon," *TEAS* 21 (1937), 37–44.

Wills and Inventories Illustrative... of the Northern Counties, Surtees Society 2, London, 1835.

Wilson, Edward, "A Middle English Manuscript at Coughton Court, Warwickshire, and British Library MS Harley 4012," *Notes and Queries* 222 (1977), 295–303.

Wilson, R. M., "The Contents of the Mediaeval Library," in Francis Wormald and C. E. Wright (eds.), *The English Library before 1700* (London, 1958), pp. 85–112.

Wogan-Browne, Jocelyn, "Rerouting the Dower: The Anglo-Norman Life of St. Audrey by Marie (of Chatteris)," in J. Carpenter and S. B. MacLean (eds.), *Power of the Weak: Studies on Medieval Women* (Urbana, Ill., 1995), pp. 27–56.

Saints' Lives and Women's Literary Culture c. 1150–1300: Virginity and Its Authorizations, Oxford, 2001.

Woodforde, Christopher, *The Norwich School of Glass-Painting in the Fifteenth Century*, Oxford, 1950.

Woolgar, C. M., *Household Accounts from Medieval England*, Records of Social and Economic History n.s. 18, Oxford, 1993.

Wright, C. E., *Fontes Harleiana*, London, 1972.

Wylie, James Hamilton, *History of England under Henry the Fourth*, London, 1896.

The Reign of Henry V, 3 vols., Cambridge, 1914–29.

Young, C. R., *The Making of the Neville Family in England 1166–1400*, Woodbridge, Suffolk, 1990.

Index of manuscripts

Page numbers set in *italics* indicate illustrative material.

Index of manuscripts

Index of manuscripts

General index

Page numbers in *italics* refer to illustrative material; titles of works are listed under names of authors where known.

CAMBRIDGE STUDIES IN MEDIEVAL LITERATURE

Lightning Source UK Ltd.
Milton Keynes UK
UKOW050134220612

194820UK00001B/27/A